Celebrity recipes
At my Mother's Knee
A patchwork of food memories

Supporter 2012

ACP Books is donating $10,000 from the sale of this cookbook to Make-A-Wish® Australia to help support their work in granting the wishes of children and young people with life-threatening medical conditions.

THE AUSTRALIAN Women's Weekly

Celebrity recipes

At my Mother's Knee

A patchwork of food memories

acp books

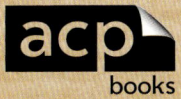

contents

Foreword 8
Our First Foodie 10
The 60s 24
The 70s 42
Italian 54
Greek 68
French 84
Asian 96
Modern Mums 120
Lazy Sundays 140
Lunch Box Days 160
Family Traditions 170
Down on the Farm 186
Mum's Little Secrets 202
Recipes to Pass Down 212
Glossary 218
Conversion Chart 220
Index 221

INSET, TOP: 11-year-old Oliver Biggar wished to trek the Inca Trail to Machu Picchu in Peru.
INSET, BOTTOM: 10-year-old Braydon Boggitt wished to pat a dolphin at Sea World. We enhanced his wish by having his favourite character Spider-Man meet him at the airport on his return home.

Foreword

At My Mother's Knee celebrates the special relationships between some of our best known celebrities and their precious mums, as they share their memories of culinary delights and secret recipes that bind their families together.

We all know that food created with love, sustains not only our bodies, but fills our hearts and spirits and creates everlasting memories. As a National Patron of Make-A-Wish® Australia and a volunteer Wish Granter, I know the importance of creating everlasting memories. For 25 years in Australia, we have granted the Wishes of children with life-threatening illnesses, to enrich the human experience with hope, strength and joy.

Savour these beautiful recipes, photographs and memories... and treasure every second with your family.

ACP Books is generously donating $10,000 to Make-A-Wish® Australia, so we can continue to grant Wishes which transcend the daily uncertainty that our families are facing. The Wishes can fall into four categories: "I wish I could go/meet/have or be". There are Wishes for puppies, "fairy" bedroom makeovers, visits to Gold Coast theme parks, an elephant in the backyard and even to meet the Pope! There are others for cubby houses or to be a published writer, while one four-year-old boy wished for "a big red money" (that is, a $20 note). One child wished for a party and a rainbow for all the people who had been so kind to him – those involved received a prism so they could make their own mini-rainbows forever.

These children have taught me to "live with urgency before the emergency". So this Mother's Day, my wish for you is to savour these beautiful recipes, photographs and memories... and treasure every second with your family.

Robyn Moore
A National Patron of Make-A-Wish® Australia

Our First Foodie

Post World War II was the era of the domestic goddess. Bread was baked daily in the home kitchen and meals were made from scratch. Takeaway food was non-existent and appliances had yet to transform the cooking experience.

Margaret Fulton & Suzanne Gibbs

I was brought up in the country, where countrywomen's cooking was so exciting. I am the youngest of six, so meal times were very busy. Mum wasn't a fancy cook but everything she made was really good and she liked quality food. We had lovely meals and it made us children very happy and healthy. It was hard work, but the rewards were joyful.

We all helped out in the kitchen and had our jobs. I would be stirring custard to make sure it didn't boil or shelling peas and we'd be chatting while we did it. So we were all learning in the kitchen. It made me realise that you need to have good fresh food to make good meals.

But the part I remember the most was just the happiness of it all – the nice feeling, the smells and my Mother's wisdom. Her wisdom would come out about food and then about living. She would ask what I thought about certain subjects. It was just a very happy time.

She wasn't a big baker but she made shortbread and a dundee cake every week, and they were so perfect. My two sisters and I all made shortbread and claimed that we made it the way mother made it – but they were all different. The funny thing about cooking is that you put yourself into it.

The thing that has influenced me all my life is how good it is to cook for your family and get them involved. It brings a family closer together and makes you realise there's nothing better in the world than being at home together.

RIGHT: (From left) Margaret Fulton and her daughter, Suzanne Gibbs.

LEFT: Margaret Fulton, age 2, in Nairn Scotland.

Dundee cake

180g (5½ ounces) butter, softened
¾ cup (165g) caster (superfine) sugar
5 eggs
1½ cups (225g) plain (all-purpose) flour
½ cup (75g) self-raising flour
½ teaspoon mixed spice
⅓ cup (80ml) milk
1¼ cups (200g) raisins, chopped coarsely
1½ cups (250g) dried currants
1¼ cups (200g) sultanas
⅓ cup (70g) red glacé cherries, chopped coarsely
2 tablespoons mixed peel
½ cup (80g) blanched almonds
1 tablespoon brandy

1 Preheat oven to 150°C/300°F. Line deep 20cm (8-inch) square cake pan with three layers of baking paper, extending paper 5cm (2 inches) above edges.
2 Beat butter, sugar, eggs, sifted dry ingredients and milk in large bowl with electric mixer on medium speed about 3 minutes or until mixture becomes pale in colour. Stir in fruit and half the almonds.
3 Spread mixture into pan; decorate top with remaining almonds.
4 Bake cake about 2 hours. Brush hot cake with brandy; cover tightly with foil, cool in pan.

prep + cook time 3 hours 20 minutes (+ cooling)
serves 16
nutritional count per serving
14.3g total fat (7g saturated fat); 1593kJ (381 cal); 56.3g carbohydrate; 6.4g protein; 3.3g fibre
tip Cake will keep in an airtight container, at room temperature, for up to a week.

BELOW: Margaret and Suzanne in the 70s at work on the magazine series, *Margaret Fulton Cookery Course*.

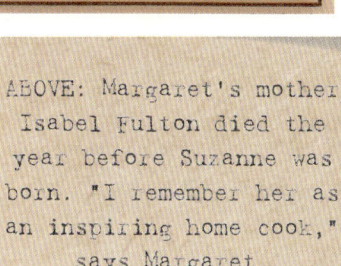

ABOVE: Margaret's mother Isabel Fulton died the year before Suzanne was born. "I remember her as an inspiring home cook," says Margaret.

My father's shears are my most precious family treasure. He brought them out from Scotland in the 1920s. When I would visit his tailor's shop, he would send for a lovely pastry to spoil me and cut it in two with these scissors. These shears are also included in the National Archives of Australia book *Keeping Family Treasures*, which features culturally-significant objects.

Our First Foodie

Beef wellington is a retro dinner party dish that has recently made its way back on the menu. Impressive and easy to prepare, it should always be served with the centre slightly pink.

Beef wellington

1 tablespoon olive oil
800g (1¾-pound) piece beef fillet
25g (¾ ounce) butter
1 small brown onion (80g), chopped finely
125g (4 ounces) button mushrooms, chopped finely
150g (5 ounces) chicken or duck liver pâté
2 sheets puff pastry
1 egg

1 Heat oil in large frying pan; cook beef until browned all over. Wrap in foil; cool.
2 Heat butter in same pan; cook onion and mushrooms, stirring, until tender and liquid has evaporated. Cool.
3 Preheat oven to 240°C/475°F. Line oven tray with baking paper.
4 Stir pâté in medium bowl until soft. Spread over top of beef; top with mushroom mixture.
5 Roll out pastry on floured surface into a rectangle large enough to enclose beef; moisten edges with water. Place beef on one end of rectangle, fold pastry over beef; trim excess pastry and press edges to seal. Place beef on tray; brush with egg then cut small slits in top of pastry.
6 Bake beef 10 minutes. Reduce oven to 200°C/400°F; bake a further 20 minutes or until browned lightly.
7 Serve beef wellington sliced thickly with a mixed leaf salad, if you like.

prep + cook time 1 hour 20 minutes
serves 4
nutritional count per serving
52.2g total fat (23g saturated fat); 3449kJ (825 cal); 31.9g carbohydrate; 56.4g protein; 2.7g fibre

Irish lamb and barley stew

2 tablespoons olive oil
1kg (2 pounds) diced lamb shoulder
1 large brown onion (200g), chopped coarsely
2 medium carrots (240g), chopped coarsely
2 stalks celery (300g), trimmed, chopped coarsely
2 cloves garlic, crushed
1 litre (4 cups) chicken stock
3 cups (750ml) water
1 cup (200g) pearl barley
4 sprigs fresh thyme
3 medium potatoes (600g), chopped coarsely
2 cups (160g) finely shredded cabbage
⅓ cup finely chopped fresh flat-leaf parsley

1 Heat half the oil in large saucepan; cook lamb, in batches, until browned. Remove from pan.
2 Heat remaining oil in same pan; cook onion, carrot, celery and garlic, stirring, until vegetables soften. Return lamb to pan with stock, the water, barley and thyme; bring to the boil. Reduce heat; simmer, covered, 1 hour, skimming fat from surface occasionally.
3 Add potato; simmer, uncovered, about 30 minutes or until potato is tender. Add cabbage; simmer, uncovered, until cabbage is just tender. Discard thyme.
4 Serve stew sprinkled with parsley.

prep + cook time 2 hours **serves** 4
nutritional count per serving 33.9g total fat (12.3g saturated fat); 3244kJ (776 cal); 56.8g carbohydrate; 60.6g protein; 12.9g fibre
serving suggestion Serve with crusty bread.

Corned beef with parsley sauce

1.5kg (3-pound) piece beef corned silverside
2 bay leaves
6 black peppercorns
1 large brown onion (200g), quartered
1 large carrot (180g), chopped coarsely
1 tablespoon brown malt vinegar
¼ cup (50g) firmly packed light brown sugar
PARSLEY SAUCE
30g (1 ounce) butter
¼ cup (35g) plain flour
2½ cups (625ml) milk
⅓ cup (40g) grated cheddar cheese
⅓ cup finely chopped fresh flat-leaf parsley
1 tablespoon mild mustard

1 Place beef, bay leaves, peppercorns, onion, carrot, vinegar and half the sugar in large saucepan. Add enough water to just cover beef; simmer, covered, about 2 hours or until beef is tender. Cool beef 1 hour in liquid in pan.
2 Remove beef from pan; discard liquid. Sprinkle sheet of foil with remaining sugar, wrap beef in foil; stand 20 minutes before serving.
3 Make parsley sauce.
4 Serve sliced corned beef with parsley sauce.
parsley sauce Melt butter in small saucepan, add flour; cook, stirring, until bubbling. Gradually stir in milk; cook, stirring, until sauce boils and thickens. Remove from heat; stir in cheese, parsley and mustard.

prep + cook time 2 hours 30 minutes (+ standing & cooling)
serves 4
nutritional count per serving 35.8g total fat (19.3g saturated fat); 3520kJ (842 cal); 31g carbohydrate; 97g protein; 2.5g fibre

Lamingtons

6 eggs
⅔ cup (150g) caster (superfine) sugar
⅓ cup (50g) cornflour (cornstarch)
½ cup (75g) plain (all-purpose) flour
⅓ cup (50g) self-raising flour
2 cups (160g) desiccated coconut
CHOCOLATE ICING
4 cups (640g) icing (confectioners') sugar
½ cup (50g) cocoa powder
15g (½ ounce) butter, melted
1 cup (250ml) milk

1 Preheat oven to 180°C/350°F. Grease 20cm x 30cm (8-inch x 12-inch) rectangular pan; line base and long sides with baking paper, extending paper 5cm (2 inches) over sides.
2 Beat eggs in large bowl with electric mixer about 10 minutes or until thick and creamy; gradually add sugar, beating until dissolved between additions. Triple-sift flours; fold into egg mixture. Spread mixture into pan.
3 Bake cake about 35 minutes. Turn cake immediately onto baking-paper-covered wire rack to cool.
4 Meanwhile, make chocolate icing.
5 Cut cake into 16 pieces. Dip each piece in icing; drain off excess. Place coconut into medium bowl; toss squares in coconut. Place lamingtons on wire rack to set.
chocolate icing Sift icing sugar and cocoa in medium heatproof bowl; stir in butter and milk. Set bowl over medium saucepan of simmering water; stir until icing is of a coating consistency.

prep + cook time 50 minutes **makes** 16
nutritional count per lamington
7.9g total fat (5g saturated fat); 1344kJ (321 cal); 59.4g carbohydrate; 4.9g protein; 1.4g fibre

Our First Foodie

Bread and butter pudding

6 slices white bread (270g)
40g (1½ ounces) butter, softened
½ cup (80g) sultanas
¼ teaspoon ground nutmeg
CUSTARD
1½ cups (375ml) milk
2 cups (500ml) pouring cream
⅓ cup (75g) caster (superfine) sugar
½ teaspoon vanilla extract
4 eggs

1 Preheat oven to 160°C/325°F. Grease shallow 2-litre (8-cup) ovenproof dish.
2 Make custard.
3 Trim crusts from bread. Spread each slice with butter; cut into four triangles. Layer bread, overlapping, in dish; sprinkle with sultanas. Pour custard over bread; sprinkle with nutmeg.
4 Place dish in large baking dish; add enough boiling water to come halfway up sides of dish.
5 Bake pudding about 45 minutes or until set. Remove pudding from baking dish; stand 5 minutes before serving.
custard Bring milk, cream, sugar and extract in medium saucepan to the boil. Whisk eggs in large bowl; whisking constantly, gradually add hot milk mixture to egg mixture.

prep + cook time 1 hour 10 minutes **serves** 6
nutritional count per serving 48.6g total fat (30.4g saturated fat); 2859kJ (684 cal); 49.3g carbohydrate; 12.4g protein; 1.8g fibre

Our First Foodie

The 60s

As supermarkets sprang up, pre-packaged foods, frozen vegetables and storage options freed up our homemaker mums. Their cake recipes dazzled, and casseroles and chicken appeared more frequently on our plates. Coffee too, gave tea a run for its money.

Kerri-Anne Kennerley

I have two brothers and a sister and we were very much the fabulous family at home. Dad had a hobby farm and another business so we were busy and Mum cooked for us all and looked after the household. It wasn't gourmet, but it was healthy fare. Carpetbag steak – steak with oysters stuffed in it – was one of her specialties.

There were lots of roasts with veg in those days and Mum was also very healthy – she was very much ahead of her time. Everything was fresh, there was no such thing as frozen stuff really in those times, nor was there a lot of takeaway. I announced to my Mother very early on that I was never going to learn to sew or cook because I didn't really like it. But I do remember, when I was really young, the white Pyrex mixmaster bowl mum would make a cake in and I would just hang around to lick the beaters. I was the youngest so mum would make one while the others were at school and I didn't have to fight anyone for them.

For my birthday in September – and I still have flashbacks today – Mum always made my favourite sponge cake; made from scratch with proper cream and fresh strawberries, being the start of the strawberry season then. That's all I ever wanted; a strawberry and cream sponge cake. That or frangipani pie. It's made of Golden Circle pineapple and meringue and it is just a quintessential Queensland 60s dessert; it's just fabulous.

Pears can be replaced with apples, peaches, plums, apricots or blueberries. This flan can be stored in an airtight container for up to 2 days.

Almond pear flan

1¼ cups (185g) plain (all-purpose) flour
90g (3 ounces) butter
¼ cup (55g) caster (superfine) sugar
2 egg yolks
3 firm ripe medium pears (690g), peeled, cored, quartered
2 tablespoons apricot jam, warmed, strained
ALMOND FILLING
125g (4 ounces) butter
⅓ cup (75g) caster (superfine) sugar
2 eggs
1 cup (120g) ground almonds
1 tablespoon plain (all-purpose) flour

1 Blend or process flour, butter, sugar and egg yolks until just combined. Knead on floured surface until smooth. Enclose in plastic wrap; refrigerate 30 minutes.
2 Meanwhile, make almond filling.
3 Preheat oven to 180°C/350°F. Grease 24cm (9½-inch) round loose-based flan tin.
4 Roll dough between sheets of baking paper until large enough to line tin. Lift pastry into tin, press evenly into base and side; trim edge. Spread filling into pastry case; arrange pears over filling.
5 Bake flan about 45 minutes. Brush top of flan with jam.
almond filling Beat butter and sugar in small bowl with electric mixer until just combined. Beat in eggs, one at a time. Fold in ground almonds and flour.

prep + cook time 1 hour (+ refrigeration)
serves 10
nutritional count per serving 26.7g total fat (12.7g saturated fat); 1751kJ (419 cal); 38.4g carbohydrate; 6.9g protein; 2.8g fibre

RIGHT: (From left) Kerri-Anne's sister, Jan Kehoe, their Mum Grace Wright and Kerri-Anne caught up for lunch at Summit restaurant in Sydney.

The 60s

Potato gratin with caramelised onion

1 tablespoon olive oil
2 large brown onions (400g), sliced thinly
1 tablespoon light brown sugar
3 teaspoons balsamic vinegar
2 tablespoons coarsely chopped fresh flat-leaf parsley
1kg (2 pounds) potatoes
1 tablespoon plain (all-purpose) flour
1¾ cups (430ml) pouring cream
¼ cup (60ml) milk
20g (¾ ounce) butter, chopped finely
¾ cup (90g) coarsely grated gruyère cheese
¾ cup (50g) stale breadcrumbs

1 Heat oil in frying pan over low heat; cook onion, stirring occasionally, about 20 minutes or until onion softens. Add sugar and vinegar; cook, stirring occasionally, about 10 minutes or until onion is caramelised. Remove from heat; stir in parsley.
2 Preheat oven to 180°C/350°F. Oil 1.5-litre (6-cup) ovenproof dish.
3 Using mandoline or V-slicer, cut potatoes into paper thin slices; pat dry with absorbent paper. Layer half the potato in dish; top with caramelised onion, then remaining potato.
4 Blend flour with a little of the cream in medium jug; stir in remaining cream and milk. Pour cream mixture over potato mixture; dot with butter.
5 Bake, covered with foil, 1¼ hours. Uncover; sprinkle with combined cheese and breadcrumbs. Bake, uncovered, 15 minutes or until potato is tender. Stand 5 minutes before serving.

prep + cook time 1 hour 45 minutes **serves** 6
nutritional count per serving 42.1g total fat (25.8g saturated fat); 2337kJ (559 cal); 32.9g carbohydrate; 11.5g protein; 3.5g fibre
tip We used sebago potatoes in this recipe.

Salmon patties

1kg (2 pounds) lasoda potatoes, peeled
440g (14 ounces) canned red salmon
1 small brown onion (80g), chopped finely
1 tablespoon finely chopped fresh flat-leaf parsley
1 teaspoon finely grated lemon rind
1 tablespoon lemon juice
½ cup (75g) plain (all-purpose) flour
1 egg
2 tablespoons milk
½ cup (50g) packaged breadcrumbs
½ cup (35g) stale breadcrumbs
vegetable oil, for deep-frying

1 Boil, steam or microwave potatoes until tender; drain. Mash potato in large bowl.
2 Drain salmon; discard any skin and bones. Add flaked salmon to potato with onion, parsley, rind and juice; mix well. Cover; refrigerate 30 minutes.
3 Using floured hands, shape salmon mixture into eight patties. Toss patties in flour; shake away excess. Dip patties, one at a time, in combined egg and milk, then in combined breadcrumbs.
4 Heat oil in large saucepan; deep-fry patties, in batches, until browned lightly. Drain patties on absorbent paper.

prep + cook time 40 minutes (+ refrigeration)
makes 8
nutritional count per patty 12.3g total fat (1.8g saturated fat); 1183kJ (283 cal); 33.8g carbohydrate; 7.3g protein; 3.6g fibre
tips You can also use coliban or nicola potatoes for this recipe. Patties can be prepared a day ahead and kept, covered, in the refrigerator.

The 60s

Pamela Clark

My love of cooking started when I was around 11; I started high school and discovered home science. My Mother, Grandmother and Great Grandmother all encouraged me. Mum was a lovely cook, but Nana was a very good cook who had a real passion for it and was taught by a woman trained at Le Cordon Bleu, way back around the 1930s.

Nana could whip up soufflés and things that nobody else could. She was taught by the woman who owned the station where she worked as a cook, so she could take care of my Mother after splitting up with my Grandfather. The owner was a rich French lady and she taught Nana what she wanted to eat. My Great Grandmother was a champion scone-maker and I have vivid memories of her making them. She taught me about scone dough; that it had to be soft and sticky.

My favourite recipe of Mum's would have to be her apple pie. I've played with the recipe and got it as close as I can to the memory of Mum's one, but it's not the same. She always went out of her way for us. I remember cooking a roast chicken was quite a rarity back then and only for special occasions. I can still see Mum plucking the feathers off the chicken and she was an animal lover so I know she hated doing it, but she knew we loved it.

If there is one thing I have inherited from Mum it's that she was a tidy freak. I'm a bit the same with my granddaughters now! We were allowed to watch the cooking, but not really help until we were much older.

RIGHT: (From left) Pamela with her son Robby and granddaughters Isobel and Elspeth (front).

Mum's favourite china tea set was a wedding gift, it was only brought out when very special people were invited to afternoon tea. I inherited what was left of the tea set and have since added to it. It holds very dear memories for me.

Apple pie slice

8 medium apples (1.5kg)
⅔ cup (150g) caster (superfine) sugar
½ cup (125ml) water
2 tablespoons white (granulated) sugar, optional
PASTRY
3 cups (450g) self-raising flour
¼ cup (40g) icing (confectioners') sugar
125g (4 ounces) cold butter, chopped coarsely
1 egg, beaten lightly
½ cup (125ml) milk, approximately
PASSIONFRUIT ICING
1½ cups (240g) icing (confectioners') sugar
2 passionfruit

1 Peel, quarter and core apples; slice thickly. Place apples, caster sugar and the water in large saucepan; cover, bring to the boil. Reduce heat; simmer about 10 minutes or until the apples are just tender. Gently turn the apple mixture into a large colander or strainer to drain; cool to room temperature.
2 Preheat oven to 200°C/400°F. Grease 20cm x 30cm (8-inch x 12-inch) lamington pan; line base with baking paper, extending paper 5cm (2 inches) over two long sides.
3 Make pastry.
4 Roll two-thirds of the pastry on floured surface until large enough to line pan, with 1cm (½ inch) extending over sides. Lift pastry into pan, ease into base and sides. Spread cold apple mixture into pastry case; brush edges with a little extra milk. Roll out remaining pastry until large enough to generously cover pie. Place pastry over filling; press edges to seal, trim edges. Brush top with a little milk; sprinkle with white sugar. Cut about six holes in pastry.
5 Bake pie 45 minutes. Stand in pan 10 minutes; turn, right-side up, on wire rack to cool.
6 Meanwhile, make passionfruit icing.
7 Spread icing over pie; serve cut into squares.
pastry Sift flour and icing sugar into large bowl; rub in butter. Make a well in centre. Using a knife, 'cut' combined egg and enough milk through flour mixture to make a soft dough.
passionfruit icing Sift icing sugar into medium heatproof bowl, stir in passionfruit pulp, then enough water to make a stiff paste. Place bowl over medium saucepan of simmering water; stir icing until spreadable.

prep + cook time 1 hour 40 minutes (+ cooling) **serves** 8
nutritional count per serving 14.9g total fat (9.2g saturated fat); 2658kJ (636 cal); 114.1g carbohydrate; 7.6g protein; 5.3g fibre

Steak diane

1 tablespoon olive oil
4 x 180g (5½-ounce) beef fillet steaks
⅓ cup (80ml) brandy
2 cloves garlic, crushed
¼ cup (60ml) worcestershire sauce
1 cup (250ml) pouring cream
1 tablespoon finely chopped fresh flat-leaf parsley

1 Heat oil in large frying pan; cook steaks. Remove from pan; cover to keep warm.
2 Add brandy to pan; bring to the boil. Add garlic, sauce and cream; cook, stirring, about 3 minutes or until sauce thickens slightly. Remove from heat; stir in parsley.
3 Serve steaks with sauce, and accompany with shoestring chips and a mixed leaf salad, if you like.

prep + cook time 20 minutes **serves** 4
nutritional count per serving 42.4g total fat (23g saturated fat); 2495kJ (597 cal); 5.2g carbohydrate; 39.5g protein; 0.4g fibre

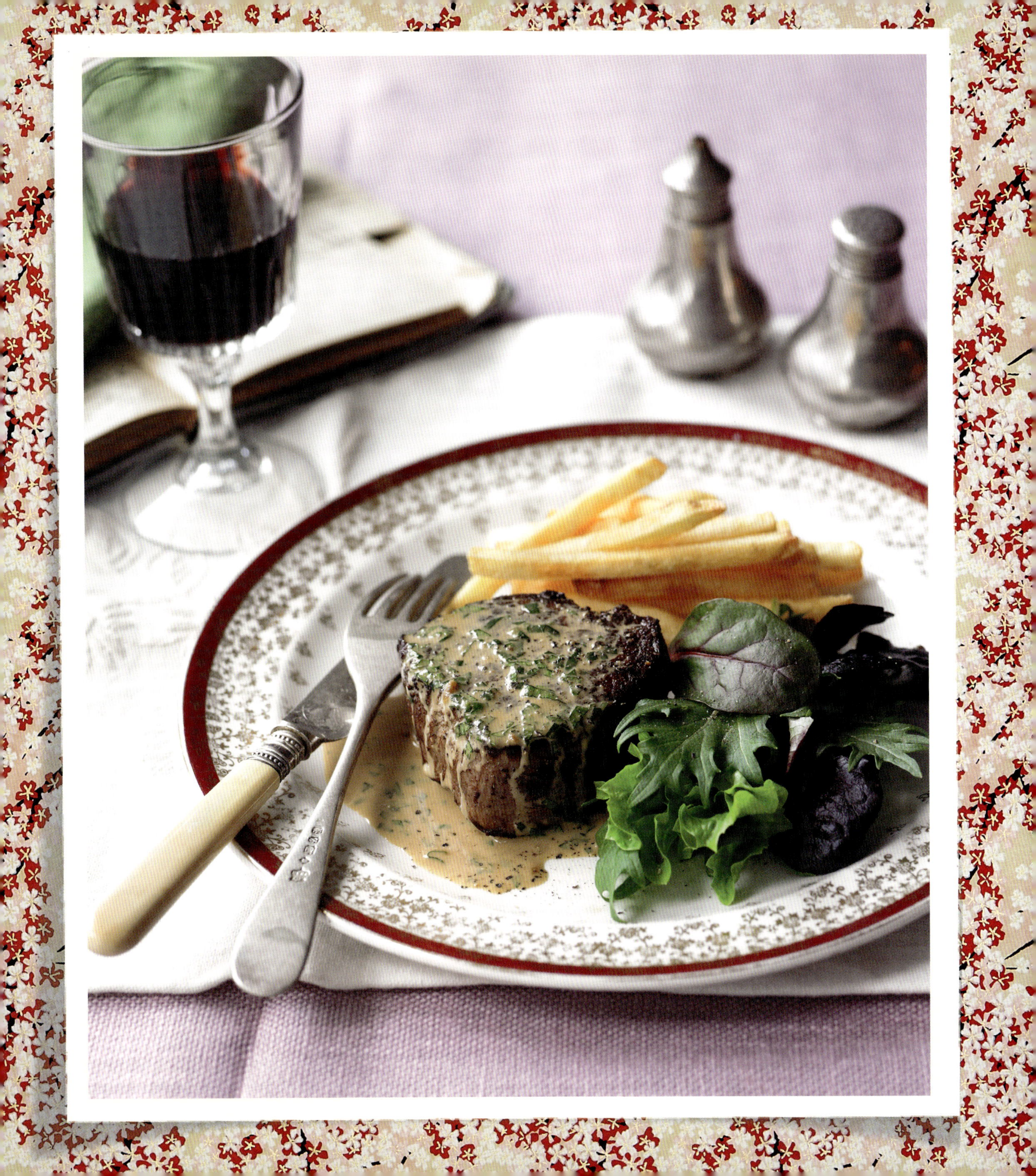

RIGHT: Les (middle row, second from right) aged 12 years old, in his football team at Berkeley High School, Berkeley, NSW.

Les Murray

Back in those days in Hungary, we'd queue up for hours for ham. We were poor, so couldn't always eat what we craved. We had meat once a week and chicken, strangely enough, once a year and in between pasta and vegetables. There was no ready-made pasta then, so Mum made everything from scratch. How she managed it while having a day job, I'll never know.

My earliest memory is having coffee with hot milk, with pastry for breakfast. I didn't taste bacon and eggs until I came to Australia, as eggs were also very expensive. I really only saw them at Easter when the painted boiled eggs were put on display. I used to steal them when mum and dad weren't looking! My favourite recipe of mum's without a doubt is paprika chicken. I still have it a couple of times a month. My other big favourite was Hungarian bean soup or Jókai Bableves, a thickened soup flavoured with smoked pork. Yummy.

ABOVE: (from left) Brothers and mates Joe, Les and Andrew celebrating Joe's birthday at dinner.

The 60s

Lyndey Milan

My parents lived and breathed the hospitality of the table. Mum was a good cook and Dad believed her baked dinner was better than any fancy restaurant's. Having grown up in the Great Depression, Mum loved to pile the plates high. I'll never forget the smell for days of her famous boiled fruitcake, as she prepared it for Christmas. She would soak the fruit, then boiled it and left it to cool. When I made it available on radio, the station was inundated with callers. We later printed it in *The Australian Women's Weekly*. I don't remember spending much time in the kitchen when I was small – I really started cooking around 16 years old. She once said to me that she was amazed that I ended up in a career with cooking. But I loved so many of her recipes, like chicken a la king, sweet lamb curry made from leftover roast lamb, and veal casserole.

ABOVE, TOP: Lyndey and her Mum, Isabel Hall.
ABOVE: Lyndey today.

The 60s

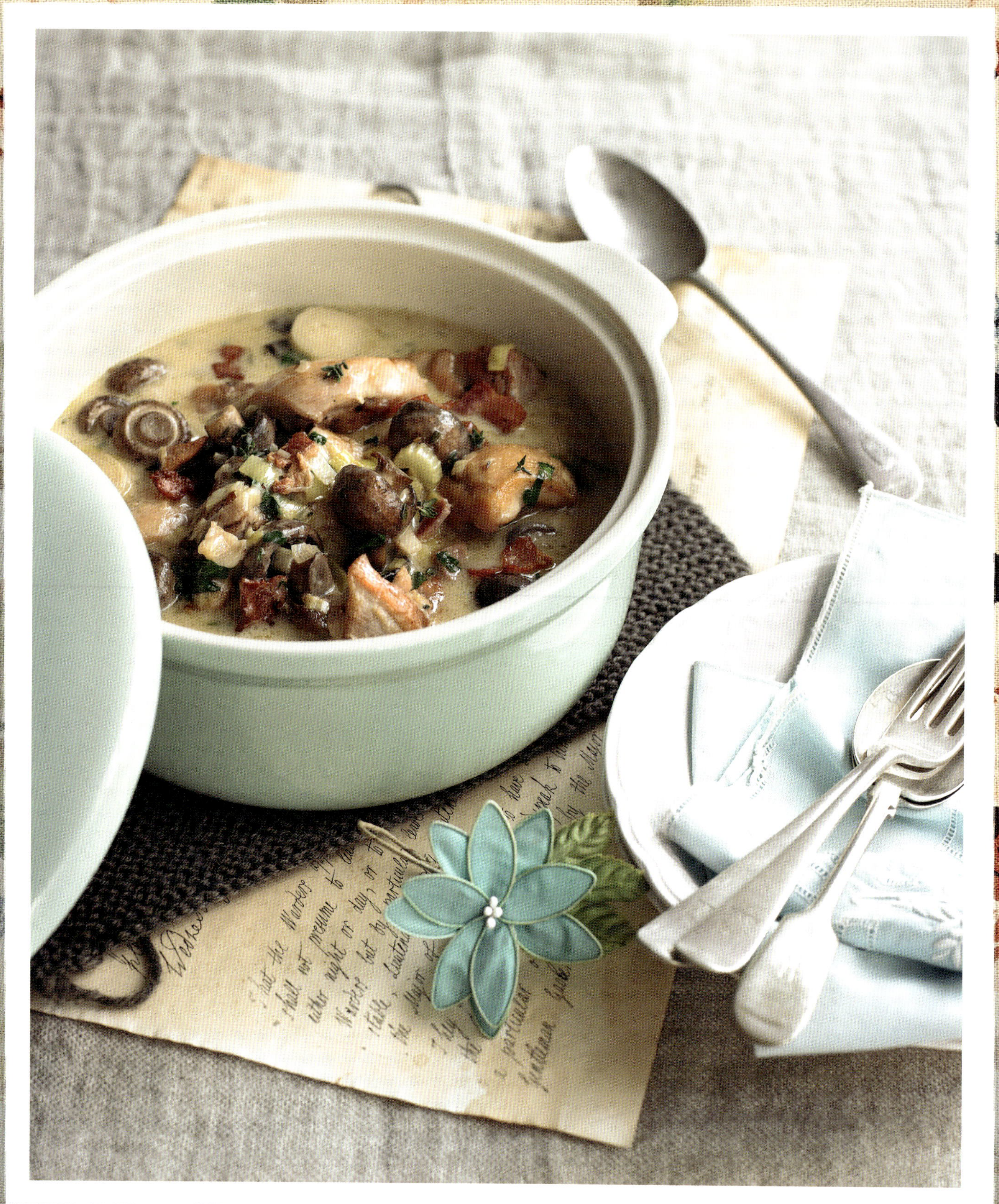

Chicken, mushroom and leek fricassee

2 tablespoons olive oil
1.5kg (3 pounds) chicken thigh fillets, quartered
3 rindless bacon slices (195g), chopped coarsely
40g (1½ ounces) butter
3 medium leeks (1kg), trimmed, sliced thinly
3 stalks celery (450g), trimmed, sliced thinly
3 cloves garlic, crushed
¼ cup loosely packed fresh thyme sprigs
2 bay leaves
2 tablespoons plain (all-purpose) flour
1½ cups (375ml) dry white wine
1½ cups (375ml) chicken stock
400g (12½ ounces) button mushrooms
¼ cup (60ml) pouring cream
½ cup coarsely chopped fresh flat-leaf parsley

1 Preheat oven to 160°C/325°F.
2 Heat oil in large heavy-based flameproof dish; cook chicken, in batches, until browned all over. Remove from pan.
3 Cook bacon in same dish, stirring, until browned lightly.
4 Add butter and leek to dish; cook, stirring occasionally, until leek softens. Stir in celery, garlic, thyme and bay leaves. Stir in flour, then wine and stock; bring to the boil, stirring. Stir in chicken and mushrooms.
5 Transfer dish to oven; cook about 20 minutes or until chicken is cooked through and sauce has thickened slightly.
6 Return dish to stove top, discard bay leaves; stir in cream and parsley. Simmer, uncovered, until heated through.
7 Serve fricassee sprinkled with extra fresh thyme leaves, if you like.

prep + cook time 50 minutes **serves** 6
nutritional count per serving
39.2g total fat (14.6g saturated fat); 2805kJ (671 cal); 8.6g carbohydrate; 59.1g protein; 6.2g fibre

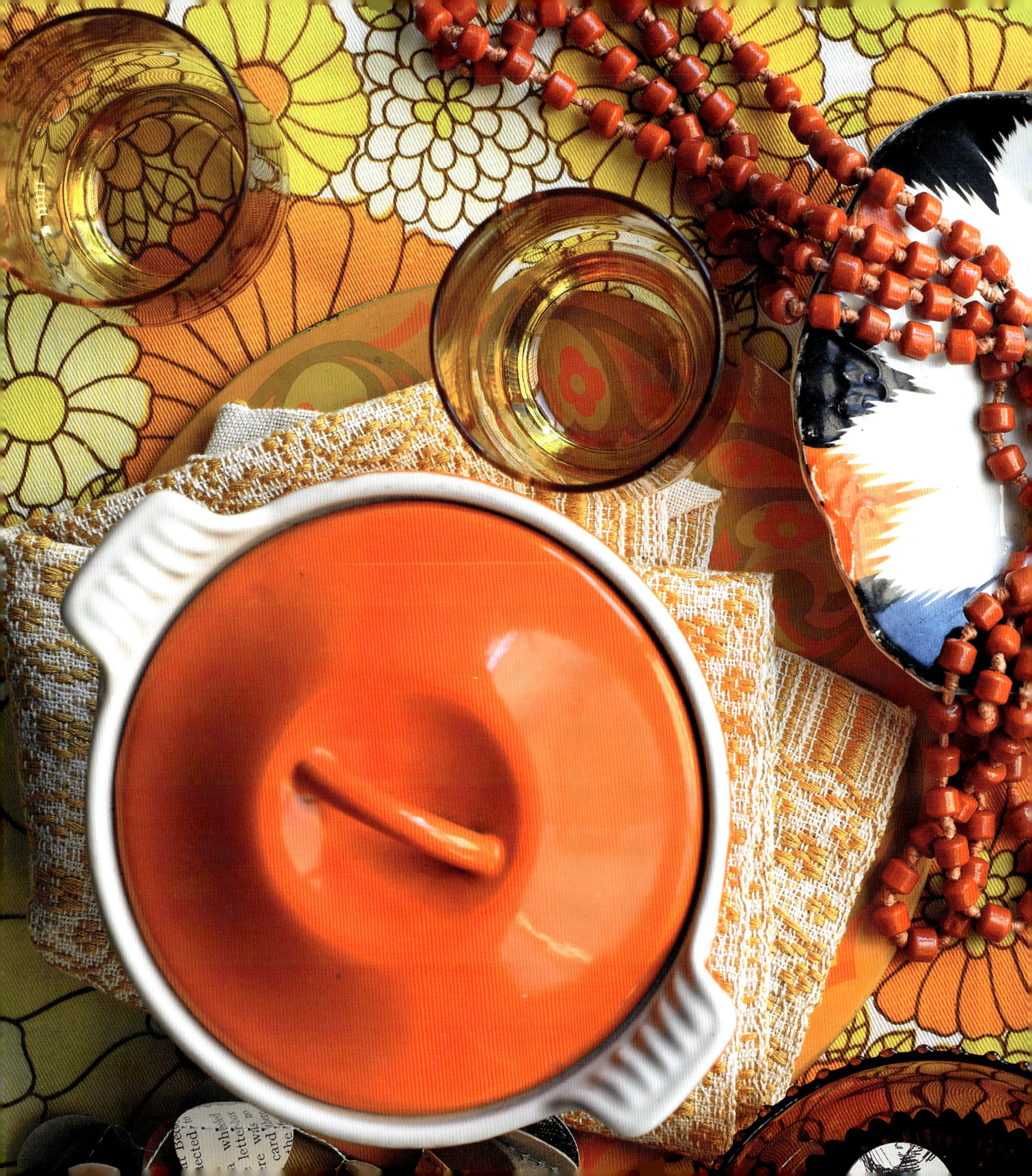

The 70s

Our ultimate dinner party hostesses started to experiment with ingredients. The barbecue cemented its place in Australian folklore and fast food had definitely arrived. Mum snapped up cookbooks and began to serve more exotic dishes to the family.

Tracey Spicer

I grew up in the era of "Cocktail". That was the food culture of Redcliffe, Brisbane. Mum was a classy lady and quite the gourmet, so we did have prawn cocktail, and spaghetti bolognese was also on the rise. I remember many a night having a spag bol. Or, the other big thing – and this was fancy then – was the tuna casserole.

In retrospect, it was basically just a whole bunch of leftovers; pasta, vegetables, tomato sauce, cheesy sauce and a tin of tuna. But it's something I cook for my kids now and in actual fact it's very healthy.

Mum was also into those kitschy 70s canapés, so we had a lot of devils and angels on horseback at parties. She'd come out in a lovely frock with the canapés and Dad would be there searing some meat on the barbie.

Mum was also a terrific baker: she made incredible biscuits, cakes and melting moments. I've still got her melting moments recipe; they were to die for. Eating them is one of my favourite childhood memories. They literally did melt in your mouth.

Another favourite childhood memory is licking the beaters and bowls; it's so nice because it's the kind of thing that I do with my kids now, though I'm a rotten baker! I still bake dreadful hard cakes with my kids, but it's about spending time with them. Sitting there, seeing them lick the beaters, just brings me back to when I was a kid.

Mum passed away 11 years ago but every time I'm cooking something I've forgotten how to do, I literally go and pick up the phone to call her. Those are the times that I miss her the most.

RIGHT: (From left) Tracey enjoys quality time in the kitchen with her kids, Taj (6) and Grace (5).

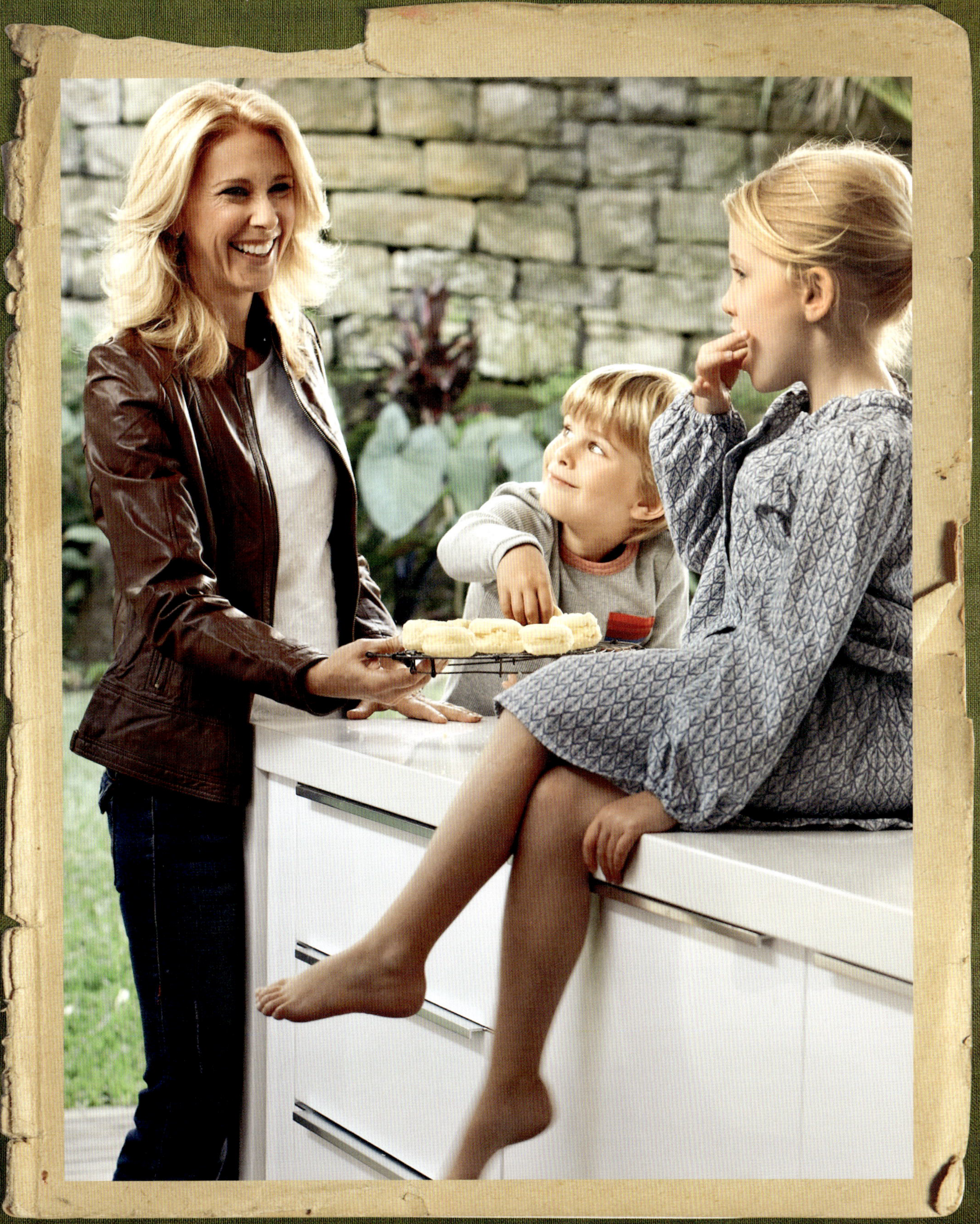

RIGHT: Tracey's Mum, Marcia Spicer, did some modelling from her late teens. "I thought she was so glamorous," said Tracey. Marcia won the Capricornia division of Miss Australia, in the 1960s.

Melting moments

250g (8 ounces) butter, softened
1 teaspoon vanilla extract
½ cup (80g) icing (confectioners') sugar
1½ cups (225g) plain (all-purpose) flour
½ cup (75g) cornflour (cornstarch)
BUTTER CREAM
90g (3 ounces) butter, softened
¾ cup (120g) icing (confectioners') sugar
1 teaspoon finely grated lemon rind
1 teaspoon lemon juice

1 Preheat oven to 160°C/325°F. Line oven trays with baking paper.
2 Beat butter, extract and sifted icing sugar in small bowl with electric mixer until light and fluffy. Transfer mixture to large bowl; stir in sifted flours, in two batches.
3 With floured hands, roll rounded teaspoons of mixture into balls; place about 2.5cm (1 inch) apart on trays. Flatten slightly with a floured fork.
4 Bake biscuits about 15 minutes. Stand biscuits on trays 5 minutes; transfer to wire racks to cool.
5 Meanwhile, make butter cream.
6 Sandwich biscuits with butter cream. Dust with extra sifted icing sugar before serving, if you like.
butter cream Beat butter, sifted icing sugar and rind in small bowl with electric mixer until light and fluffy; beat in juice.

prep + cook time 40 minutes **makes** 25
nutritional count per biscuit 11.3g total fat (7.4g saturated fat); 694kJ (166 cal); 15.6g carbohydrate; 1.1g protein; 0.4g fibre
tip Unfilled biscuits will keep in an airtight container, at room temperature, for up to a week. Filled biscuits will keep for a few days in an airtight container in the fridge.

ABOVE: (From left) Tracey's eight-year-old sister Suzanne, Tracey's Mum and an 11-year-old Tracey in the 70s, "sporting an interesting wingnut hair-style!"

The 70s

Caesar salad

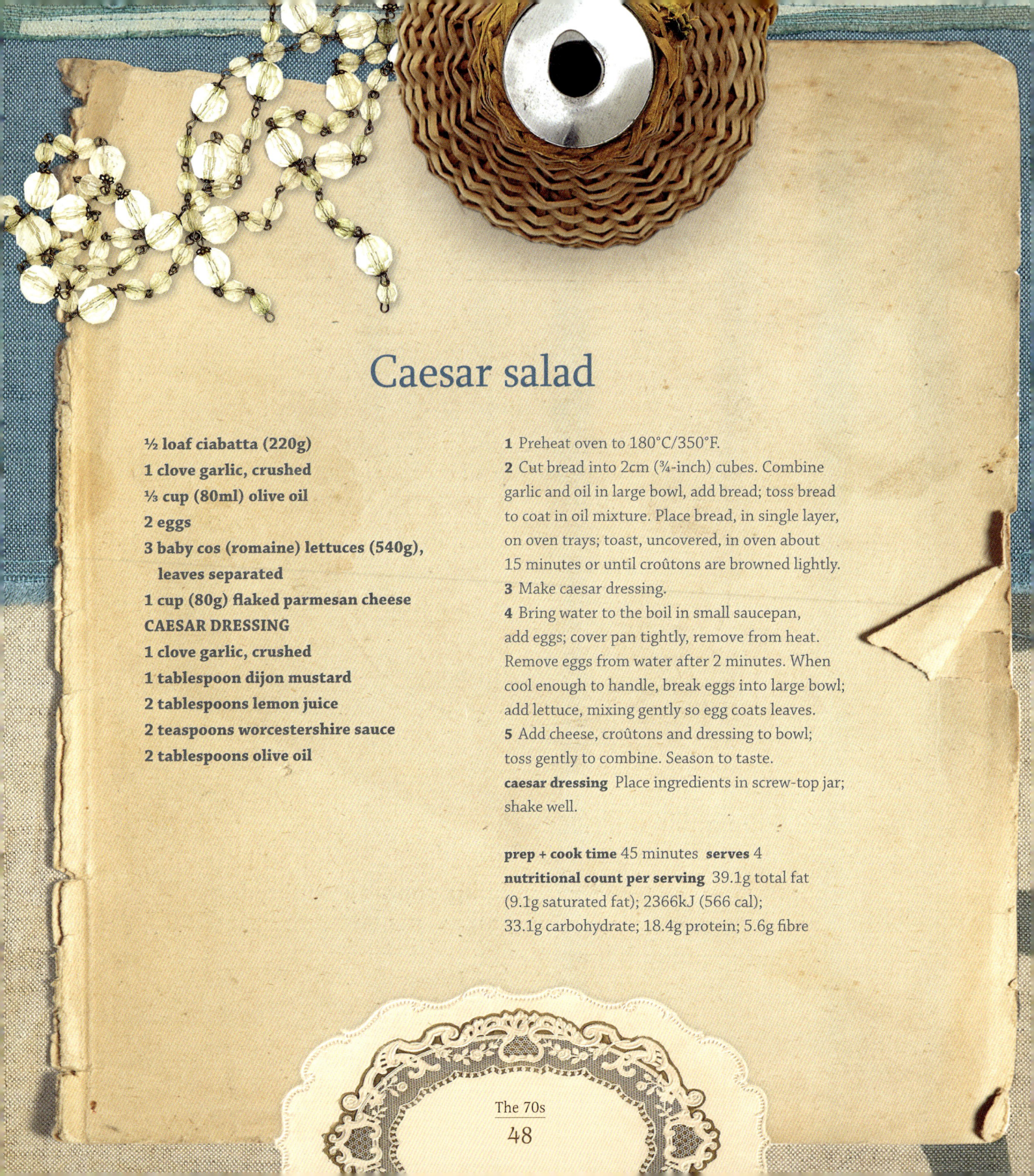

½ loaf ciabatta (220g)
1 clove garlic, crushed
⅓ cup (80ml) olive oil
2 eggs
3 baby cos (romaine) lettuces (540g), leaves separated
1 cup (80g) flaked parmesan cheese
CAESAR DRESSING
1 clove garlic, crushed
1 tablespoon dijon mustard
2 tablespoons lemon juice
2 teaspoons worcestershire sauce
2 tablespoons olive oil

1 Preheat oven to 180°C/350°F.
2 Cut bread into 2cm (¾-inch) cubes. Combine garlic and oil in large bowl, add bread; toss bread to coat in oil mixture. Place bread, in single layer, on oven trays; toast, uncovered, in oven about 15 minutes or until croûtons are browned lightly.
3 Make caesar dressing.
4 Bring water to the boil in small saucepan, add eggs; cover pan tightly, remove from heat. Remove eggs from water after 2 minutes. When cool enough to handle, break eggs into large bowl; add lettuce, mixing gently so egg coats leaves.
5 Add cheese, croûtons and dressing to bowl; toss gently to combine. Season to taste.
caesar dressing Place ingredients in screw-top jar; shake well.

prep + cook time 45 minutes **serves** 4
nutritional count per serving 39.1g total fat (9.1g saturated fat); 2366kJ (566 cal); 33.1g carbohydrate; 18.4g protein; 5.6g fibre

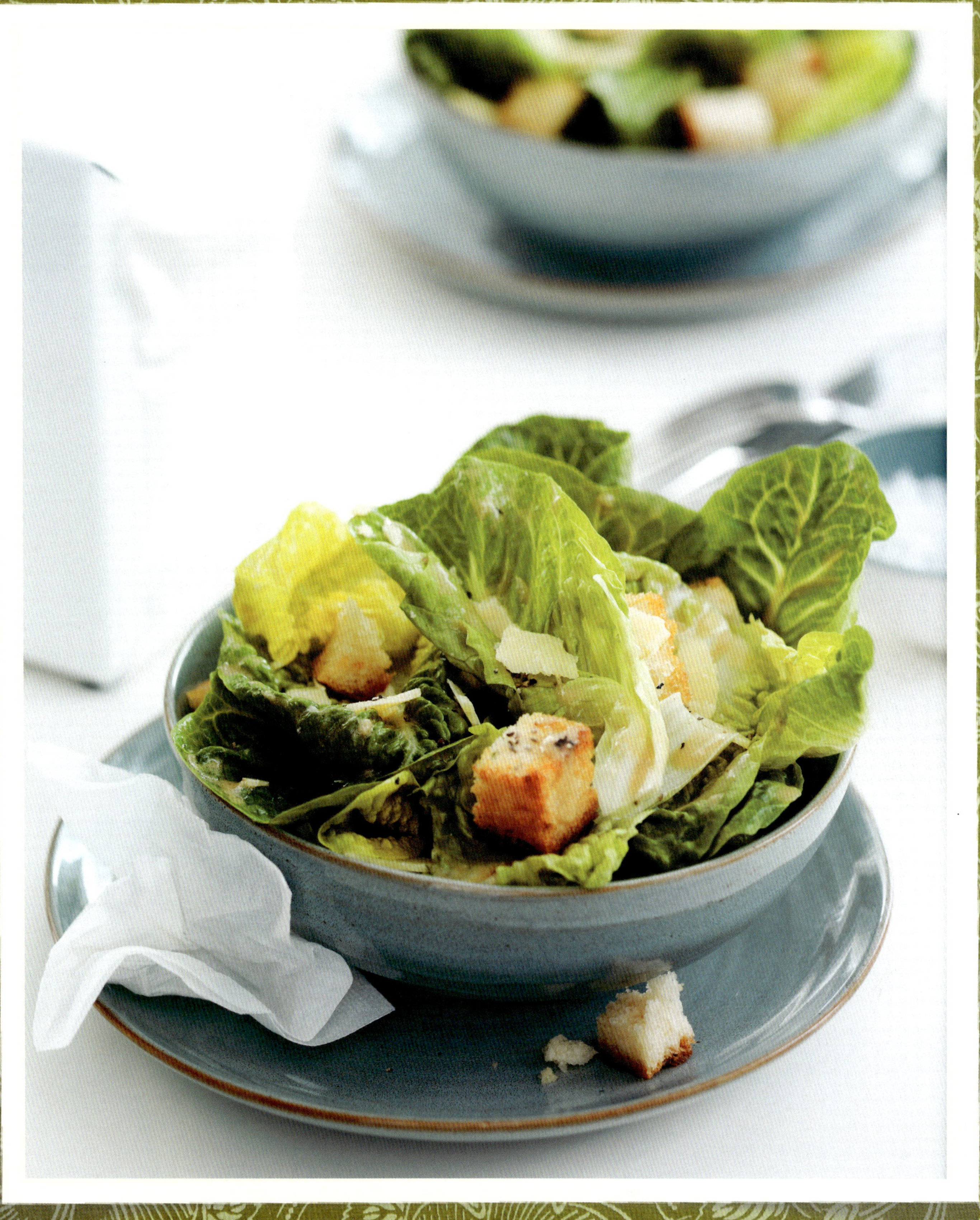

Tuna mornay

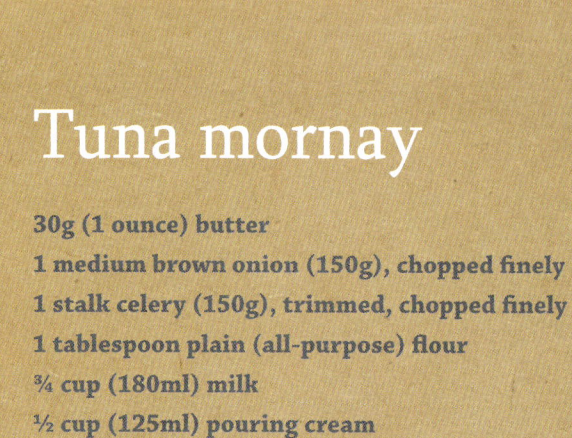

30g (1 ounce) butter
1 medium brown onion (150g), chopped finely
1 stalk celery (150g), trimmed, chopped finely
1 tablespoon plain (all-purpose) flour
¾ cup (180ml) milk
½ cup (125ml) pouring cream
⅓ cup (40g) grated cheddar cheese
130g (4 ounces) canned corn kernels, drained
2 x 185g (6 ounces) canned tuna, drained
1 cup (70g) stale breadcrumbs
¼ cup (30g) grated cheddar cheese, extra

1 Preheat oven to 180°C/350°F.
2 Melt butter in medium saucepan; cook onion and celery, stirring, until onion is soft. Add flour; cook, stirring, 1 minute. Gradually stir in combined milk and cream; cook, stirring, until mixture boils and thickens. Remove pan from heat, add cheese, corn and tuna; stir until cheese is melted.
3 Spoon mornay mixture into four 1½-cup (375ml) ovenproof dishes. Sprinkle with combined breadcrumbs and extra cheese.
4 Bake mornay about 15 minutes or until heated through.

prep + cook time 35 minutes **serves** 4
nutritional count per serving 30.2g total fat (18.8g saturated fat); 2031kJ (486 cal); 23.4g carbohydrate; 29.3g protein; 2.5g fibre

Beef bourguignon

300g (9½ ounces) baby brown onions
2 tablespoons olive oil
2kg (4 pounds) gravy beef, trimmed, chopped coarsely
30g (1 ounce) butter
4 rindless bacon slices (260g), chopped coarsely
400g (12½ ounces) button mushrooms, halved
2 cloves garlic, crushed
¼ cup (35g) plain (all-purpose) flour
1¼ cups (310ml) beef stock
2½ cups (625ml) dry red wine
2 bay leaves
2 sprigs fresh thyme
½ cup coarsely chopped fresh flat-leaf parsley

1 Peel onions, leaving root end intact so onion remains whole during cooking.
2 Heat oil in large flameproof dish; cook beef, in batches, until browned. Remove beef from dish.
3 Add butter to same dish; cook onions, bacon, mushrooms and garlic, stirring, until onions are browned lightly.
4 Sprinkle flour over onion mixture; cook, stirring, until flour mixture thickens and bubbles. Gradually add stock and wine; stir over heat until mixture boils and thickens.
5 Return beef and any juices to dish, add bay leaves and thyme; bring to the boil. Reduce heat; simmer, covered, 2 hours or until beef is tender, stirring every 30 minutes.
6 Remove dish from heat; discard bay leaves. Serve beef bourguignon sprinkled with parsley.

prep + cook time 2 hours 45 minutes **serves** 6
nutritional count per serving 31.4g total fat (12.1g saturated fat); 2658kJ (636 cal); 6.6g carbohydrate; 80.3g protein; 2.8g fibre

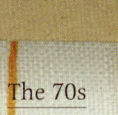

The 70s

Flour, Teas, Molasses, Spices, Tobacco, Butter, Cheese,

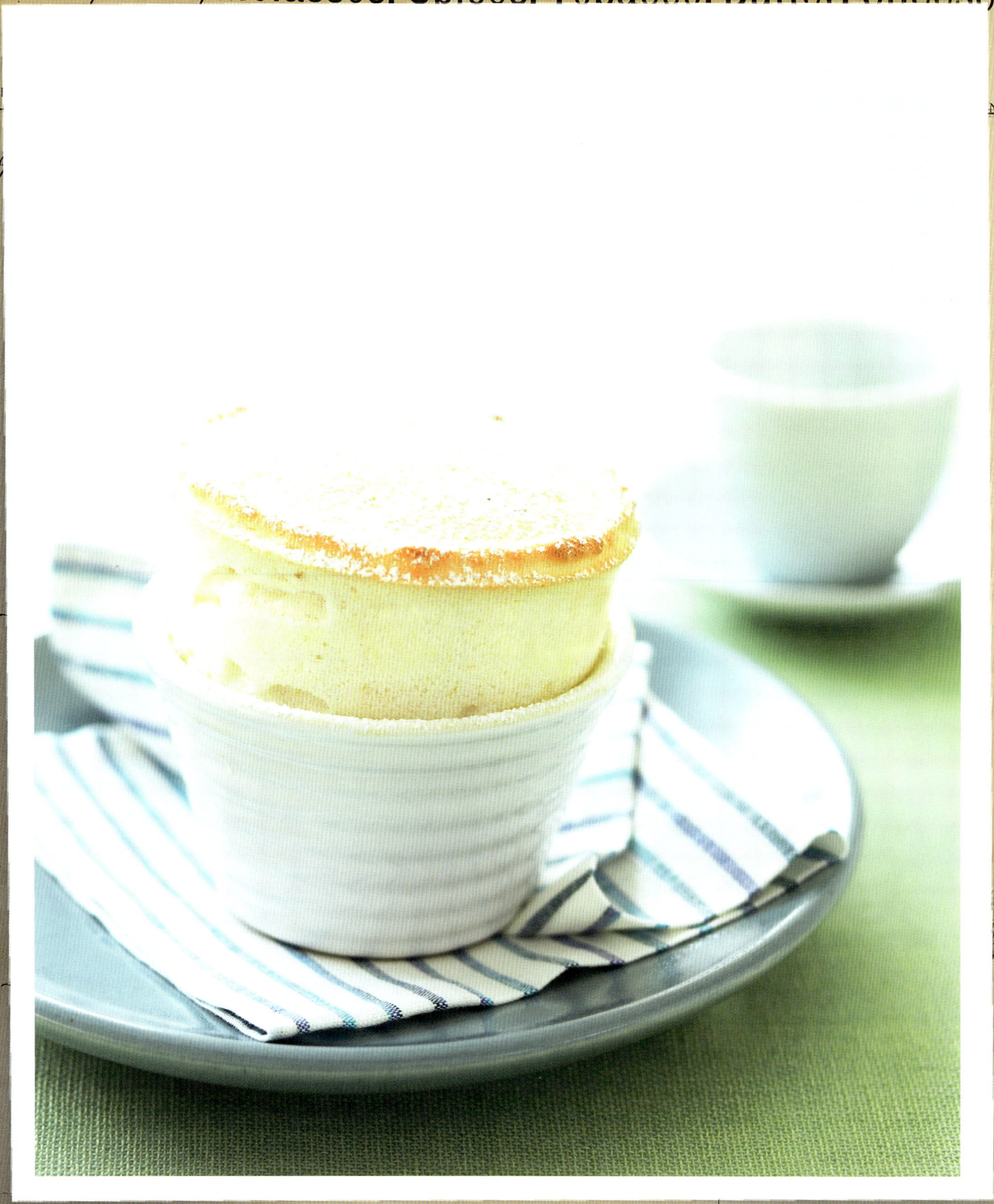

Apricot and honey soufflés

¼ cup (55g) caster (superfine) sugar
4 fresh medium apricots (200g)
¼ cup (60ml) water
2 tablespoons honey
4 egg whites
1 tablespoon icing (confectioners') sugar

1 Preheat oven to 180°C/350°F. Grease six ¾-cup (180ml) soufflé dishes. Sprinkle inside of dishes with a little of the caster sugar; shake away excess. Place dishes on oven tray.
2 Place apricots in small heatproof bowl, cover with boiling water; stand 2 minutes. Drain; cool 5 minutes. Peel and seed apricots; chop flesh finely.
3 Place apricots in small saucepan with remaining caster sugar, the water and honey; bring to the boil. Reduce heat; simmer, uncovered, about 10 minutes or until apricots softens to a jam-like consistency.
4 Beat egg whites in small bowl with electric mixer until soft peaks form. With motor operating, gradually add hot apricot mixture, beating until just combined. Spoon mixture into dishes.
5 Bake soufflés 15 minutes. Serve immediately, dusted with icing sugar.

prep + cook time 35 minutes **serves** 6
nutritional count per serving 0.1g total fat (0g saturated fat); 397kJ (95 cal); 21.3g carbohydrate; 2.6g protein; 0.6g fibre

512 - VENEZIA - RIO DELL'ABBAZIA

Italian

Food and family are undeniably intertwined in Italian culture. Start cooking and the family will come – invite the family and a feast will be prepared. Simple, humble ingredients are cooked with passion by Italian mums who respect tradition.

Armando Percuoco

Some of my earliest memories were at home in the kitchen with my Mother. The kitchen is the centre of most homes and in our Italian family, Mum always cooked all the time. There was no such thing as takeaway food back then. Food was very important to me growing up for the simple reason that my family was in the restaurant business.

Our family had seven generations in the kitchen. I remember being very little and sitting at the table with Mum, Dad and cousins who were all talking about food and customers.

My generation also lived through the war, so I grew up with Mum and Dad, as well as all the families in Italy having suffered. Whether you had money or not, everybody suffered because there was no food. So after the war, food was extremely important in the minds of everyone. I remember Mum and Dad telling me, "You eat everything, because there are millions of people who don't have anything. Finish what's on your plate!" I like the taste of all foods now because my mother forced me to eat everything or otherwise we starved.

I watched my Mum do lots of things in the kitchen because there was no TV then. So we were always there around her and smelled and tasted a lot more because of it. I remember with a dish like scaloppine alla pizzaiola, Mum would fry the garlic in oil followed by a little tomato, then add the veal and then the oregano. At the end of summer too, I'd help my Mother bottle tomatoes in a 44-gallon drum with bricks and fire underneath it. And those were the tomatoes for winter.

RIGHT: Armando and family (from left): granddaughter, Freya; Armando's partner, Gemma Cunningham; grandson, Dante; (standing) eldest son, Mario; Armando; son, Sascha; grandson, Christian; daughter-in-law, Katina.

CITTA DEL VATICANO
Basilica di S. Pietro
Die Hlg. Peterskirche
512 - VENEZIA - RIO DELL'ABBAZIA

Pasta Fagioli
(Pasta with beans)

100g (3½ ounces) dried cannellini beans
2 medium onions (300g), chopped coarsely
1 medium carrot (120g), chopped coarsely
1 stalk celery (150g), trimmed, chopped coarsely
2 tablespoon olive oil
1 medium tomato (150g), chopped coarsely
2 cloves garlic, peeled
200g (6½ ounces) tubetti pasta
45g (1½ ounces) freshly grated parmesan cheese
1 tablespoon finely chopped fresh flat-leaf parsley

1 Soak beans in saucepan of water about 6 hours.
2 Drain beans, replace the water; bring to the boil. Reduce heat; simmer about 45 minutes or until beans are soft. Drain; reserve cooking liquid.
3 Heat oil in large saucepan; cook onion, stirring, about 10 minutes. Add carrot and celery; cook, stirring, 5 minutes. Add beans, tomato and garlic; cook, stirring, 2 minutes. Add 1 cup of the reserved cooking liquid; bring to the boil. Remove pan from heat. Discard garlic.
4 Meanwhile, cook pasta in large saucepan salted boiling water about 5 minutes. Drain.
5 Add pasta to soup. Return pan to heat; simmer 3 minutes. (If it seems too dry, add another cup of reserved cooking liquid.) Season to taste.
6 Serve sprinkled with cheese and parsley, drizzle with a little extra virgin olive oil, if you like.

prep + cook time 1 hour 35 minutes (+ standing)
serves 4
nutritional count per serving 14.2g total fat (3.8g saturated fat); 1733kJ (414 cal); 50.2g carbohydrate; 7.7g protein; 8.5g fibre

ABOVE: (From left) Armando's sons, Mario and Sascha with Armando.
RIGHT: Baby Armando, held by his Mother at his christening in Naples, Italy in 1946.

Italian
59

Spaghetti with clams

1kg (2 pounds) clams
¼ cup (60ml) dry white wine
500g (1 pound) spaghetti
½ cup (125ml) extra virgin olive oil
2 cloves garlic, crushed
2 fresh medium red chillies, chopped
½ cup coarsely chopped fresh flat-leaf parsley

1 Rinse clams. Place in large bowl of cold water; stand 1 hour. Drain.
2 Bring wine to the boil in large saucepan. Add clams to pan; simmer, covered, until shells open. Remove clams from pan; cover to keep warm. Strain cooking liquid through a fine sieve into a jug; reserve ½ cup of the liquid.
3 Meanwhile, cook spaghetti in large saucepan of boiling water until tender; drain. Return spaghetti to pan.
4 Heat oil in large frying pan; cook garlic and chilli, stirring, until fragrant.
5 Add clams to spaghetti with oil mixture, parsley and enough of the reserved cooking liquid to moisten; toss gently to combine.

prep + cook time 30 minutes (+ standing) **serves** 4
nutritional count per serving 14.4g total fat (2.1g saturated fat); 1455kJ (348 cal); 41.2g carbohydrate; 11g protein; 2.3g fibre

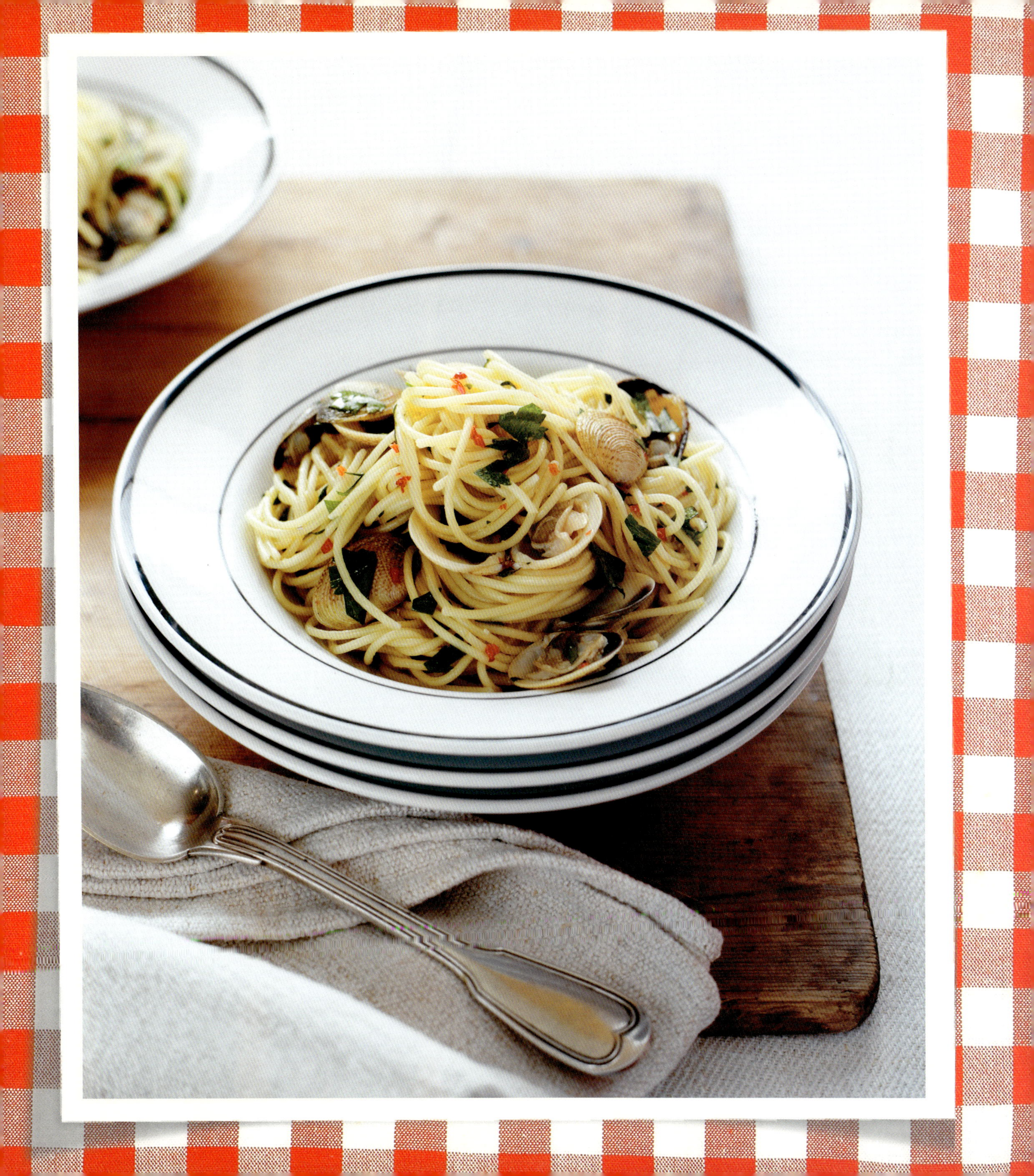

Isabella & Sofia Bliss

Cooking is a big party for our family. We'd make pasta and pizza with Mum, Nonna and Zie (our Aunties) and they would show us things like cleaning fish. Every Christmas we make maccaruni, a Sicilian pasta. It takes time, but has a beautiful meat sauce. We all pinch and roll the maccaruni, talking and laughing.

Mum's pizza recipe is our favourite. We love the smell of fresh pizza dough, rising out of the pot like an alien life form. Paste di mandorla is our favourite sweet. Mum makes these with almond meal and they look very cute when they are dusted with icing sugar. We share them in traditional boxes from Sicily and love how you can shape them into little pears. Nonna makes the traditional falsomagro in sugo or sauce and it always tastes so good. We also enjoy learning about our Italian heritage and food traditions.

RIGHT: (From left) Three-year-old twins Sofia and Isabella would stand on stools to reach the kitchen bench.

ABOVE: (From left) Isabella and Sofia wearing diamantes.

Adriano Zumbo

Growing up with Italian heritage and a family supermarket, food was very important in our house. I only spent a little bit of time in the kitchen with mum as a child as I was always off playing sports or out with friends — and trying to avoid being lectured. But I have great memories of it, including mostly being chased around with a wooden spoon! My earliest memory in the kitchen is making chicken Rice a Riso in the microwave.

It was always the same traditional Italian dishes in our house; meatballs, gnocchi, crumbed chicken, seafood, trifle, ravioli and involtini. My favourite recipe of Mum's though was her meatballs and involtini and she was the one who taught me to add a splash of sherry when frying meatballs.

LEFT (TOP): Adriano and his Mother, Annunziata Zumbo today.
LEFT: A ten-year-old Adriano poses with his Mum.

Italian

Meatballs napoletana

500g (1 pound) minced (ground) beef
1 egg
½ cup (50g) packaged breadcrumbs
¼ cup (20g) finely grated parmesan cheese
¼ cup finely chopped fresh flat-leaf parsley
2 tablespoons olive oil
1 small brown onion (80g), chopped finely
1 clove garlic, crushed
2½ cups (625ml) bottled tomato pasta sauce
½ cup (60g) frozen peas
¼ cup coarsely chopped fresh basil

1 Combine beef, egg, breadcrumbs, cheese and parsley in medium bowl. Using wet hands, roll level tablespoons of beef mixture into balls.
2 Heat half the oil in large frying pan; cook meatballs, in batches, until browned and cooked through. Remove from pan.
3 Heat remaining oil in same pan; cook onion and garlic, stirring, until onion softens. Add sauce; bring to the boil. Add meatballs, reduce heat; simmer, uncovered, about 10 minutes or until sauce thickens slightly. Add peas and basil; simmer, uncovered, until peas are tender.
4 Serve meatballs and sauce with crusty bread, if you like.

prep + cook time 1 hour **makes** 26
nutritional count per meatball 3.9g total fat (1.2g saturated fat); 305kJ (73 cal); 4.1g carbohydrate; 4.9g protein; 0.8g fibre

Italian

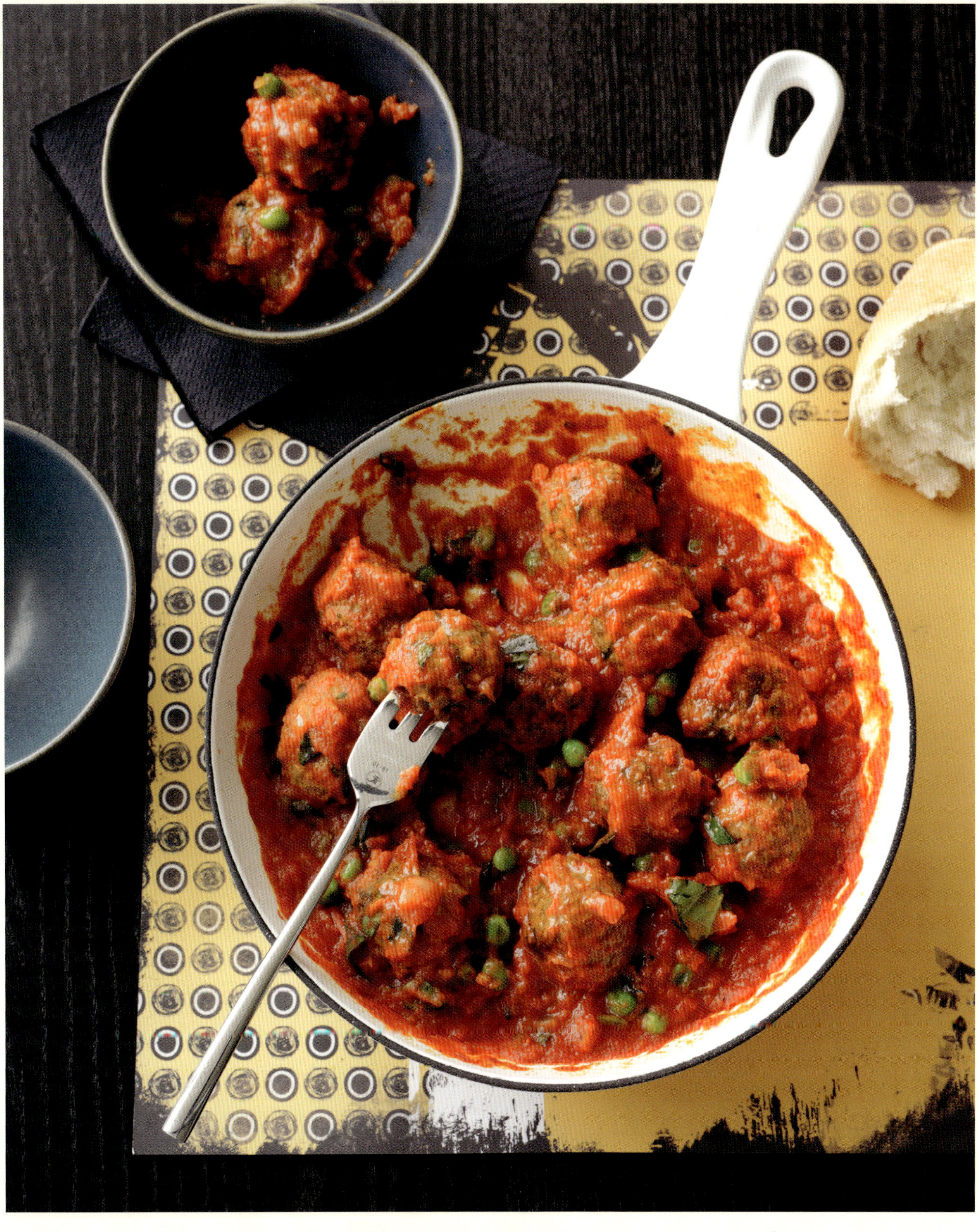

Wild mushroom risotto

15g (½ ounce) dried chanterelle mushrooms
15g (½ ounce) dried porcini mushrooms
1 litre (4 cups) chicken or vegetable stock
2 cups (500ml) water
50g (2 ounces) butter
125g (4 ounces) chestnut mushrooms, trimmed
125g (4 ounces) button mushrooms, sliced thickly
2 flat mushrooms (160g), halved, sliced thickly
4 shallots (100g), chopped finely
2 cloves garlic, crushed
2 cups (400g) arborio rice
½ cup (125ml) dry white wine
½ cup (40g) finely grated parmesan cheese
2 tablespoons finely chopped fresh chives

1 Bring chanterelle and porcini mushrooms, stock and the water to the boil in medium saucepan. Reduce heat; simmer, covered.
2 Meanwhile, melt 30g (1 ounce) of the butter in large saucepan, add remaining mushrooms; cook, stirring, until mushrooms are tender and liquid evaporates. Remove from pan.
3 Melt remaining butter in same pan; cook shallots and garlic, stirring, until shallots soften. Add rice; stir to coat rice in butter mixture. Return mushrooms cooked in butter to pan with wine; bring to the boil. Reduce heat; simmer, uncovered, until liquid has almost evaporated. Add 1 cup simmering mushroom stock mixture; cook, stirring, over low heat, until stock is absorbed. Continue adding stock mixture, in 1-cup batches, stirring, until absorbed between additions. Total cooking time should be about 25 minutes or until rice is tender. Stir in cheese and chives.

prep + cook time 40 minutes **serves** 4
nutritional count per serving 15.4g total fat (9.4g saturated fat); 2391kJ (572 cal); 82.2g carbohydrate; 17.9g protein; 4.4g fibre

Italian ricotta cheesecake

90g (3 ounces) butter, softened
¼ cup (55g) caster (superfine) sugar
1 egg
1¼ cups (185g) plain (all-purpose) flour
¼ cup (35g) self-raising flour
FILLING
1kg (2 pounds) ricotta cheese
1 tablespoon finely grated lemon rind
¼ cup (60ml) lemon juice
1 cup (220g) caster (superfine) sugar
5 eggs
¼ cup (40g) sultanas
¼ cup (80g) finely chopped glacé fruit salad

1 Beat butter, sugar and egg in small bowl with electric mixer until combined. Stir in half the sifted flours; then work in remaining flour with your hand. Knead pastry on floured surface until smooth. Wrap in plastic; refrigerate 30 minutes.
2 Grease 28cm (11¼-inch) springform tin. Press pastry over base of tin; prick with fork. Place on oven tray; refrigerate another 30 minutes.
3 Preheat oven to 200°C/400°F.
4 Line pastry with baking paper, fill with dried beans or rice; bake 10 minutes. Remove paper and beans; bake 15 minutes or until browned lightly. Cool.
5 Reduce oven to 160°C/325°F.
6 Make filling by processing cheese, rind, juice, sugar and eggs until smooth. Stir in sultanas and glacé fruit. Pour filling into tin.
7 Bake cheesecake about 50 minutes. Cool in oven with door ajar. Refrigerate cheesecake 3 hours or overnight. Serve dusted with sifted icing sugar, if you like.

prep + cook time 1 hour 35 minutes (+ refrigeration)
serves 16
nutritional count per serving
13.8g total fat (8.2g saturated fat); 1262kJ (302 cal); 33.2g carbohydrate; 10.7g protein; 0.7g fibre

ΜΑΣΤΙΧΑ
670 ml
PRODUCT OF GREECE · PRODUCED AND BOTTLED
BY KALOYANNIS BROS. LTD. ATHENS, GREECE
15
POSTES
RF

Greek

Food is central to the relaxed, social Greek way of life – it's an experience to be shared with family and friends. With ingredients such as olive oil, meats, cheeses and vegetables, it's no wonder dishes like dolmades and moussaka are on tables the world over.

George Houvardas

Mum was always cooking. Having three boys in the family, there was always plenty of food going around. The good old stuffed vine leaves or even lamb on the spit is probably my earliest memory. Because Mum was always working and we were all very independent, we learned to cook early – you know, slap a steak on or make spaghetti bolognese. Being into restaurants too, we all love our good portions of food.

Mum had us three boys and even when I come home now, she's always cooking something. At least one of us is always popping in at home at any time. I've been in restaurants since I was 13 and at the moment I'm the barista king. I can't see myself becoming a chef, but definitely running a restaurant and dealing with suppliers.

Being from Greek heritage we always enjoy having our big family dinners and Greek food is very hands-on. We love our stuffed vine leaves and nice roast lamb. One of my earliest memories would be me making stuffed vine leaves with Mum; it's a very child-friendly meal, although it took me a long time to make them perfectly. It was either stuffed vine leaves or the good old Greek-style casserole with beans, carrots, vegies, tomato sauce, fresh tomato, stock, lamb and beef.

One of the best cooking tips Mum ever gave me was how to finish pasta. We call it burning the olive oil. Once you have cooked the pasta, take it out of the pot and put the same pot back on the hot plate. Throw in some olive oil and unsalted butter, let it simmer and just as the bubbles are dying down, throw the pasta back in. It gives the pasta a really nice flavour. It's a simple trick, but works so well.

RIGHT: George and his Mum, Annette Houvardas.

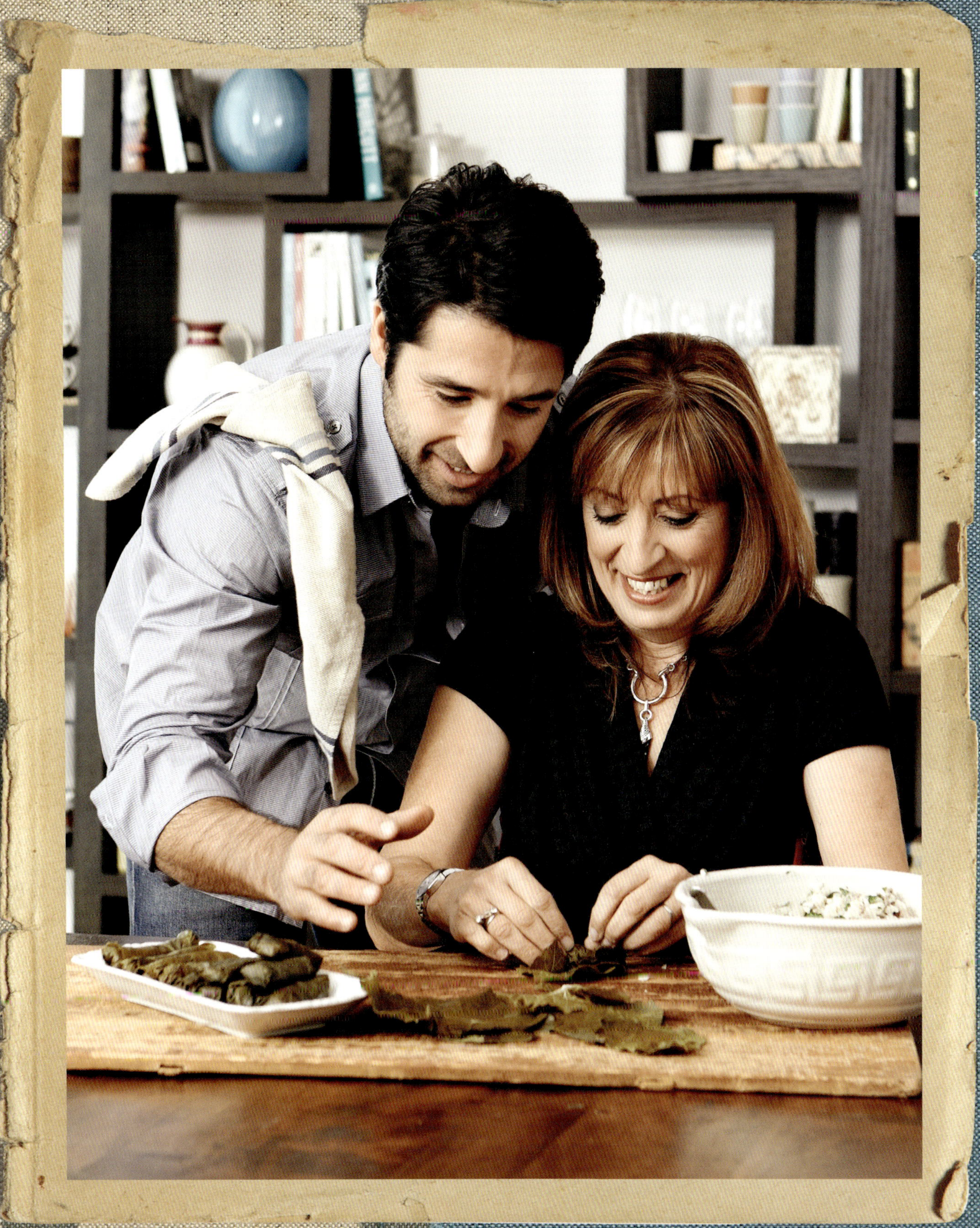

Preserved vine leaves are packed in brine so should be rinsed and dried before use. Fresh leaves should be softened in boiling water for a minute until pliable, then dried.

RIGHT: (From left) George's big brother Steve, birthday boy, George, and Mum Annette Houvardas.

Dolmades (Stuffed vine leaves)

2 tablespoons olive oil
2 medium brown onions (300g), chopped finely
155g (5 ounces) lean minced (ground) lamb
¾ cup (150g) white long-grain rice
2 tablespoons pine nuts
½ cup finely chopped fresh flat-leaf parsley
2 tablespoons each finely chopped fresh dill and mint
¼ cup (60ml) lemon juice
2 cups (500ml) water
500g (1 pound) preserved vine leaves
¾ cup (200g) yogurt

1 Heat oil in large saucepan; cook onion, stirring, until softened. Add lamb; cook, stirring, until browned. Stir in rice and pine nuts. Add herbs, 2 tablespoons of the juice and half the water; bring to the boil. Reduce heat; simmer, covered, 10 minutes or until water is absorbed and rice is partially cooked. Cool.
2 Rinse vine leaves in cold water. Drop leaves into a large saucepan of boiling water, in batches, for a few seconds, transfer to colander; rinse under cold water, drain well.
3 Place a vine leaf, smooth-side down on bench, trim large stem. Place a heaped teaspoon of rice mixture in centre. Fold stem end and sides over filling, roll up firmly. Line medium heavy-based saucepan with a few vine leaves; place rolls, close together, seam-side down, on leaves.
4 Add the remaining water; cover rolls with any remaining leaves. Place a plate on top of leaves to weigh down rolls. Cover pan tightly, bring to the boil. Reduce heat; simmer, over very low heat, 1½ hours. Remove from heat; stand, covered, about 2 hours or until liquid has been absorbed.
5 Combine yogurt and remaining juice.
6 Serve dolmades with yogurt mixture.

prep + cook time 3 hours (+ standing)
serves 10
nutritional count per serving
7.6g total fat (1.6g saturated fat); 690kJ (165 cal); 14.9g carbohydrate; 7.7g protein; 3.2g fibre

ABOVE: "After almost 16 years in the hospitality industry, here I am working (or rather posing!) at one of our past restaurants, Spitlers Waterfront, Mosman," explains George.

Greek

Greek salad

¼ cup (60ml) olive oil
1 tablespoon lemon juice
1 tablespoon white wine vinegar
1 tablespoon finely chopped fresh oregano
1 clove garlic, crushed
3 medium tomatoes (450g), cut into wedges
2 lebanese cucumbers (260g), chopped coarsely
200g (6½ ounces) fetta cheese, chopped coarsely
1 small red capsicum (bell pepper) (150g), sliced thinly
1 small red onion (100g), sliced thinly
½ cup (75g) seeded black olives

1 Place oil, juice, vinegar, oregano and garlic in screw-top jar; shake well.
2 Place tomato, cucumber and remaining ingredients in large bowl with dressing; toss gently to combine.

prep time 20 minutes **serves** 4
nutritional count per serving 25.8g total fat (9.6g saturated fat); 1359kJ (325 cal); 10.8g carbohydrate; 11.5g protein; 3.2g fibre

Greek
74

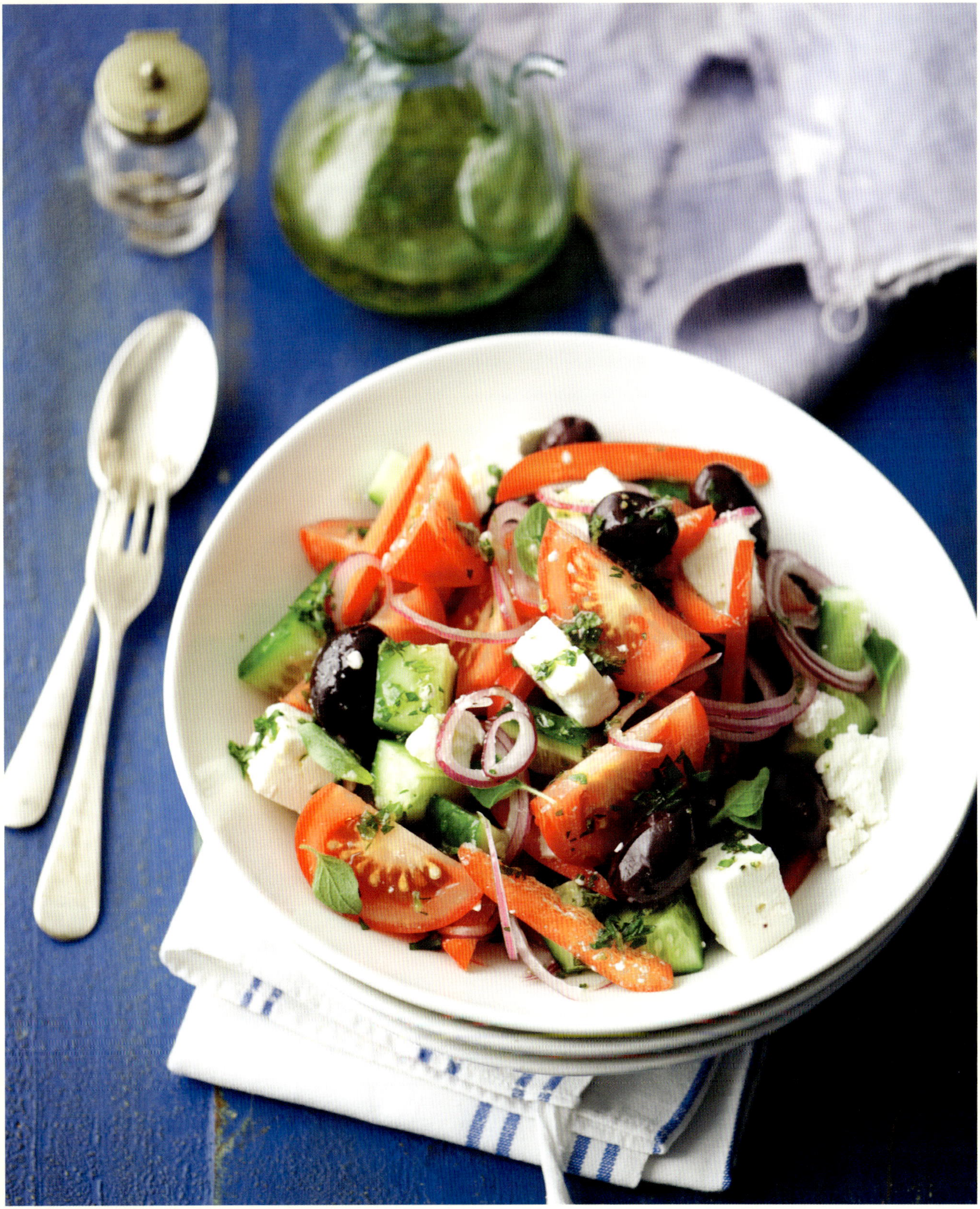

Mary Coustas

For the Greeks, food provides a way of socialising, sharing, expressing and being creative. It's such a universal language. My Grandmother always had a spare plate for somebody who didn't have anything to eat. It was a way of showing your love and a sense of community, which Greeks are big on. We had a very social household and always had people over.

If my Mother was sent to a deserted island, the first thing she'd take is the sink! She was always in the kitchen and it was the place my Dad would come to as soon as he got home from work, to see what we were having for dinner. It was her way of giving back to him.

On Sunday, Mum would make Greek donuts – Loukoumades – as a treat. You eat them with honey syrup and crushed walnuts and we always looked forward to them.

I spent a lot of time in the kitchen watching Mum and I think it made me a paranoid cook, because I felt like I couldn't quite live up to her talent.

Mum didn't work off a recipe much. When I ask her how long something stays in the oven for, she'll always say, "I don't know". "Well is it 10 minutes or is it an hour and a half?" I ask and she will reply, "when it's ready, it's done."

The part of Greece that we are from is known for beans. Not green beans, but lima beans. My mother does this fantastic side dish and it's a bean bake. It's really big flat beans done with tomato, capsicum and onion. Some people have it for lunch on the side and some people have it on toast.

RIGHT: Mary with her Mum, Fani Coustas.

Freybourg
MONACO
VIENNA
Stokach
BUDA
Lucerna
Alessand
BOSNIA
Utovo
Ragusa
Bocche di
Monopoli
Sassari

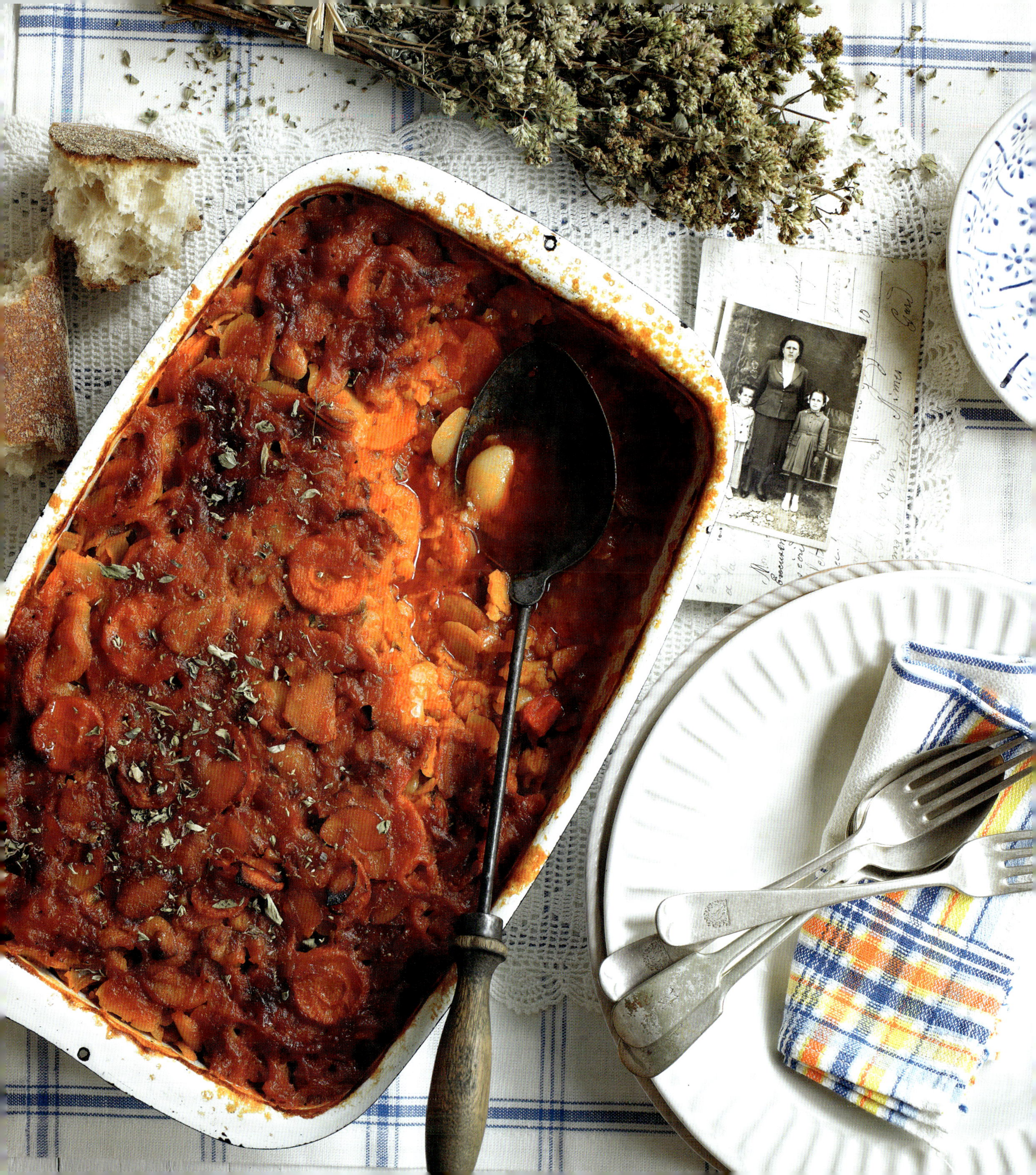

Tradition is something that Greeks celebrate wholeheartedly. So much of how we socialise is based around comforting traditions that we have grown up with. That, married with the Australian influence, makes for something pretty unique and at times culturally schizophrenic. The evil eye is worn to protect from negative energy and to look good of course, which is almost as important.

Baked lima beans

2¾ cups (520g) dried lima beans
½ medium red capsicum (bell pepper) (100g), diced
2 stalks celery (300g), trimmed, diced
1 medium carrot (120g), sliced thinly
2 medium brown onions (300g), sliced thinly
1 cup (250ml) extra virgin olive oil
1.5 litres (6 cups) water
½ cup (140g) tomato paste
1 cup (280g) tomato puree
1 tablespoon dried oregano
1 tablespoon caster (superfine) sugar
2 chicken stock cubes

1 Wash beans well under cold water; drain. Place beans in large saucepan with about 2 litres (8 cups) of cold water; bring to the boil. Boil, uncovered, 10 minutes. Drain beans; rinse under cold water two or three times. Discard skins that float to the surface; peel away any skins remaining.
2 Combine beans, capsicum, celery, carrot, onions, oil and the water in large saucepan; bring to the boil. Reduce heat. Add tomato paste, tomato puree, oregano, sugar and stock cubes; simmer, uncovered, stirring occasionally, about 35 minutes or until beans are tender. Season to taste.
3 Meanwhile, preheat oven to 200°C/400°F.
4 Transfer bean mixture to large baking dish; cook, in oven, uncovered, 1 hour. Sprinkle with a little extra dried oregano.

prep + cook time 2 hours 15 minutes **serves** 6
nutritional count per serving 40.1g total fat (5.6g saturated fat); 2744kJ (656 cal); 46.5g carbohydrate; 21.8g protein; 19.8g fibre

ABOVE: "My Mother left Greece at 18. She went back, married with two children, a year after this picture was taken of me as a six year old, with Mum in Collingwood, Victoria," tells Mary.

Spanakopita

1.5kg (3 pounds) silver beet (swiss chard), trimmed
1 tablespoon olive oil
1 medium brown onion (150g), chopped finely
2 cloves garlic, crushed
1 teaspoon ground nutmeg
200g (6½ ounces) fetta cheese, crumbled
1 tablespoon finely grated lemon rind
¼ cup each coarsely chopped fresh mint, fresh flat-leaf parsley and fresh dill
4 green onions (scallions), chopped finely
16 sheets fillo pastry
125g (4 ounces) butter, melted
2 teaspoons sesame seeds

1 Boil, steam or microwave silver beet until just wilted; drain. Squeeze out excess moisture; drain on absorbent paper. Chop silver beet coarsely; spread out on absorbent paper.
2 Heat oil in small frying pan; cook brown onion and garlic, stirring, until onion is soft. Add nutmeg; cook, stirring, until fragrant. Combine onion mixture and silver beet in large bowl with fetta, rind, herbs and green onion.
3 Preheat oven to 180°C/350°F. Oil oven trays.
4 Brush 1 sheet of pastry with some of the butter; fold lengthways into thirds, brushing with butter between each fold. Place rounded tablespoon of silver beet mixture at the bottom of one narrow edge of folded pastry sheet, leaving a border. Fold one corner of pastry diagonally over filling to form a large triangle. Continue folding to end of pastry sheet, retaining triangular shape. Repeat with remaining ingredients to make 16 triangles in total.
5 Place triangles, seam-side down, on trays. Brush with remaining butter; sprinkle with sesame seeds. Bake about 15 minutes or until browned lightly.

prep + cook time 50 minutes **makes** 16
nutritional count per triangle 11.1g total fat (6.4g saturated fat); 690kJ (165 cal); 11g carbohydrate; 4.7g protein; 1.5g fibre
tips When working with the first sheet of fillo pastry, cover remaining pastry with a sheet of baking paper then a damp tea towel to prevent it from drying out.

Moussaka

¼ cup (60ml) olive oil
2 large eggplants (1kg), sliced thinly
1 large brown onion (200g), chopped finely
2 cloves garlic, crushed
1kg (2 pounds) minced (ground) lamb
410g (13 ounces) canned crushed tomatoes
½ cup (125ml) dry white wine
1 teaspoon ground cinnamon
¼ cup (20g) finely grated kefalotyri cheese
WHITE SAUCE
75g (2½ ounces) butter
⅓ cup (50g) plain (all-purpose) flour
2 cups (500ml) milk

1 Heat oil in large frying pan; cook eggplant, in batches, until browned both sides. Drain on absorbent paper.
2 Cook onion and garlic in same pan, stirring, until onion softens. Add lamb; cook, stirring, until lamb changes colour. Stir in undrained tomatoes, wine and cinnamon; bring to the boil. Reduce heat; simmer, uncovered, about 30 minutes or until liquid has evaporated.
3 Meanwhile, preheat oven to 180°C/350°F. Oil shallow 2-litre (8-cup) rectangular baking dish.
4 Make white sauce.
5 Place one-third of the eggplant, overlapping slices slightly, in dish; spread half the meat sauce over eggplant. Repeat layering with another third of the eggplant, remaining meat sauce and remaining eggplant. Spread white sauce over top layer of eggplant; sprinkle with cheese.
6 Bake moussaka about 40 minutes or until top browns lightly. Cover; stand 10 minutes before serving.
white sauce Melt butter in medium saucepan, add flour; cook, stirring, until mixture bubbles and thickens. Gradually add milk; stir until mixture boils and thickens.

prep + cook time 1 hour 50 minutes **serves** 6
nutritional count per serving 36.6g total fat (16.5g saturated fat); 2420kJ (579 cal); 18g carbohydrate; 41.8g protein; 5.3g fibre

Greek

Milopita

3 medium apples (450g), peeled, cored, quartered
¼ cup (60ml) lemon juice
60g (2 ounces) butter
¼ cup (55g) firmly packed light brown sugar
1 teaspoon ground cinnamon
125g (4 ounces) butter, softened, extra
1 cup (220g) caster (superfine) sugar
1 tablespoon finely grated lemon rind
1 teaspoon vanilla extract
2 eggs, separated
1 cup (150g) self-raising flour
¼ cup (60ml) milk
1 tablespoon icing (confectioners') sugar
BRANDY YOGURT
1½ tablespoons brandy
3 teaspoons light brown sugar
1 cup (280g) Greek-style yogurt

1 Preheat oven to 160°C/325°F. Grease 24cm (9½-inch) fluted pie dish.
2 Slice apple thinly; combine with juice in medium bowl.
3 Stir butter, brown sugar and cinnamon in small saucepan over heat until sugar dissolves.
4 Beat extra butter, caster sugar, rind, extract and egg yolks in small bowl with electric mixer until light and fluffy. Stir in sifted flour and milk, in two batches.
5 Beat egg whites in small bowl with electric mixer until soft peaks form; fold into cake mixture, in two batches. Spread mixture into dish.
6 Drain apples; discard juice, return apples to bowl. Stir warm brown sugar mixture into apples. Arrange apple slices over cake mixture in dish; drizzle with brown sugar mixture. Bake about 45 minutes.
7 Meanwhile, make brandy yogurt.
8 Dust milopita with sifted icing sugar; serve warm with brandy yogurt.
brandy yogurt Stir brandy and sugar in small bowl until sugar dissolves; stir in yogurt.

prep + cook time 1 hour 30 minutes **serves** 8
nutritional count per serving 22.5g total fat (14.2g saturated fat); 1962kJ (470 cal); 61.1g carbohydrate; 6.2g protein; 1.8g fibre

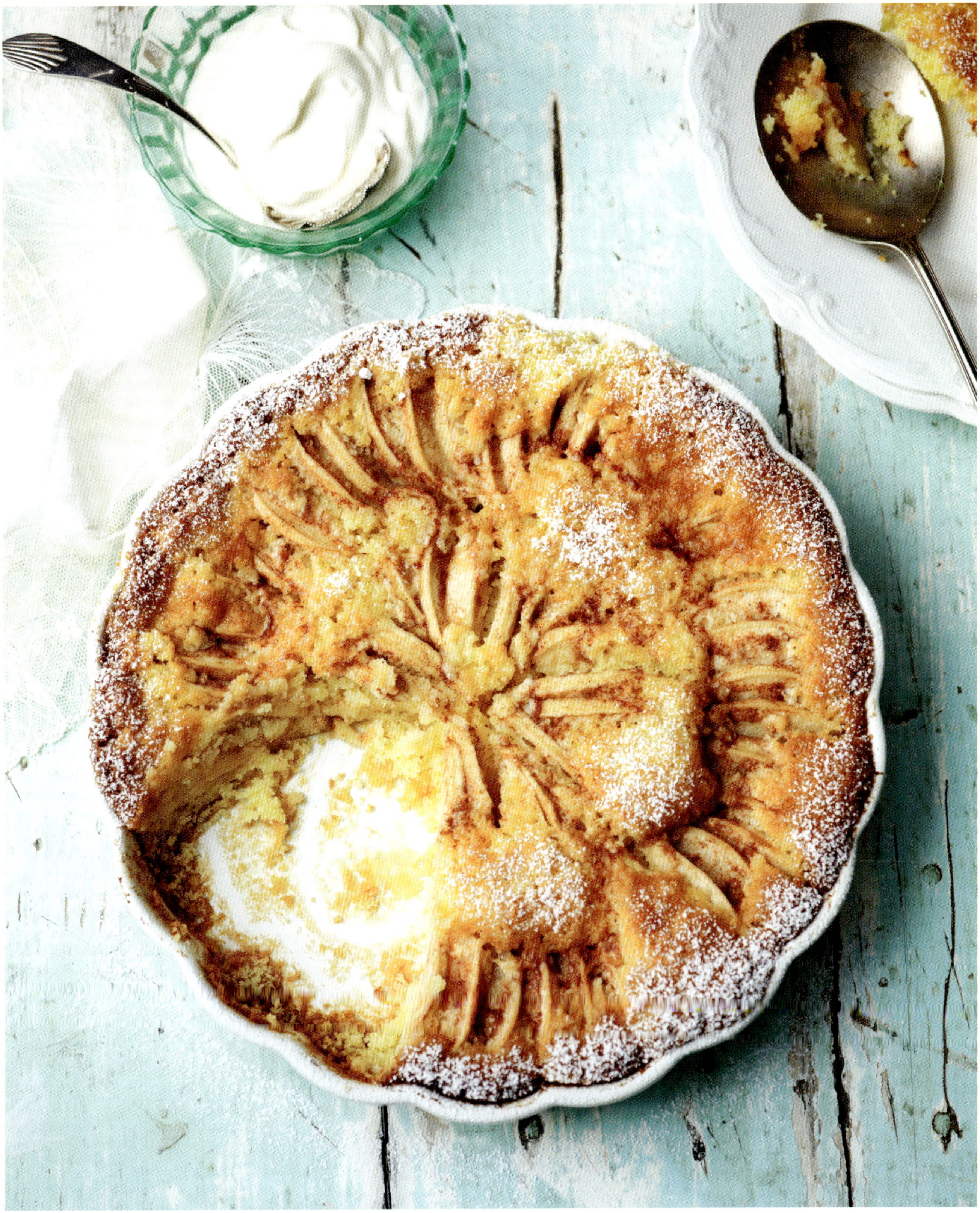

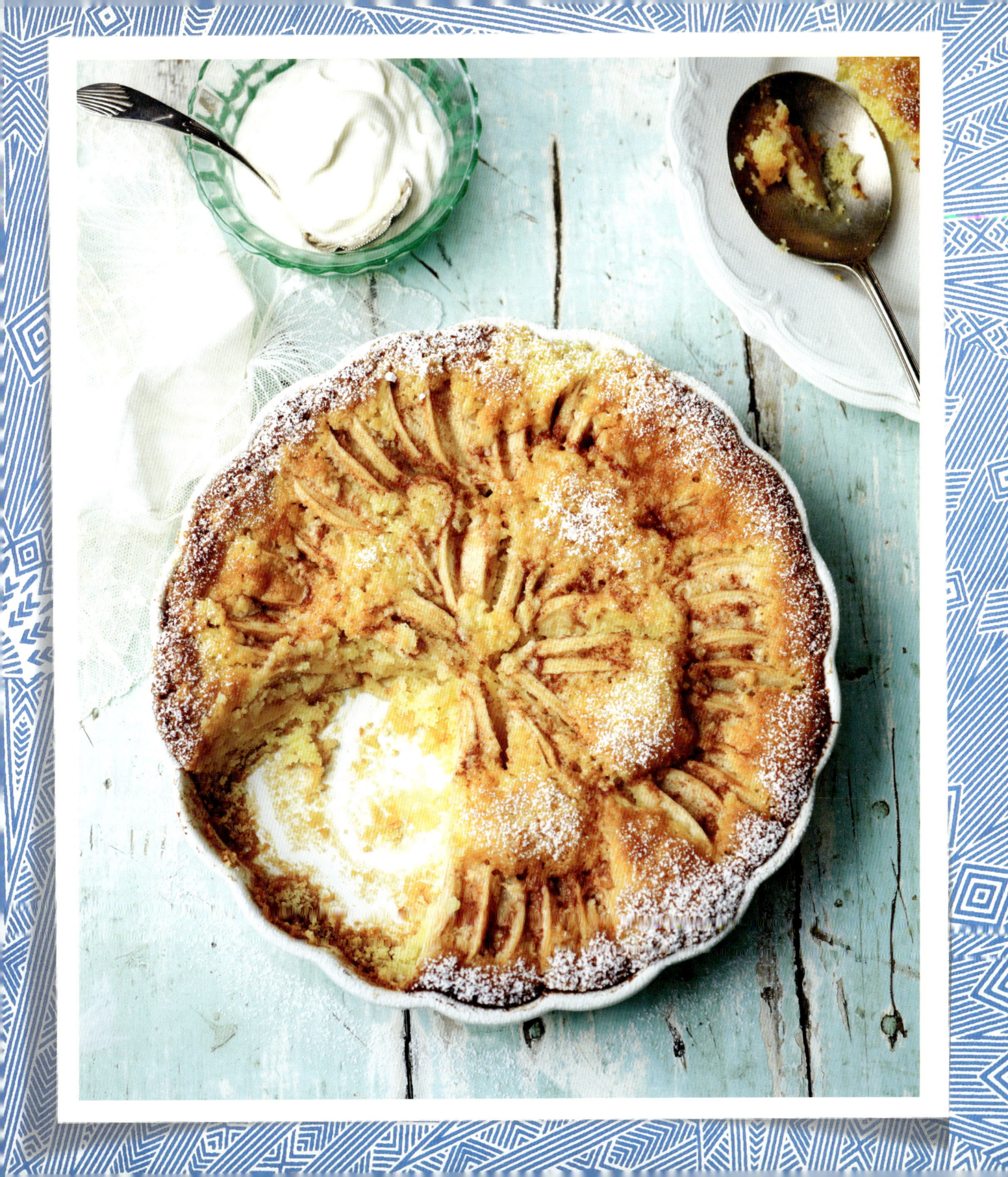

DÉPARTEMENS :

UN AN : 66 FR.
SIX MOIS . .
TROIS MOIS

DIRECTEUR
GUSTAVE NICOT

La Gazette

TOUT POUR LE PEUPLE

NAL DE L'APPE

PARIS, 10 SEPTEMBRE

Le Congrès d
nève, a tenu
mière séance
sident d'ho
M. Johsain
présidence
Chauff
du bu
nève
» pri
» de

aussi
puiss
propo
me pa
sidence
fession,
neur qu
homme q
l'admir
nature,
fiée la lutte
Ce congrès
prêcher la conc
des luttes pacifi
tement que l'heur
tions de remettre
d'un tribunal arbitr
brutale, le soin de pro
férends, et il a mis une
clamer le chef des chemises
jamais compris et pratiqué, qu
prend et ne prétend encore pratiquer a
tre apostolat que celui du sabre et du
volver!
Ce congrès, — s'il faut l'en croire, —
ambitionne de fonder la paix perpétuelle
sur la fraternité universelle, et le fantôm

French

French cooking has influenced the culinary world for centuries. The food is beautiful, sophisticated and full of passion – just like the people. Good food is a part of family tradition, from a hearty cassoulet to a silky smooth crème caramel. Bon appétit.

Manu Feildel

My Mum and Grandmother were great cooks while Dad and Grandfather were chefs – so food was very important at home and I was a fat baby. We often had very cheap food, cooked very well. I remember Mum's simple dishes, which were done so well, like her stuffed tomatoes and cauliflower soup that I just loved in winter.

I was lucky as a child because I was surrounded by food and it was a way of life; I'm happy that I was brought up that way. My Mother always had friends over on the weekend and she always organised dinners and we have always been hands-on. Whatever needed to be done, we always did together and we always spend time in the kitchen together. The only thing I didn't enjoy doing was the washing up.

One of Mum's dishes I really enjoyed was braised witlof, wrapped in ham with a béchamel sauce and cheese over the top and baked in the oven. That is one of the memories in my head that will always be there.

The difference between a cook and a professional chef is that Mum just cooks "by feel". When you look at my Mum cooking a tart, it's all by feel; like Italian mamas cooking a pasta. And that's the best cooking in the whole world because there are no rules, it's just ingrained into your brain and even though I've tried to make my Mum's apple tart a million times, it never tastes the same as hers. It's a secret you can't share because you don't know you have that secret.

RIGHT: Manu with his Mum, Evelyne.

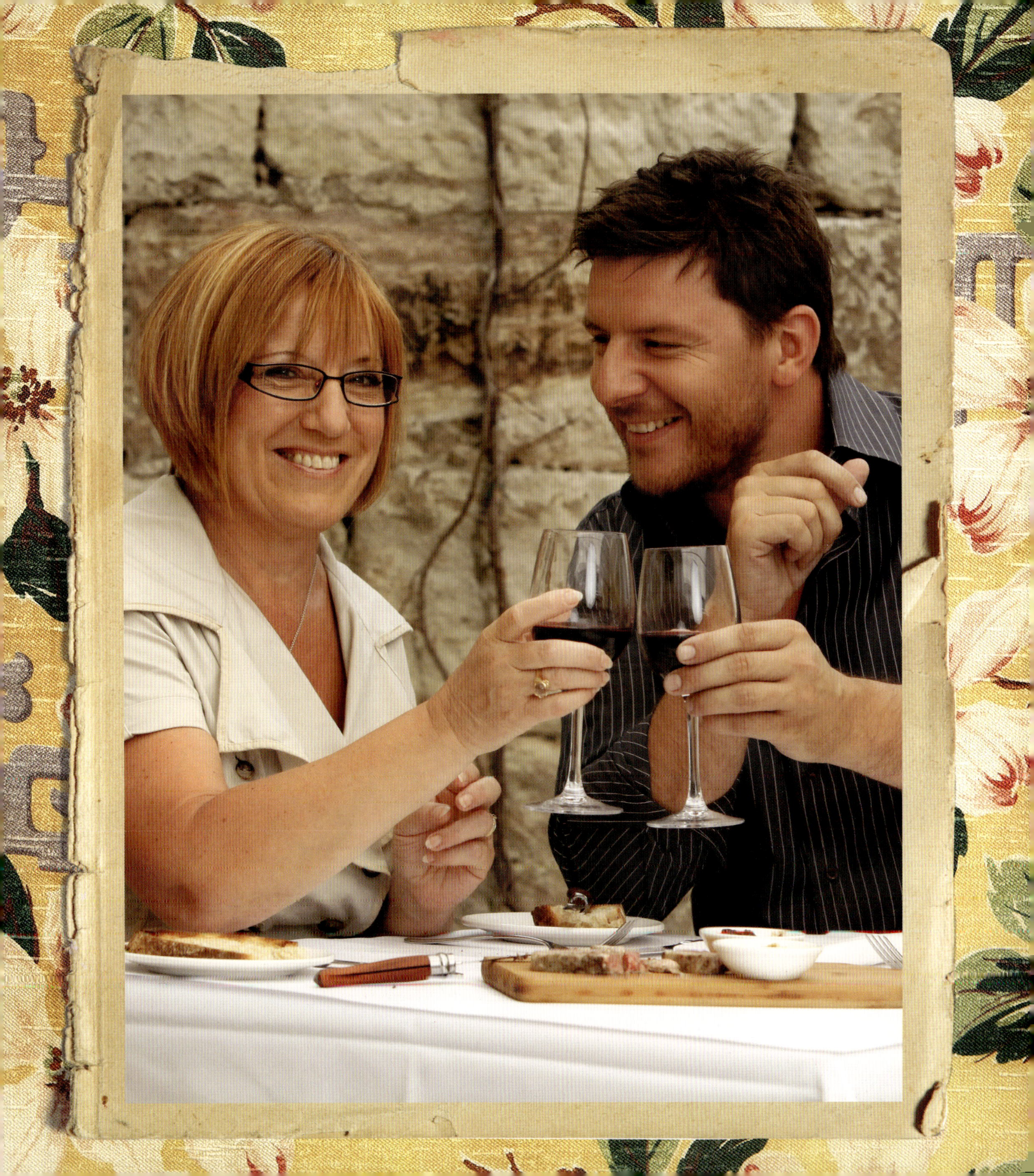

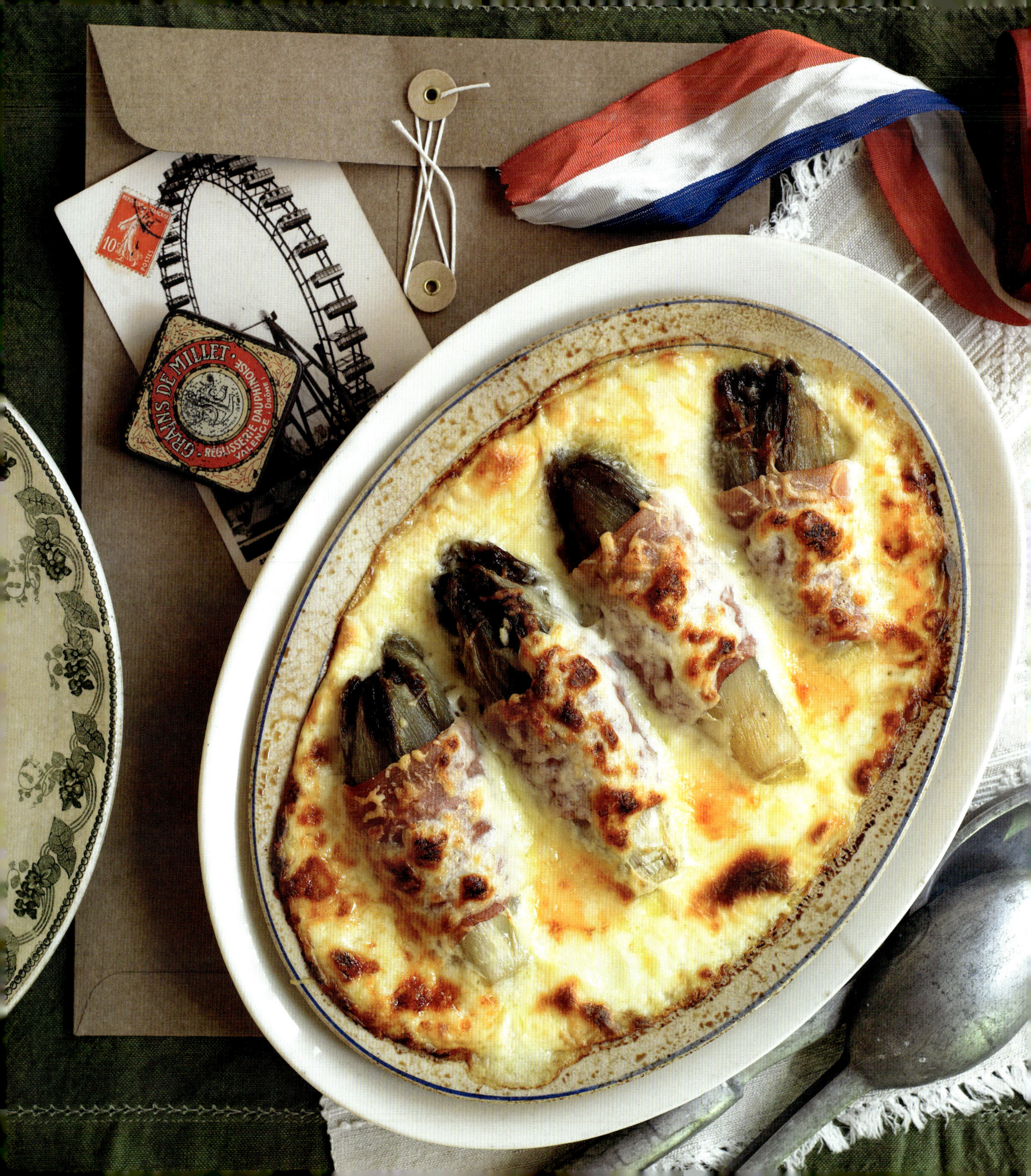
GRAINS DE MILLET
RÉGLISSERIE DAUPHINOISE
VALENCE · DRÔME

ABOVE: A teenage Manu serves a delighted table.

RIGHT: One-year-old Manu stirs the pot.

Witlof and ham bake (gratin d'endives au jambon)

4 witlof (belgian endive) (500g)
1 teaspoon caster (superfine) sugar
60g (2 ounces) butter
1 medium brown onion (150g), chopped finely
2 cloves garlic, crushed
1¼ cups (310ml) chicken stock
4 slices (90g) leg ham
50g (1½ ounces) gruyére cheese, grated
BECHAMEL SAUCE
30g (1 ounce) butter
¼ cup (35g) plain (all-purpose) flour
2 cups (500ml) milk
pinch ground nutmeg
50g (1½ ounces) gruyére cheese, grated

1 Remove outer leaves from witlof; chop leaves finely. Reserve whole and chopped witlof, separately.
2 Melt butter in medium frying pan over medium heat. Add whole witlof, in single layer, sprinkle with sugar and season with salt and pepper; cook witlof until browned lightly on all sides. Add onion, garlic, stock and chopped witlof leaves. Reduce heat; simmer, covered, over low heat about 30 minutes.
3 Preheat oven to 180°C/350°F.
4 Remove witlof from pan; drain on absorbent paper.
5 Meanwhile, make béchamel sauce.
6 Pour half the béchamel sauce into medium shallow ovenproof dish. Roll a slice of ham around each witlof; place in dish. Pour remaining sauce over witlof; sprinkle with cheese.
7 Bake witlof about 20 minutes or until golden.
béchamel sauce Melt butter in medium saucepan. Add flour and whisk mixture 2 minutes until well combined. Gradually add milk, whisking mixture to avoid any lumps. Add nutmeg, salt and pepper; cook, whisking constantly, 10 minutes. Stir in cheese.

prep + cook time 1 hour 20 minutes **serves** 4
nutritional count per serving 32.4g total fat (20.6g saturated fat); 1848kJ (442 cal); 16.8g carbohydrate; 20g protein; 3.8g fibre

French

Chicken liver pâté

1kg (2 pounds) chicken livers
200g (6½ ounces) ghee (clarified butter)
4 rindless bacon slices (260g), chopped finely
1 small brown onion (80g), chopped finely
¼ cup (60ml) brandy
½ cup (125ml) pouring cream
2 teaspoons finely chopped fresh thyme
pinch ground nutmeg

1 Cut any sinew from livers; pull each lobe away from connecting tissue.
2 Heat a quarter of the ghee in large frying pan; cook half the livers, stirring, until browned and barely cooked. Remove from pan. Repeat with another quarter of the ghee and remaining livers.
3 Heat 1 tablespoon of the remaining ghee in same pan; cook bacon and onion, stirring, until onion softens. Add brandy; bring to the boil.
4 Blend livers, bacon mixture, cream, thyme, nutmeg and 2 tablespoons of the remaining ghee until smooth (you may need to do this in batches). Press pâté into 1-litre (4-cup) dish.
5 Melt remaining ghee; pour over pâté in dish. Refrigerate 3 hours or overnight.

prep + cook time 45 minutes (+ refrigeration)
makes 4 cups
nutritional count per teaspoon 1.7g total fat (1g saturated fat); 88kJ (21 cal); 0.1g carbohydrate; 1.2g protein; 0g fibre
serving suggestion Serve with crusty baguette, lavosh crispbread, melba toast or water crackers.

French

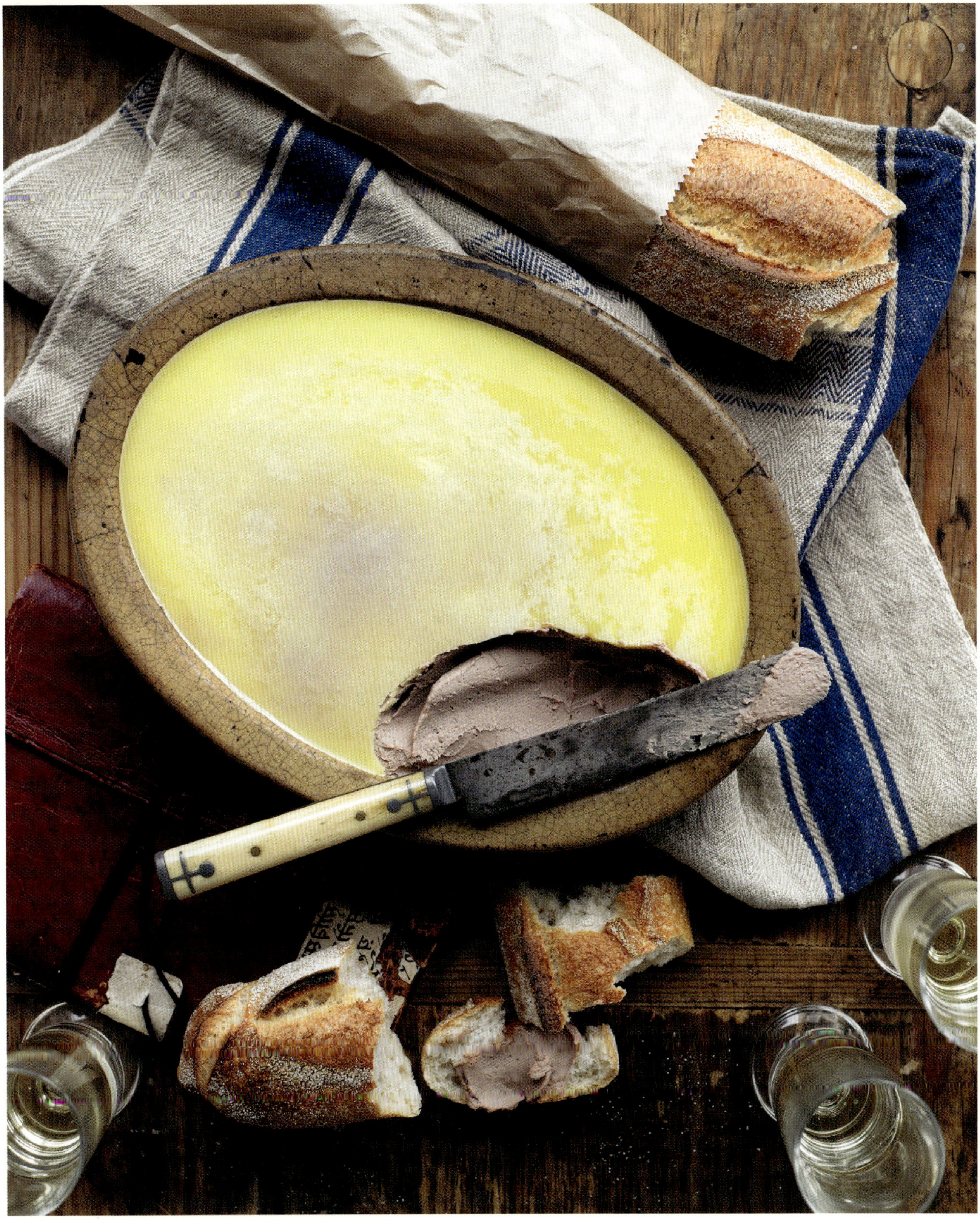

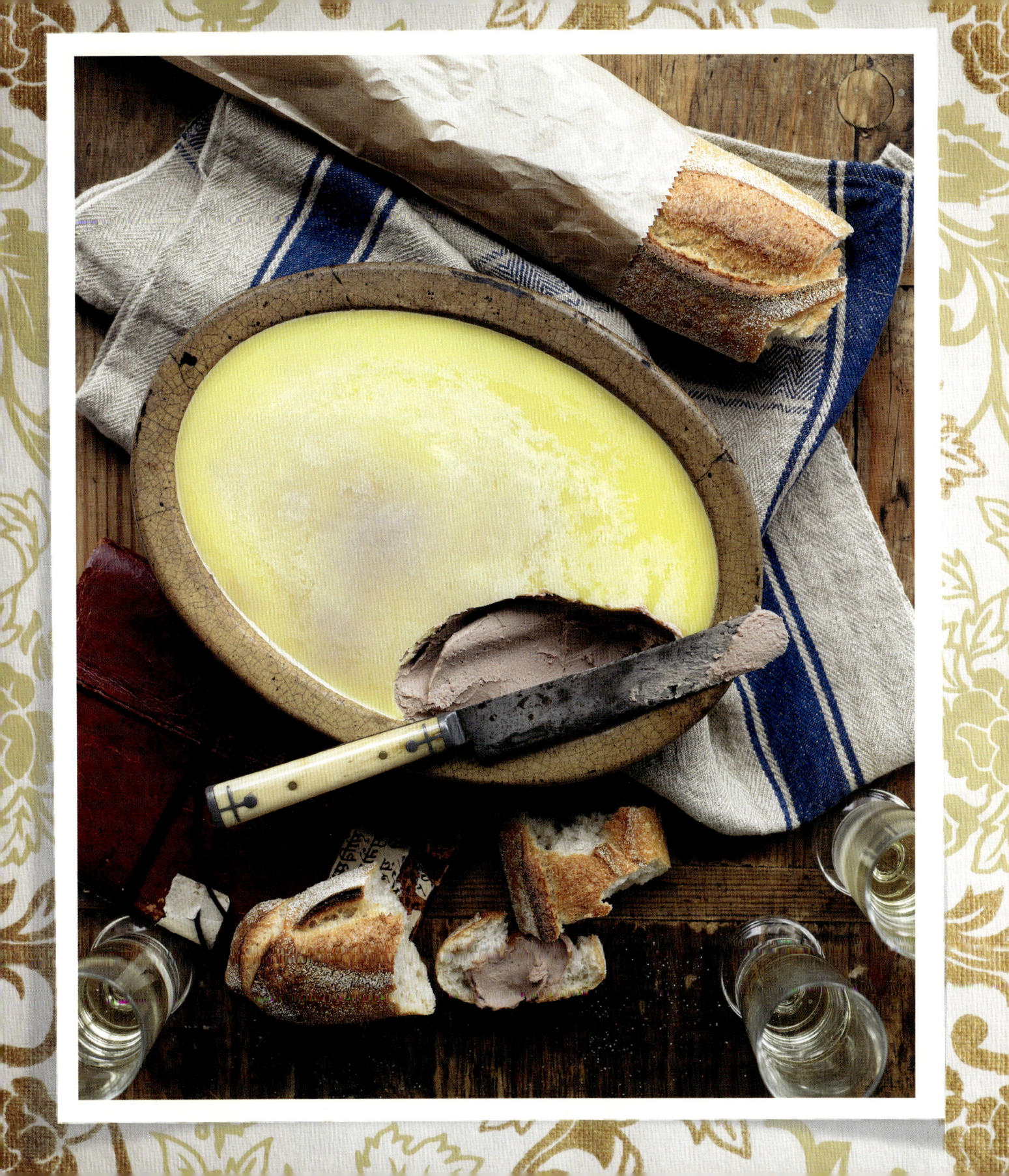

This is a traditional recipe from the Languedoc region in the south west of France. There are many variations: with duck or goose fat, with or without lamb, tomato, toulouse sausages or duck confit.

Cassoulet

- 1½ cups (300g) dried white beans
- 300g (9½ ounces) boned pork belly, rind removed, sliced thinly
- 150g (4½-ounce) piece streaky bacon, rind removed, cut into 1cm (½-inch) pieces
- 800g (1½-pound) piece boned lamb shoulder, cut into 2.5cm (1-inch) pieces
- 1 large brown onion (200g), chopped finely
- 1 small leek (200g), sliced thinly
- 2 cloves garlic, crushed
- 3 sprigs fresh thyme
- 400g (12½ ounces) canned crushed tomatoes
- 2 dried bay leaves
- 1 cup (250ml) water
- 1 cup (250ml) chicken stock
- 2 cups (140g) stale breadcrumbs
- ⅓ cup coarsely chopped fresh flat-leaf parsley

1 Place beans in medium bowl, cover with cold water; stand overnight. Drain; rinse under cold water, drain. Cook beans in medium saucepan of boiling water about 15 minutes or until tender; drain.
2 Preheat oven to 160°C/325°F.
3 Cook pork in large flameproof dish, pressing down with back of spoon on pork until browned; remove from dish. Cook bacon in same pan, stirring, until crisp; remove from dish. Cook lamb, in batches, in same pan, until browned. Remove from dish.
4 Cook onion, leek and garlic in same dish, stirring, until onion softens. Return meat to dish with thyme, undrained tomatoes, bay leaves, the water, stock and beans; bring to the boil. Cover; cook, in oven, 45 minutes. Remove from oven; season to taste. Sprinkle with combined breadcrumbs and parsley; cook, uncovered, in oven, about 45 minutes or until liquid is nearly absorbed and beans are tender.

prep + cook time 2 hours 50 minutes (+ standing)
serves 6
nutritional count per serving 28.2g total fat (10.5g saturated fat); 2750kJ (658 cal); 38.5g carbohydrate; 55.8g protein; 12.4g fibre

French

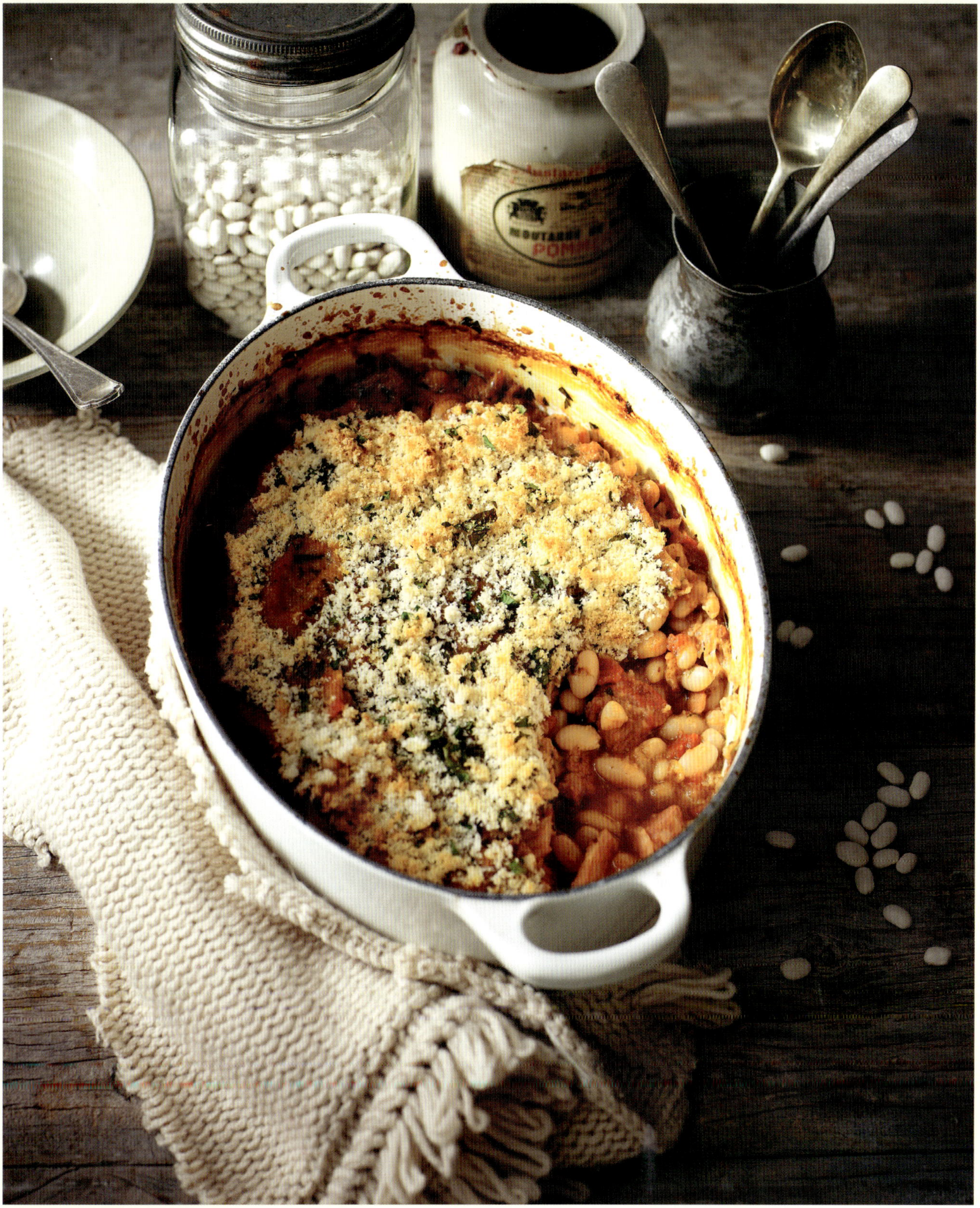

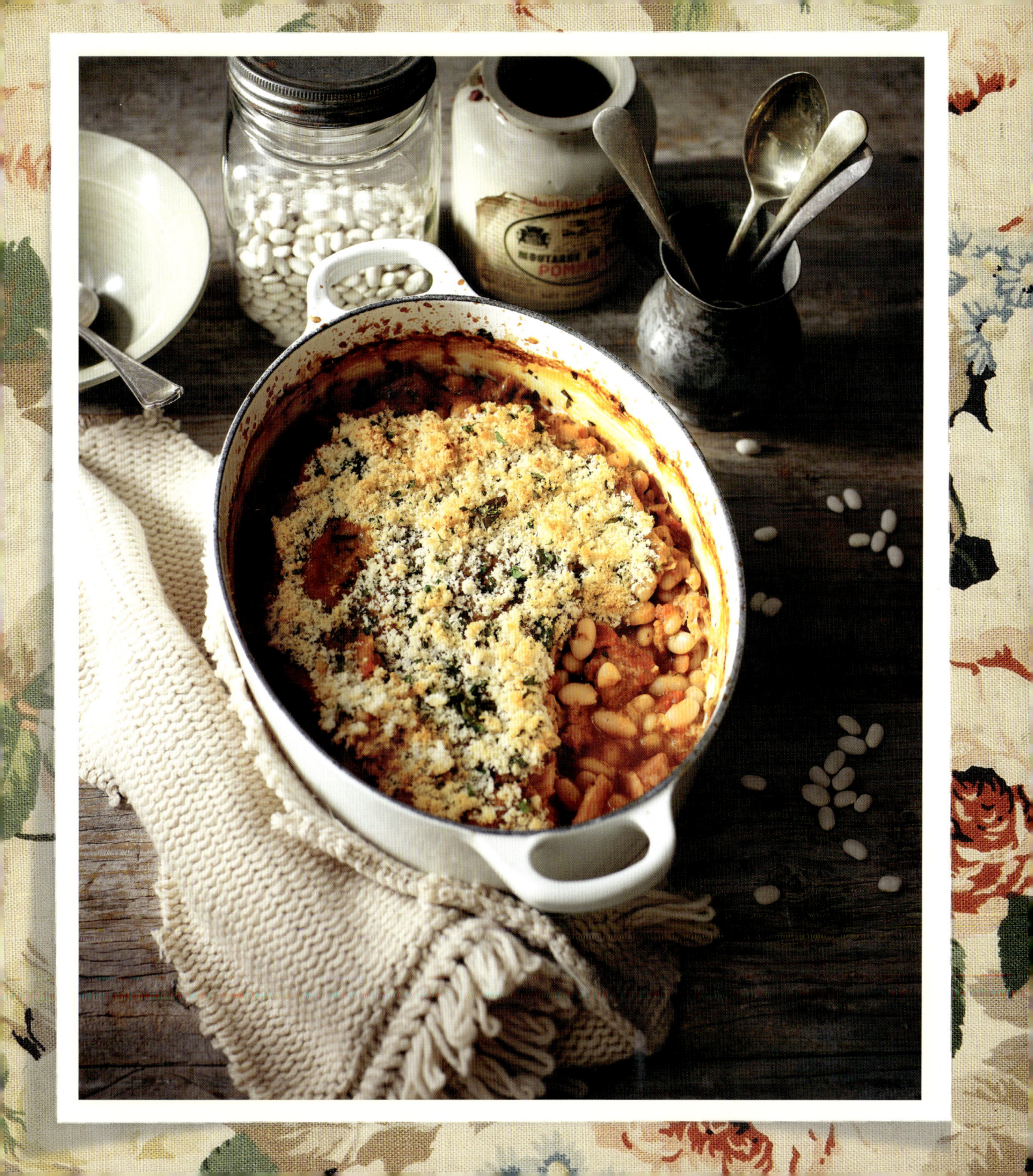

Pressure-cooked navarin of lamb

1 tablespoon olive oil
4 lamb neck chops (680g), trimmed
1 large brown onion (200g), chopped finely
2 cloves garlic, crushed
410g (13 ounces) canned diced tomatoes
½ cup (125 ml) water
8 baby brown onions (200g)
500g (1 pound) baby new potatoes, halved
400g (12½ ounces) baby carrots, trimmed, peeled
1 cup (120g) frozen peas
2 tablespoons coarsely chopped fresh flat-leaf parsley

1 Heat oil in 6-litre (24-cup) pressure cooker; cook lamb, in batches, until browned. Remove from cooker.
2 Cook chopped onion and garlic in cooker, stirring, until onion softens. Return lamb to cooker with undrained tomatoes and the water; secure lid. Bring cooker to high pressure. Reduce heat to stabilise pressure; cook 15 minutes.
3 Meanwhile, peel baby onions, leaving root ends intact.
4 Release pressure using the quick release method, by carefully turning the pressure valve with tongs (steam can burn) to release the steam; wait for pressure to drop, then remove lid. Stir in potato and onions, top with carrots; secure lid. Bring cooker to high pressure. Reduce heat to stabilise pressure; cook 5 minutes.
5 Release pressure by carefully turning the pressure valve with tongs (steam can burn) to release the steam; wait for pressure to drop, then remove lid. Stir in peas; season to taste. Serve sprinkled with parsley.

prep + cook time 40 minutes **serves** 4
nutritional count per serving 21.9g total fat (8.3g saturated fat); 1994kJ (477 cal); 31.2g carbohydrate; 34g protein; 9.6g fibre
tips If you have an electric pressure cooker you won't need to reduce the heat to stabilise pressure, your cooker will automatically stabilise itself. Always check with the manufacturer's instructions before using your pressure cooker. Recipe not suitable to freeze.

French

Crème caramel

¾ cup (165g) caster (superfine) sugar
½ cup (125ml) water
6 eggs
1 teaspoon vanilla extract
½ cup (75g) caster (superfine) sugar, extra
1¼ cups (310ml) thickened (heavy) cream
1¾ cups (430ml) milk

1 Preheat oven to 160°C/325°F.
2 Stir sugar and the water in medium heavy-based frying pan over heat, without boiling, until sugar dissolves. Bring to the boil; boil, uncovered, without stirring, until mixture is a deep caramel colour. Remove from heat; allow bubbles to subside. Pour toffee into deep 20cm (8-inch) round cake pan.
3 Whisk eggs, extract and extra sugar in large bowl.
4 Bring cream and milk to the boil in medium saucepan. Whisking constantly, pour hot milk mixture into egg mixture. Strain mixture into cake pan.
5 Place pan in baking dish; add enough boiling water to come half way up side of pan.
6 Bake crème caramel about 40 minutes or until set. Remove pan from baking dish. Cover; refrigerate overnight.
7 Gently ease crème caramel from side of pan; invert onto deep-sided serving plate.

prep + cook time 1 hour (+ refrigeration) **serves** 8
nutritional count per serving 22.3g total fat (13.3g saturated fat); 1526kJ (365 cal); 33.8g carbohydrate; 7.5g protein; 0g fibre
tip It is fine to use just one 300ml carton of cream for this recipe.

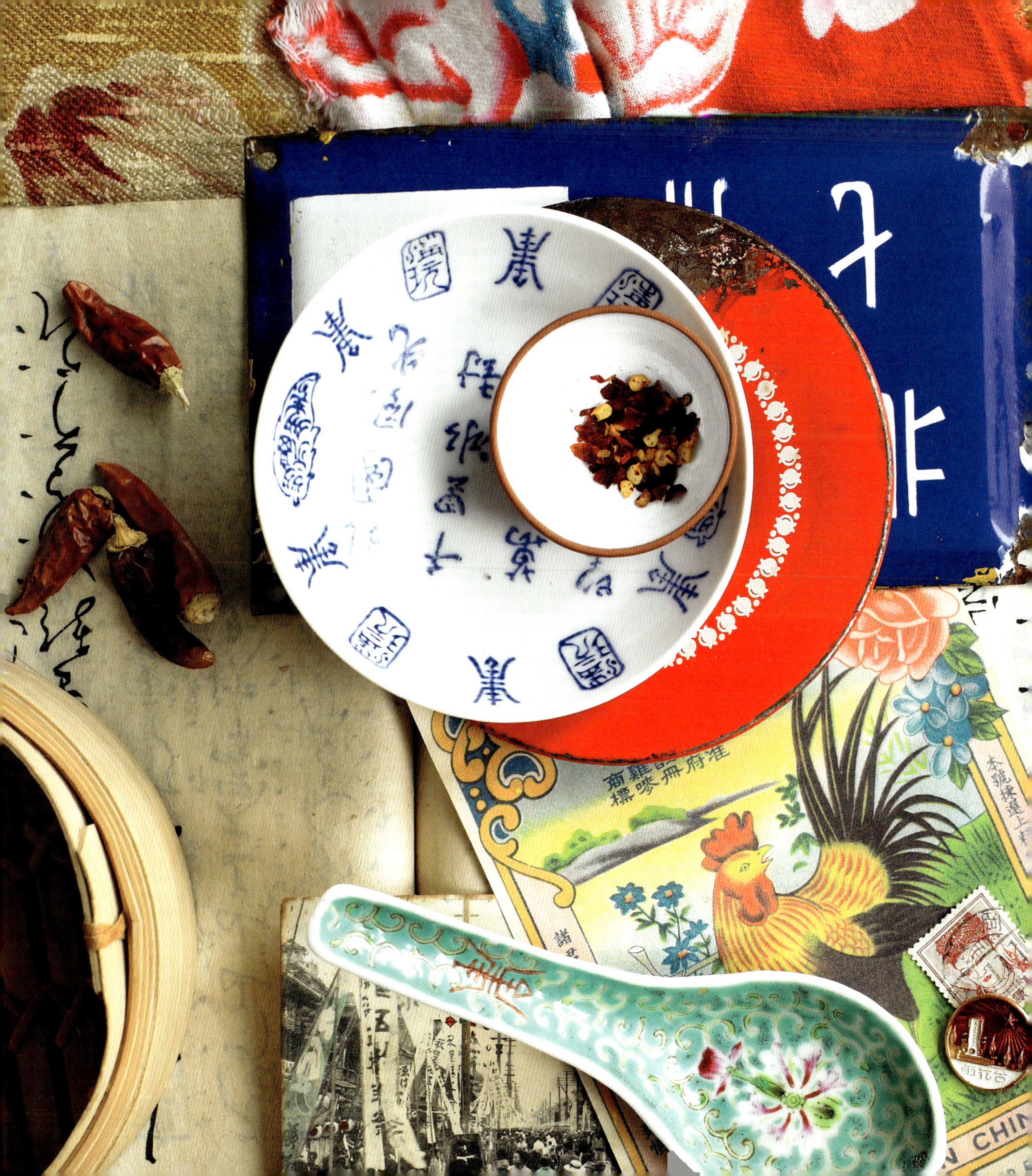

Asian

Asian mums well know why theirs is one of the world's most savoured cuisines. With so many varieties of their own spicy sauces and seasonings, few families can resist a stir-fry or curry, paired with noodles, pork or spring vegetables.

Tetsuya Wakuda

When I was growing up, my parents liked to cook. I just liked to eat though – kids are always hungry. Cooking never really captured my imagination as a child. My Mum would spend a lot of time in the kitchen and I remember watching her, thinking, "I can't wait to eat."

In Japan, we would eat lots of vegetables, chicken, pork and especially fish. When I became a cook, remembering how they were used there and cooked became very important. As a child, I loved going fishing with my family, especially during the Autumn and Winter months. But for my birthday, one of my favourite dishes was my Mum's Karaage Chicken. With all of my family still living back in Japan, I often make it for myself at home, as well as friends. It's also a firm favourite with staff at my Sydney restaurant, Tetsuya's.

I never learned Japanese cooking from my Mum, but I certainly have a Japanese palate. That background is the basis for the food I cook now. Sydney chef Tony Bilson was a big influence on my cooking career but because of where I have come from, I have my own taste and way of tasting and creating flavours.

My Mum knows I'm a chef, but I think she finds it hard to understand why I would choose this career when, as a child, I was never interested in cooking. She has seen my television programme though in Japan and she came out to Australia many years ago and ate in my restaurant. She didn't say too much, but I certainly hope she liked it.

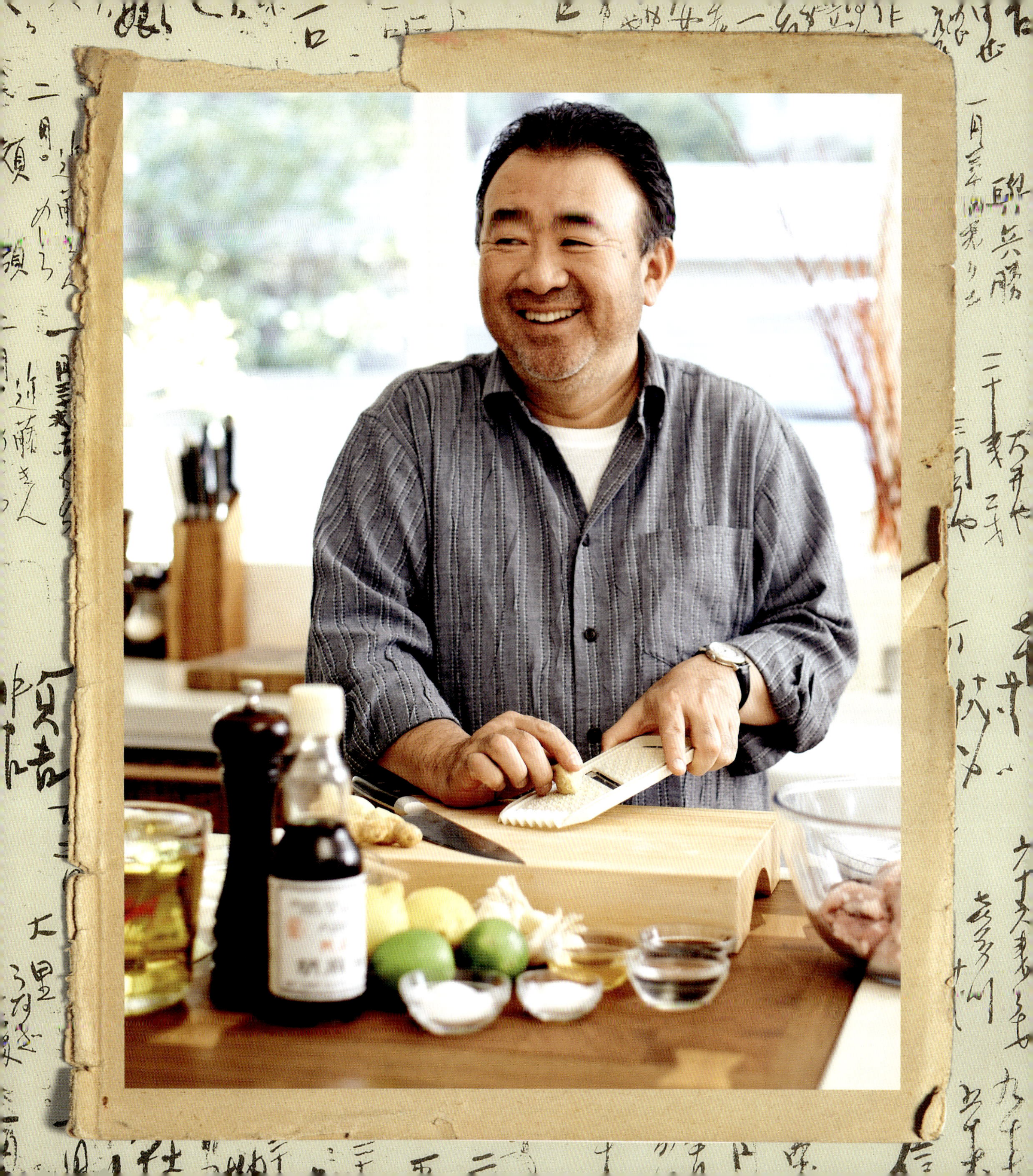

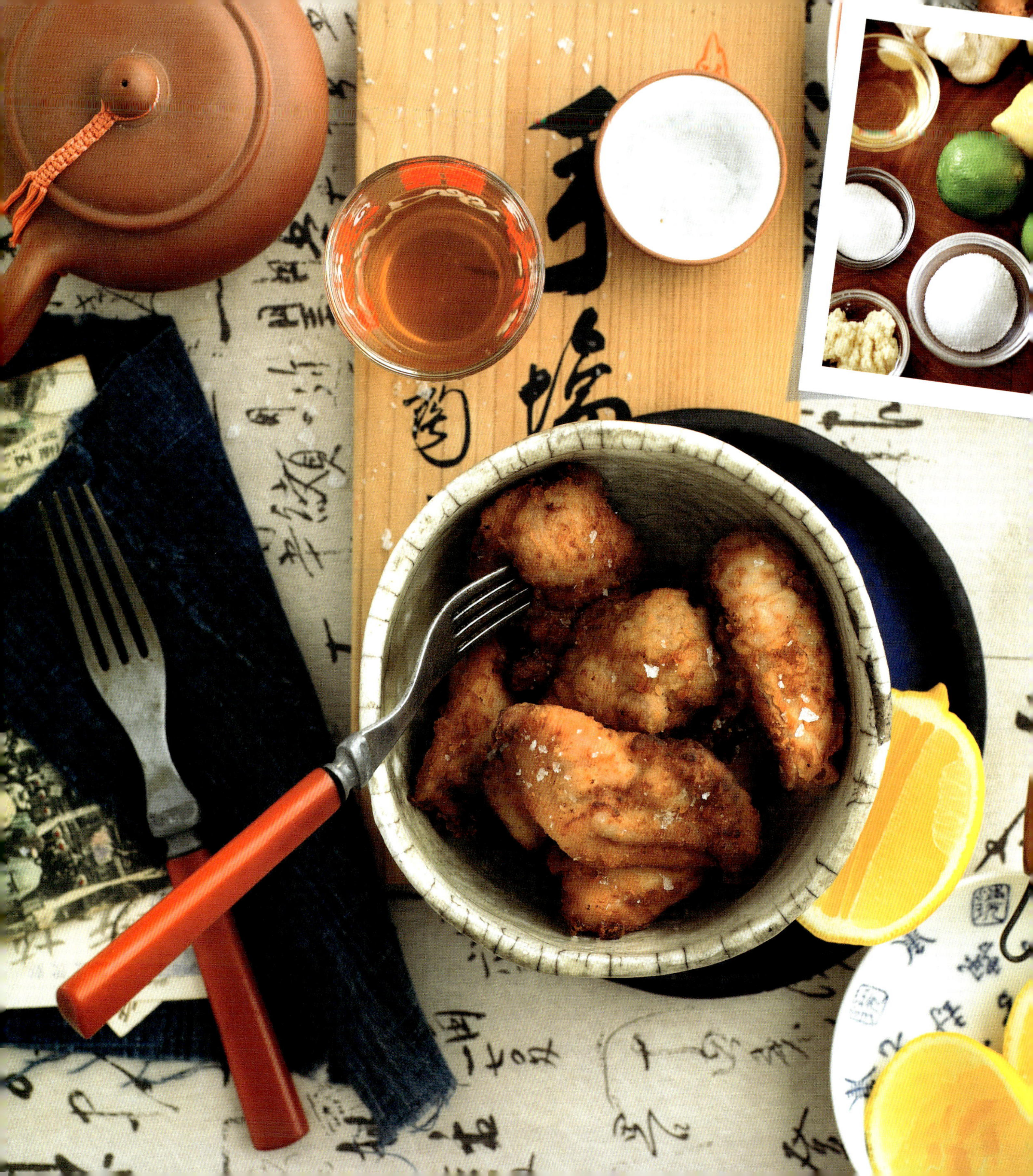

Chicken karaage

1 teaspoon caster (superfine) sugar
1 teaspoon salt
4cm (1½-inch) piece fresh ginger (20g), grated
2 tablespoons mirin
1 tablespoon sake
1 tablespoon japanese soy sauce
1 teaspoon sesame oil
500g (1 pound) chicken thigh fillets, chopped coarsely
¼ cup (35g) plain (all-purpose) flour
grape seed oil, for deep-frying

1 Combine sugar, salt, ginger, mirin, sake, sauce and sesame oil in medium bowl, add chicken; toss to coat chicken. Season with cracked black pepper. Cover; refrigerate 30 minutes.
2 Coat chicken in flour; shake off excess.
3 Heat grape seed oil in large, deep saucepan to 180°C/350°F; deep-fry chicken, in batches, until golden brown. Drain well on absorbent paper. Serve with lemon wedges.

prep + cook time 35 minutes (+ refrigeration)
serves 2
nutritional count per serving 38.1g total fat (7.7g saturated fat); 2625kJ (628 cal); 16.4g carbohydrate; 49.2g protein; 0.9g fibre

ABOVE: "It's simple and tasty," Tetsuya enthuses about the deep-fried chicken. His tip? "Use grape seed oil for frying for a better result."

My Mac knife represents a perfect fusion of Western design with traditional Japanese craftsmanship. It is beautifully balanced and retains its sharpness.

Asian
101

Vegetable tempura

250g (8 ounces) firm tofu
1 medium brown onion (150g)
1 small fresh or frozen lotus root (200g)
8 fresh shiitake mushrooms
2 sheets toasted seaweed (yaki-nori)
20g (¾ ounce) cellophane noodles, cut in half
vegetable oil, for deep-frying
plain flour, for dusting
120g (4 ounces) pumpkin, sliced
50g (1½ ounces) green beans, halved
1 small kumara (orange sweet potato) (250g), sliced thinly
1 baby eggplant (60g), sliced
1 small red capsicum (bell pepper) (150g), seeded, cut into squares
1 medium carrot (120g), sliced
1 medium lemon (140g), cut into wedges
BATTER
1 egg, beaten lightly
2 cups (500ml) iced soda water
1 cup (150g) plain (all-purpose) flour
1 cup (150g) cornflour (cornstarch)

1 Press tofu between two chopping boards with weight on top, raise one end; stand 25 minutes. Cut tofu into 2cm (¾-inch) cubes.
2 Halve onion from root end. Insert toothpicks at regular intervals to hold onion rings together and slice in between.
3 Peel lotus root and slice; place in water with a dash of vinegar to prevent browning. (If using canned lotus, drain and slice.) Discard mushroom stems; cut a cross in top of caps.
4 Cut one sheet nori into 5cm (2-inch) squares; halve other sheet, cut into 2cm (¾-inch) wide strips. Brush nori strips with water, wrap tightly around middle of 10 noodles; reserve noodle bunches.
5 Make batter.
6 Heat oil in large saucepan. Dust ingredients, except nori squares, lightly in flour; shake off excess. Dip nori squares and other ingredients in batter, drain excess; deep-fry, in small batches, until golden. Drain. Only fry in small batches and ensure oil comes back to correct temperature before adding next batch. Deep-fry noodle bundles.
7 Serve tempura and noodles immediately with lemon wedges, and a tempura dipping sauce topped with grated daikon, if you like.
batter Combine egg and soda water in bowl. Add sifted flours at once; mix lightly until just combined. Do not overmix; mixture should be lumpy.

prep + cook time 40 minutes **serves** 4
nutritional count per serving 39.6g total fat (5.7g saturated fat); 3285kJ (786 cal); 78.3g carbohydrate; 20.3g protein; 11.7g fibre

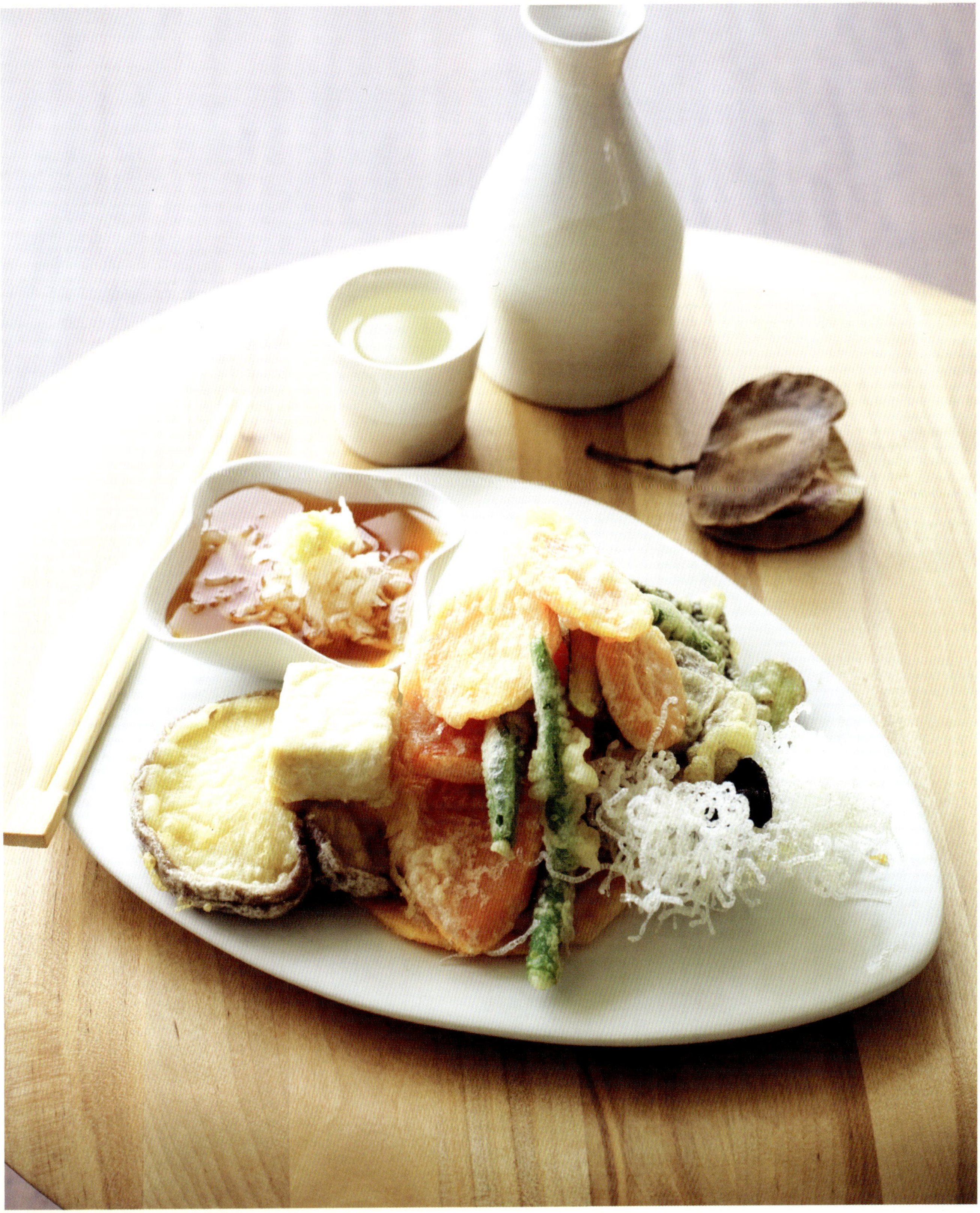

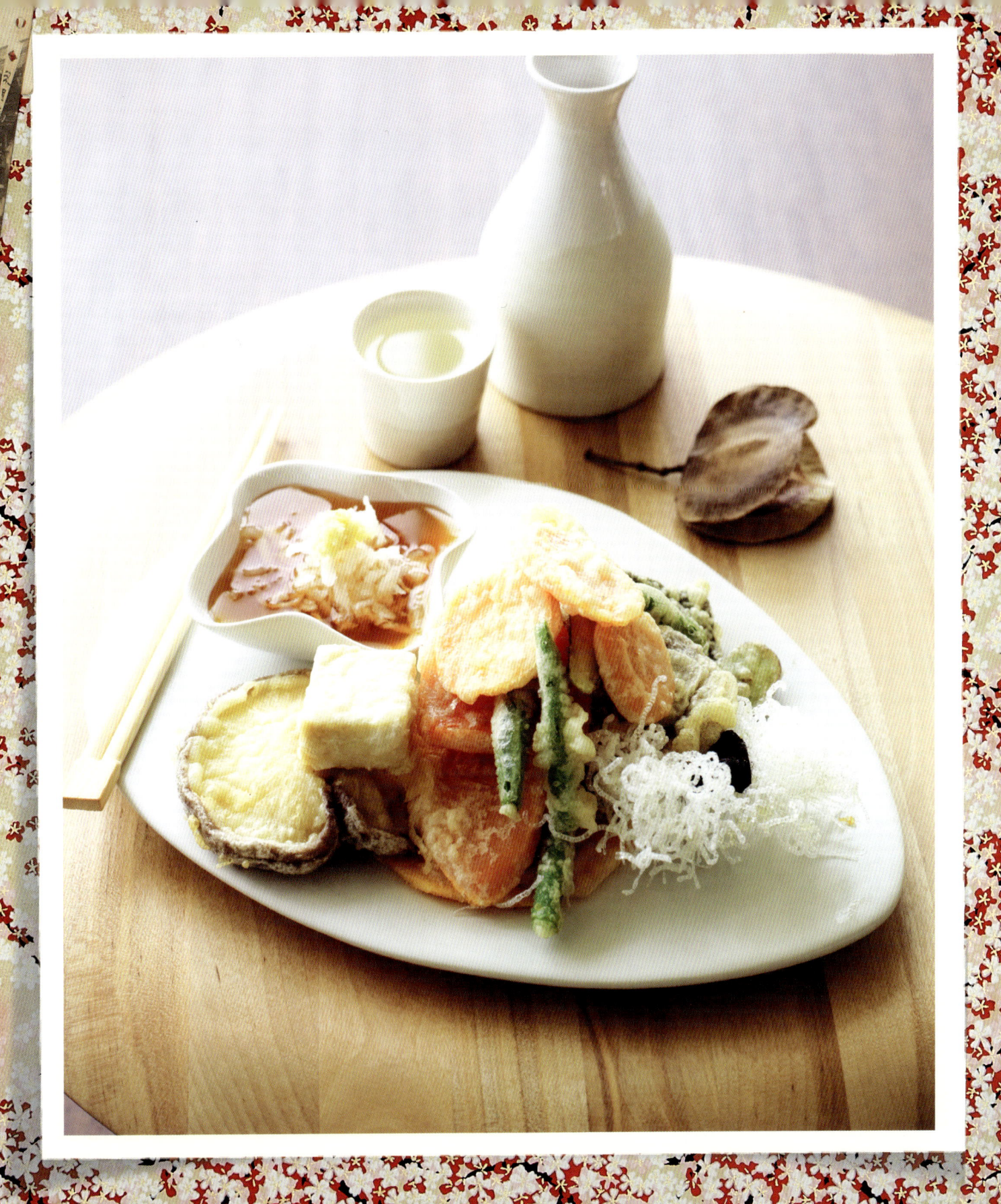

Chicken yakitori

500g (1 pound) chicken breast fillets, sliced thinly
½ cup (125ml) mirin
¼ cup (60ml) kecap manis
1 tablespoon japanese soy sauce
1 teaspoon white sesame seeds, toasted
1 green onion (scallion), sliced thinly

1 Thread chicken loosely onto skewers; place, in single layer, in large shallow dish.
2 Combine mirin, kecap manis and sauce in small jug. Pour half the marinade over skewers; reserve remaining marinade. Cover skewers; refrigerate 3 hours or overnight.
3 Simmer reserved marinade in small saucepan over low heat until reduced by half.
4 Meanwhile, cook drained skewers on heated oiled grill plate (or grill or grill pan) until cooked through.
5 Serve skewers drizzled with hot marinade; sprinkle with seeds and onion.

prep + cook time 30 minutes (+ refrigeration) **makes** 24
nutritional count per skewer 0.6g total fat (0.1g saturated fat); 121kJ (29 cal); 0.3g carbohydrate; 4.9g protein; 0g fibre
tip You need 24 bamboo skewers for this recipe. Soak them in cold water for an hour before use to prevent them splintering or scorching during cooking.

Thai beef salad with chilli and lime

500g (1 pound) beef fillet, trimmed
100g (3 ounces) rice vermicelli noodles
1 lebanese cucumber (130g), seeded, sliced thinly
½ cup firmly packed fresh coriander leaves
⅓ cup firmly packed fresh thai basil leaves
10cm (4-inch) stick lemon grass (20g), crushed, sliced thinly
2 fresh kaffir lime leaves, shredded finely
2 shallots (50g), sliced thinly
2 tablespoons fried shallots
THAI DRESSING
2 fresh small red thai (serrano) chillies, halved
1 clove garlic, quartered
¼ teaspoon caster (superfine) sugar
⅓ cup (80ml) lime juice
2 tablespoons fish sauce

1 Cook beef on heated oiled grill plate (or grill or barbecue) until cooked as desired. Cover beef; stand 5 minutes then slice thinly.
2 Meanwhile, place noodles in medium heatproof bowl, cover with boiling water; stand until tender, drain. Rinse under cold water; drain.
3 Make thai dressing.
4 Place beef and noodles in large bowl with cucumber, herbs, lemon grass, lime leaves and sliced shallot; toss gently to combine.
5 Divide salad among serving plates; drizzle with dressing, sprinkle with fried shallots.
thai dressing Using mortar and pestle, crush chilli, garlic and sugar to a paste. Combine paste with remaining ingredients in small bowl.

prep + cook time 30 minutes **serves** 4
nutritional count per serving 8.3g total fat (3.2g saturated fat); 1133kJ (271 cal); 18.6g carbohydrate; 29.5g protein; 1.5g fibre

Shrimp paste is also known as trasi or blanchan; it is a strong-scented, very firm preserved paste made of salted dried shrimp. It is used as a flavouring in many South-East Asian soups and sauces.

Prawn laksa

1 tablespoon vegetable oil
3¼ cups (800ml) canned coconut milk
1 litre (4 cups) chicken stock
1 tablespoon light brown sugar
2 teaspoons fish sauce
6 fresh kaffir lime leaves, shredded finely
1kg (2 pounds) uncooked medium king prawns (shrimp)
250g (8 ounces) fresh thin egg noodles
125g (4 ounces) dried thin rice noodles
1 cup (80g) bean sprouts
¼ cup loosely packed fresh coriander (cilantro) leaves
1 lime, quartered

LAKSA PASTE
1 medium brown onion (150g), chopped coarsely
⅓ cup (80ml) canned coconut milk
2 tablespoons lime juice
1 tablespoon shrimp paste
2cm (¾-inch) piece fresh ginger (10g), grated
1 tablespoon macadamias (10g), halved
10cm (4-inch) stick fresh lemon grass (20g), chopped finely
4 cloves garlic, quartered
2 fresh small red thai (serrano) chillies, chopped coarsely
2 teaspoons each ground coriander and ground cumin
1 teaspoon ground turmeric

1 Make laksa paste.
2 Heat oil in large saucepan; cook laksa paste, stirring, about 5 minutes or until fragrant. Add coconut milk, stock, sugar, sauce and lime leaves; bring to the boil. Reduce heat; simmer, covered, 30 minutes.
3 Meanwhile, shell and devein prawns, leaving tails intact.
4 Place egg noodles in medium heatproof bowl, cover with boiling water; separate with fork, drain. Place rice noodles in same bowl, cover with boiling water; stand until just tender, drain.
5 Add prawns to laksa; cook, uncovered, until just changed in colour.
6 Divide noodles among serving bowls; ladle hot laksa into bowls. Top with sprouts and coriander; serve with lime.
laksa paste Blend or process ingredients until mixture forms a smooth paste.

prep + cook time 1 hour 15 minutes **serves** 4
nutritional count per serving 55.2g total fat (41.6g saturated fat); 3775kJ (903 cal); 56.6g carbohydrate; 42g protein; 7.6g fibre

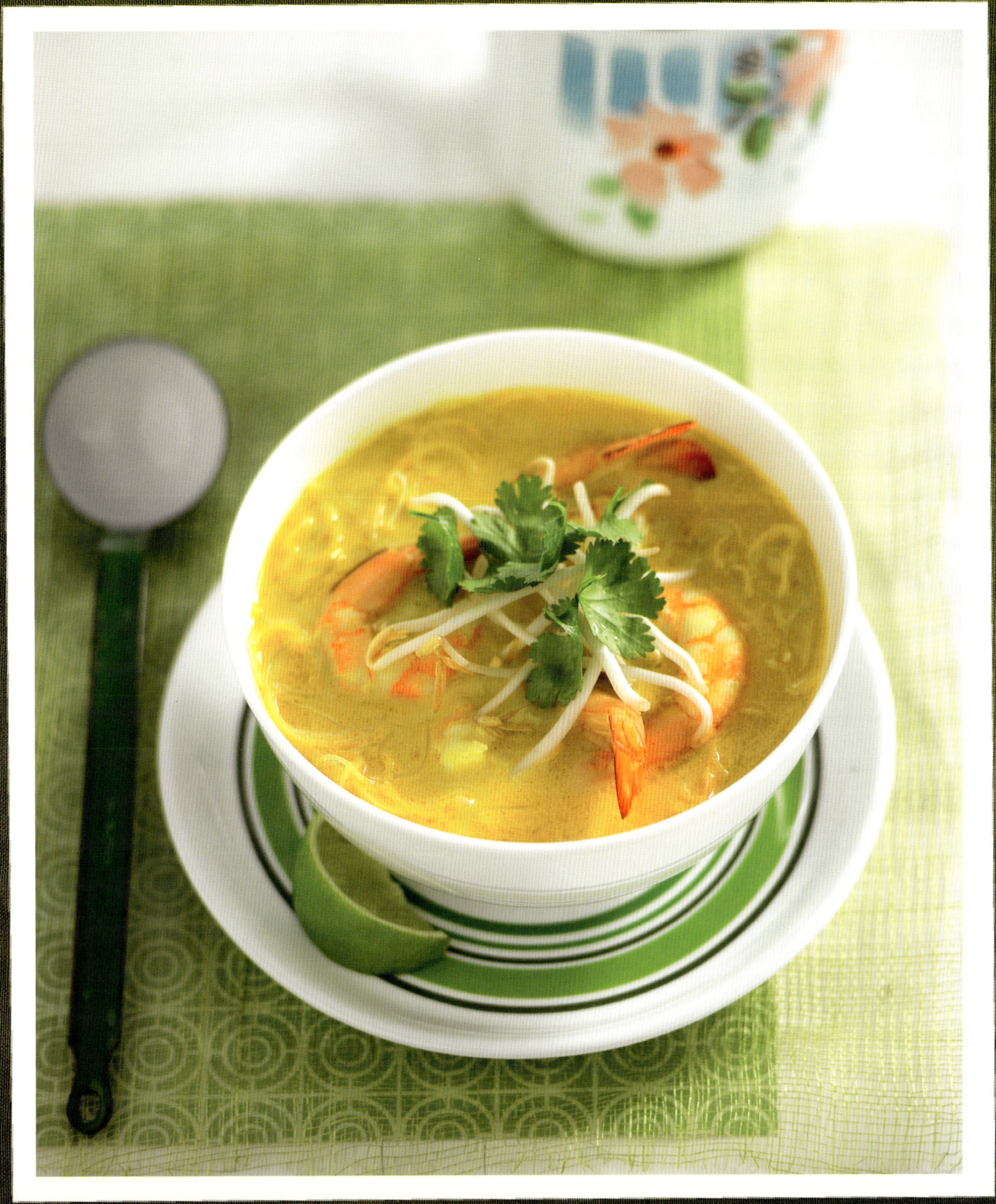

RIGHT: (From left) Marion's Mum, Noi Grasby, Marion, Marion's Grandma and Marion's Aunty Oi in Marion's Grandma's house in Noi's village, Nakhon Chum, Thailand.

Marion Grasby

Food was such an ingrained part of my life growing up and I've always loved it. It's like knowing that you've always loved your parents, even though you can't quite say when it was that you started loving them.

My mum is from Thailand and our dinners included laab salad, curries and my favourite, kai palo (soy-braised pork and egg). Laab salad is everything I love about Thai food – spicy chilli, salty fish sauce, tart lime juice and fresh herbs. I loved piling the salad up into a lettuce leaf cup. I also love wandering through an Asian market and smelling that heady mixture of herbs and ripe mangoes. My mum was a chef, so we loved to experiment. When we wanted a change we'd cook pasta. As I got older we got quite competitive too, so Dad often sat down to two separate dishes at dinner.

My fondest memory was cooking in my Mother's village in Thailand with her and her family. The village kitchen is only two outside clay pot stoves. I can't speak Thai and my mother's family can't speak English but we had a great time cooking together.

ABOVE: Marion's Mum, Noi Grasby, holds a one-year-old Marion in the driveway of their house in Darwin.

Asian
108

BELOW: Poh and her Great Aunty Kim.

Poh Ling Yeow

I come from a food-obsessed culture in Malaysia. Between the three main cultures of Malay, Indian and Chinese cuisines, there is an amazing diversity of flavours.

I had the privilege of growing up with two matriarchs in the house: my Mum and my Great Aunty Kim. My earliest food memory was probably watching my Aunty prepare Buddhist vegetarian food. When I was little I'd help with menial tasks like plucking herbs. With Mum it was much later, after we migrated to Australia, and she would let me help her bake when I was nine-years-old. My Mum's strength is in baking, so there's a strong tradition in that between us, especially at Christmas. My favourite recipe of Mum's is crème caramel – it's my all-time favourite dessert – whereas my Aunt's is a simple mint omelette. Even though it seems like one of the easiest things in the world to make, I can never make it like her. She has that elusive magic touch.

ABOVE: Poh sits between her "two mums": Great Aunty Kim (left) and Mum, Christina Yeow (right).

Asian
109

Yumi Stynes

Growing up, food was just as important as education in our house. We would sit down and eat every meal together, the television was never on and we always minded our manners, even if it was just us at the table. The kitchen was the heart of our household and my Mum was at its centre. She would tell us she loved us through her cooking.

As a native Japanese speaker, my Mother was sometimes hesitant with her English so a lot of her self-expression came through her food. A treat in my childhood was a sheet of seaweed or some sweet adzuki bean dessert with pounded rice; we thought that was terrific. And as a weeknight meal when she couldn't be bothered cooking, she'd give us a simple bowl of rice with raw egg, soya sauce and seaweed; we thought that was also brilliant.

My earliest memory in the kitchen was trying to make a fruit salad for the family dessert. Somehow I latched on to the idea that it would be a real gift to my Mother to cut the fruit into really small pieces (less chewing, maybe?!). Anyway, it looked like it had been run over by the lawnmower a couple of times, complete with lawn clippings.

It's ironic that in spite of her Japanese background and her brilliance in the kitchen, the recipe that my brother and sisters and I always love from my Mum comes from a 1970s *The Australian Women's Weekly Cookbook*. It's for Chinese chicken wings – not even Japanese! These were a regular meal at my Mum's and they're a regular at mine. Now that I'm a mum too, whenever my daughters have a birthday, I'll ask my Mum to bring over some food. She will usually bring these chicken wings and some sushi rolls – they're also excellent.

RIGHT: Yumi has a laugh with her "excellent" Mum, Yoshiko Stynes.

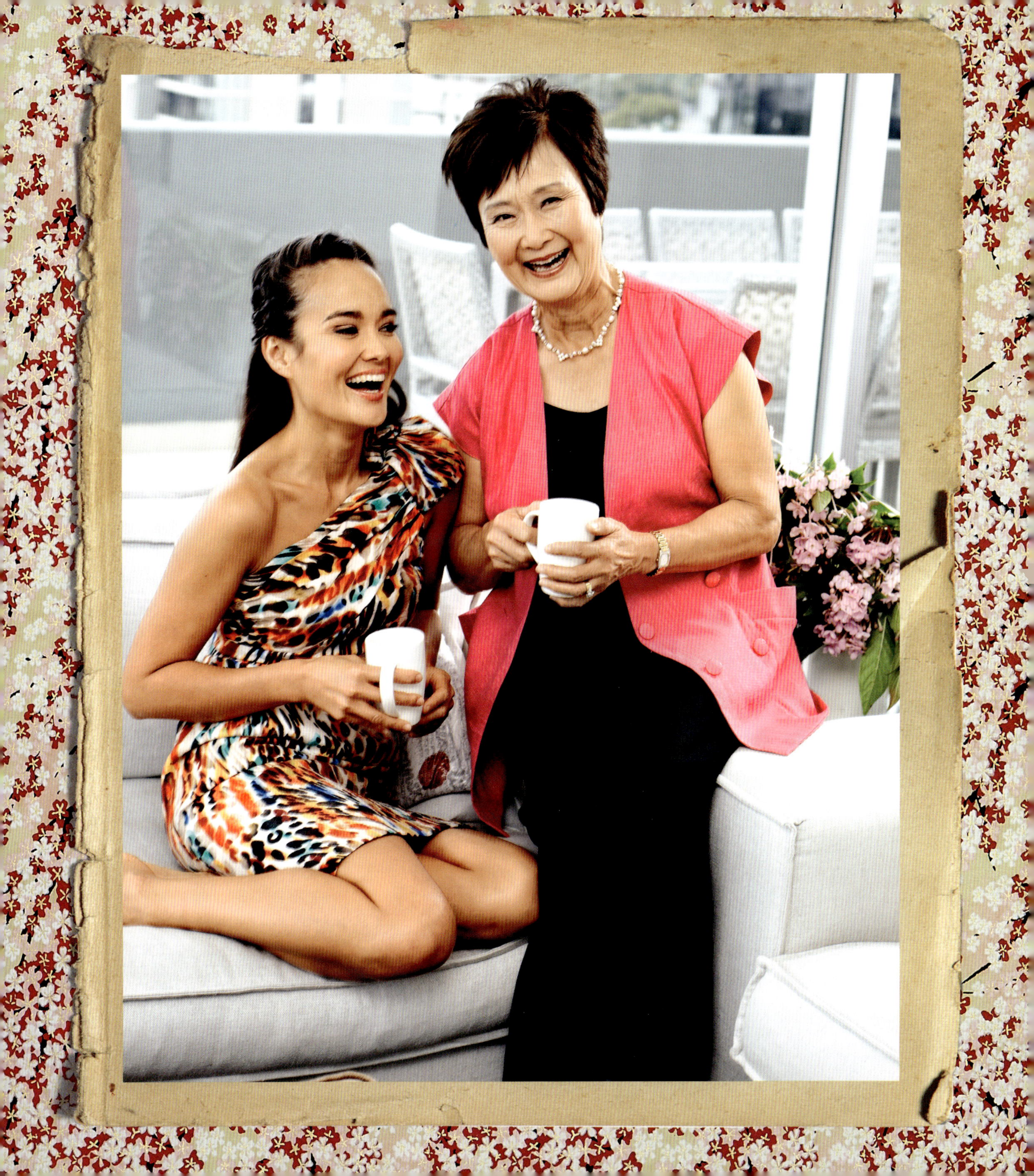

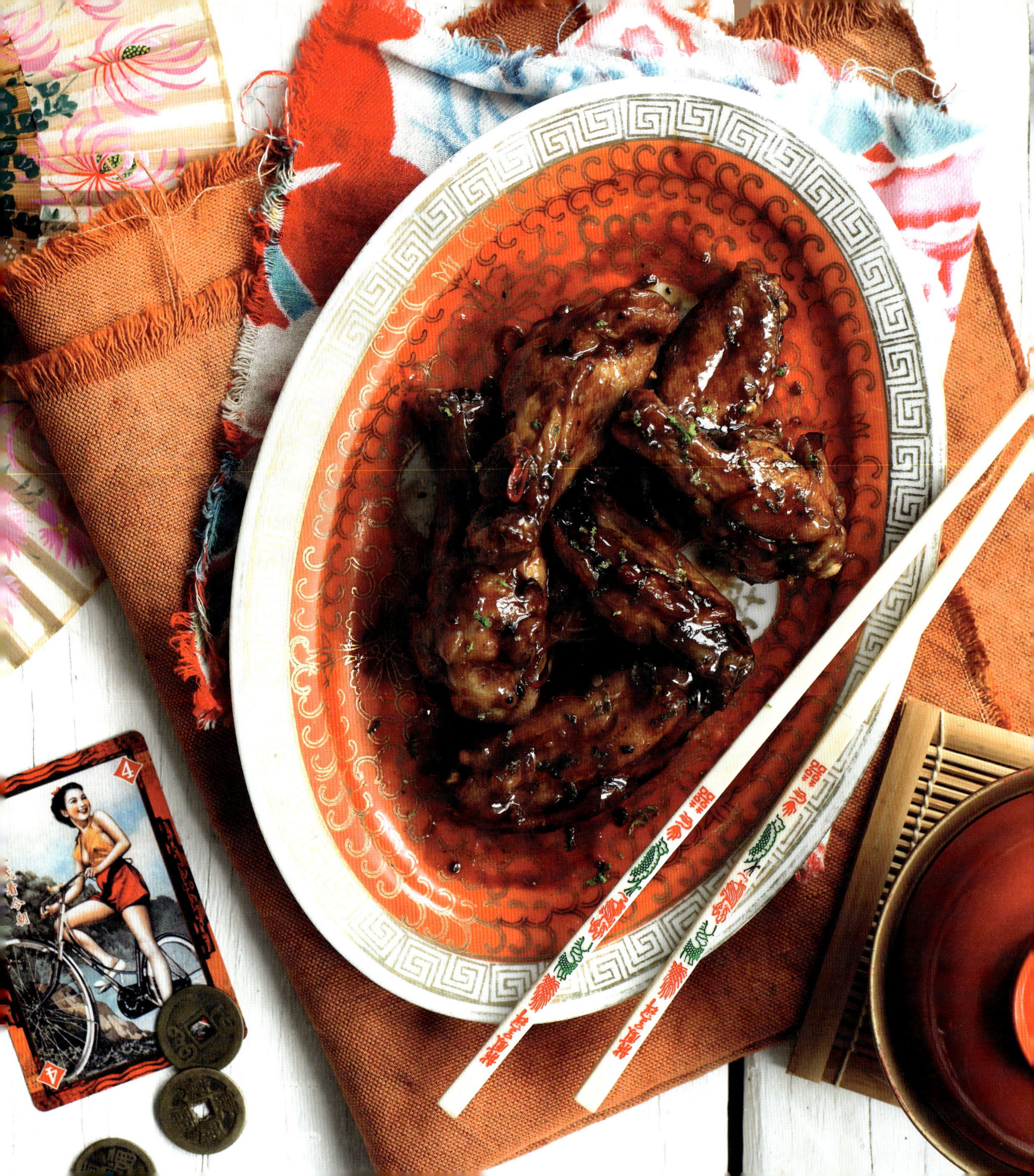

Chinese chicken wings

1.2kg (2½ pounds) chicken wings
vegetable oil, for shallow-frying
1 tablespoon peanut oil
3 cloves garlic, crushed
2cm (¾-inch) piece fresh ginger (10g), sliced finely
2 fresh small red thai (serrano) chillies, sliced finely
1 teaspoon chilli powder
1 teaspoon freshly cracked black peppercorns
2 tablespoons caster (superfine) sugar
¼ cup (60ml) chicken stock
¼ cup (60ml) salt-reduced soy sauce
2 tablespoons each oyster sauce and plum sauce
1 tablespoon rice vinegar
¼ teaspoon sesame oil
2 teaspoons grated lime rind

1 Remove and discard tips from wings. Cut remaining pieces into two sections at joint.
2 Place wings in large saucepan, cover with cold water; bring to the boil. Reduce heat; simmer, uncovered, 3 minutes. Drain wings; pat dry with absorbent paper.
3 Heat vegetable oil in frying pan; shallow-fry wings, in batches, until browned. Drain on absorbent paper.
4 Heat peanut oil in wok; stir-fry garlic and ginger until fragrant. Add chilli, chilli powder, pepper and sugar; stir in stock, sauces, vinegar and sesame oil. Bring to the boil; add wings, cook, stirring, about 3 minutes or until chicken is glazed and heated through. Serve sprinkled with rind.

prep + cook time 35 minutes **serves** 4
nutritional count per serving 31.7g total fat (6.3g saturated fat); 2257kJ (540 cal); 19.2g carbohydrate; 44.8g protein; 0.6g fibre

RIGHT: "This picture was taken in 1983. We were visiting Japan together and I was eight years old. My hair has actually never looked better!" grins Yumi.

Asian

Fresh coriander (cilantro), is also called chinese parsley; it is a bright-green-leafed herb with a pungent flavour, often stirred into or sprinkled over a dish just before serving for maximum impact. Both the stems and roots of coriander are also used in Thai cooking; wash well before chopping.

Fish curry in lime and coconut

6 fresh small red thai (serrano) chillies, chopped coarsely
2 cloves garlic, quartered
10 shallots (250g), chopped coarsely
10cm (4-inch) stick fresh lemon grass (20g), chopped coarsely
5cm (2-inch) piece fresh galangal (25g), quartered
¼ cup coarsely chopped coriander (cilantro) root and stem mixture
¼ teaspoon ground turmeric
1 tablespoon peanut oil
3¼ cups (800ml) canned coconut milk
2 tablespoons fish sauce
4 fresh kaffir lime leaves, shredded
1 tablespoon lime juice
4 x 200g (6½ ounces) kingfish fillets
½ cup loosely packed fresh coriander (cilantro) leaves

1 Blend or process chilli, garlic, shallot, lemon grass, galangal, coriander root and stem mixture, turmeric and oil until mixture forms a smooth paste.
2 Cook paste in large frying pan, stirring, over medium heat, about 3 minutes or until fragrant. Add coconut milk, sauce and lime leaves; bring to a boil. Reduce heat; simmer, uncovered, about 15 minutes or until thickened slightly. Stir in juice.
3 Add fish to pan; simmer, uncovered, about 10 minutes or until cooked. Serve curry sprinkled with coriander leaves.

prep + cook time 1 hour **serves** 4
nutritional count per serving 50.6g total fat (38.5g saturated fat); 2867kJ (686 cal); 10.6g carbohydrate; 45.9g protein; 4.9g fibre
tip We used kingfish in this curry, but you can replace it with any firm white fish with a meaty texture.
serving suggestion Serve with steamed basmati rice.

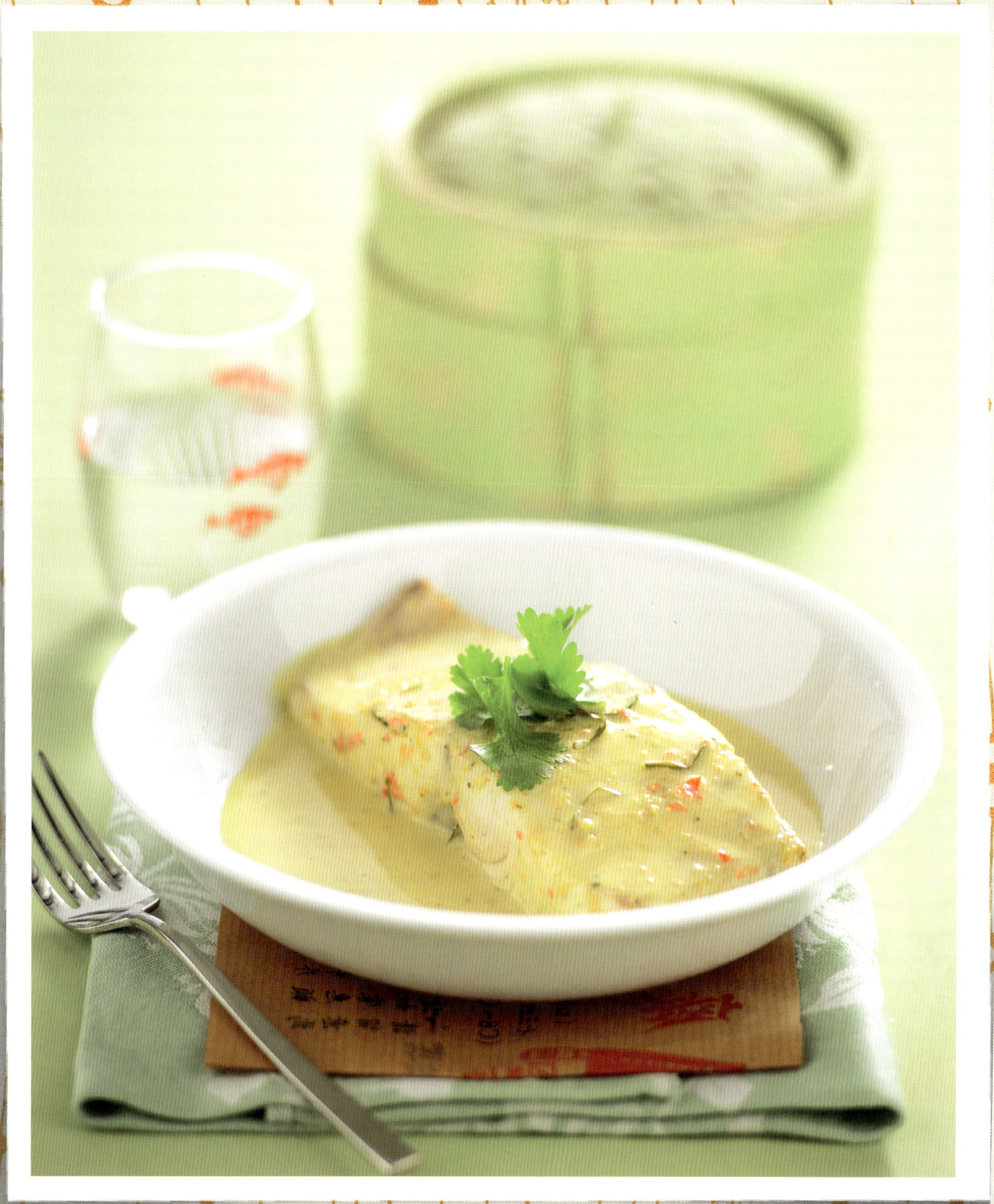

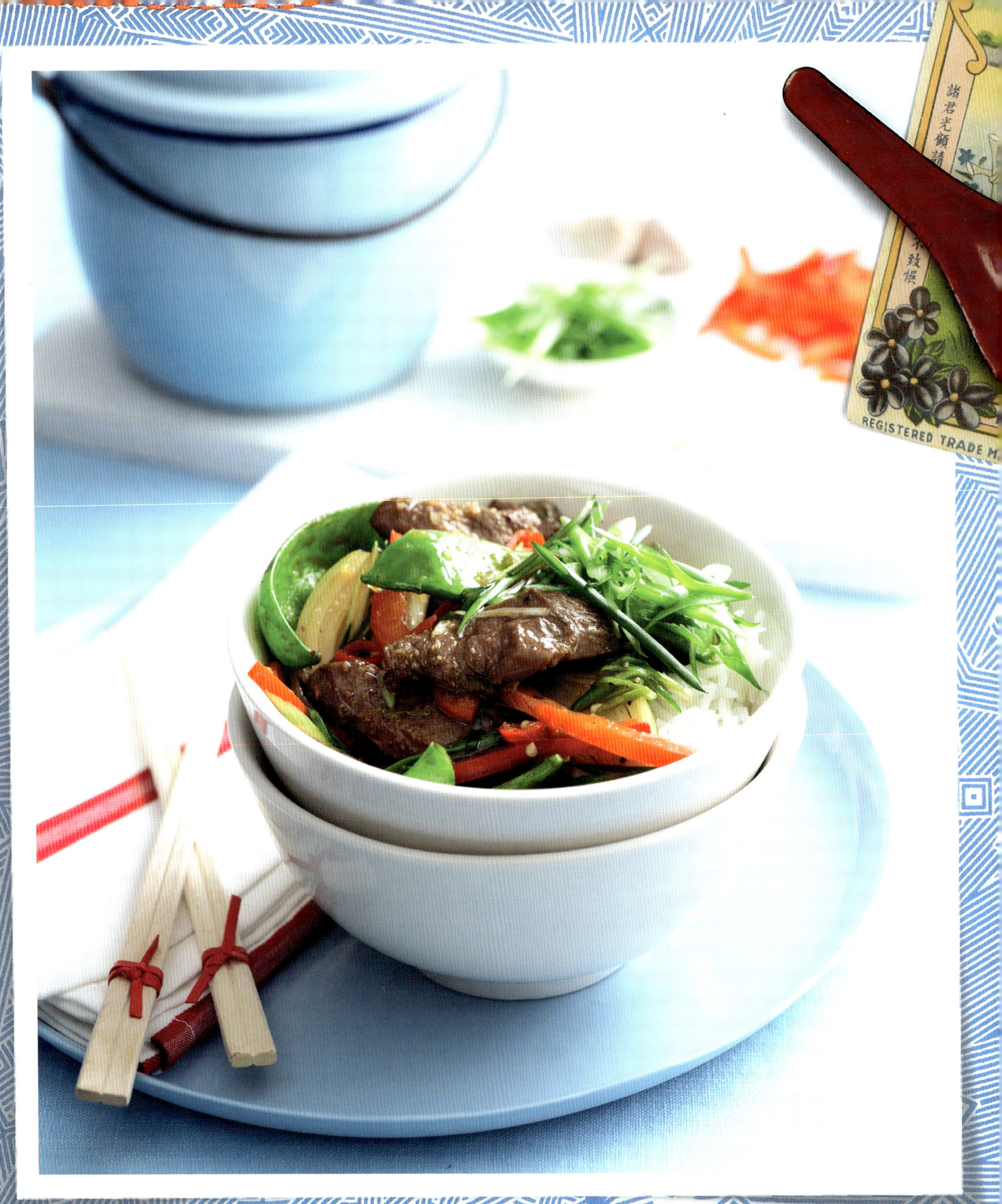
諸君光顧請
致悞
REGISTERED TRADE MA

Mongolian lamb

250g (8 ounces) lamb fillet, sliced thinly
2 teaspoons light soy sauce
2 teaspoons cornflour (cornstarch)
2cm (¾-inch) piece fresh ginger (10g), grated
1 clove garlic, crushed
1 tablespoon mirin
½ teaspoon sesame oil
1 tablespoon peanut oil
1 small brown onion (80g), cut into wedges
1 small red capsicum (bell pepper) (150g), sliced thinly
1 tablespoon hoisin sauce
2 teaspoons oyster sauce
1 tablespoon water
100g (3 ounces) snow peas, trimmed
1 fresh small red thai (serrano) chilli, chopped finely
2 green onions (scallions), sliced thinly

1 Combine lamb, soy sauce, cornflour, ginger, garlic, mirin and sesame oil in small bowl.
2 Heat half the peanut oil in wok; stir-fry lamb mixture, in batches, until browned. Remove from wok.
3 Heat remaining oil in wok; stir-fry brown onion and capsicum until tender. Return lamb to wok with hoisin and oyster sauces, the water and peas; stir-fry until hot. Remove from heat; stir in chilli and half the green onion, season. Serve sprinkled with remaining green onion.

prep + cook time 25 minutes **serves** 2
nutritional count per serving 16.5g total fat (3.7g saturated fat); 1459kJ (349 cal); 15.4g carbohydrate; 31.4g protein; 4g fibre
tip Lamb mixture can be marinated for 3 hours or overnight in the refrigerator.
serving suggestion Serve with steamed jasmine rice or rice noodles.

Asian

This pudding is also great served topped with fresh mango slices instead of the banana.

Coconut sago pudding with caramelised banana

5cm (2-inch) strip fresh lime rind
1 cup (200g) sago
¼ cup (60ml) water
½ cup (135g) firmly packed grated palm sugar
⅔ cup (160ml) canned coconut cream
4 unpeeled sugar bananas (520g), halved lengthways
1 tablespoon grated palm sugar, extra
½ teaspoon finely grated lime rind

1 Place strip of rind in large saucepan of cold water; bring to the boil. Discard rind; add sago. Reduce heat; simmer, uncovered, about 15 minutes or until sago is almost transparent. Drain; rinse under cold water. Drain.
2 Meanwhile, stir the water and sugar in small saucepan over heat, without boiling, until sugar dissolves. Bring to the boil; boil, uncovered, without stirring, 10 minutes or until toffee coloured. Remove from heat; stir in coconut cream. Cool 10 minutes.
3 Sprinkle cut side of banana with extra sugar. Place, cut-side down, on heated greased grill plate (or grill or barbecue); cook about 5 minutes or until tender.
4 Combine sago in medium bowl with coconut mixture and grated rind. Divide among serving bowls; serve with banana, and extra lime rind, if you like

prep + cook time 35 minutes **serves** 4
nutritional count per serving 7.5g total fat (6.4g saturated fat); 2065kJ (494 cal); 101.3g carbohydrate; 2.1g protein; 4.1g fibre

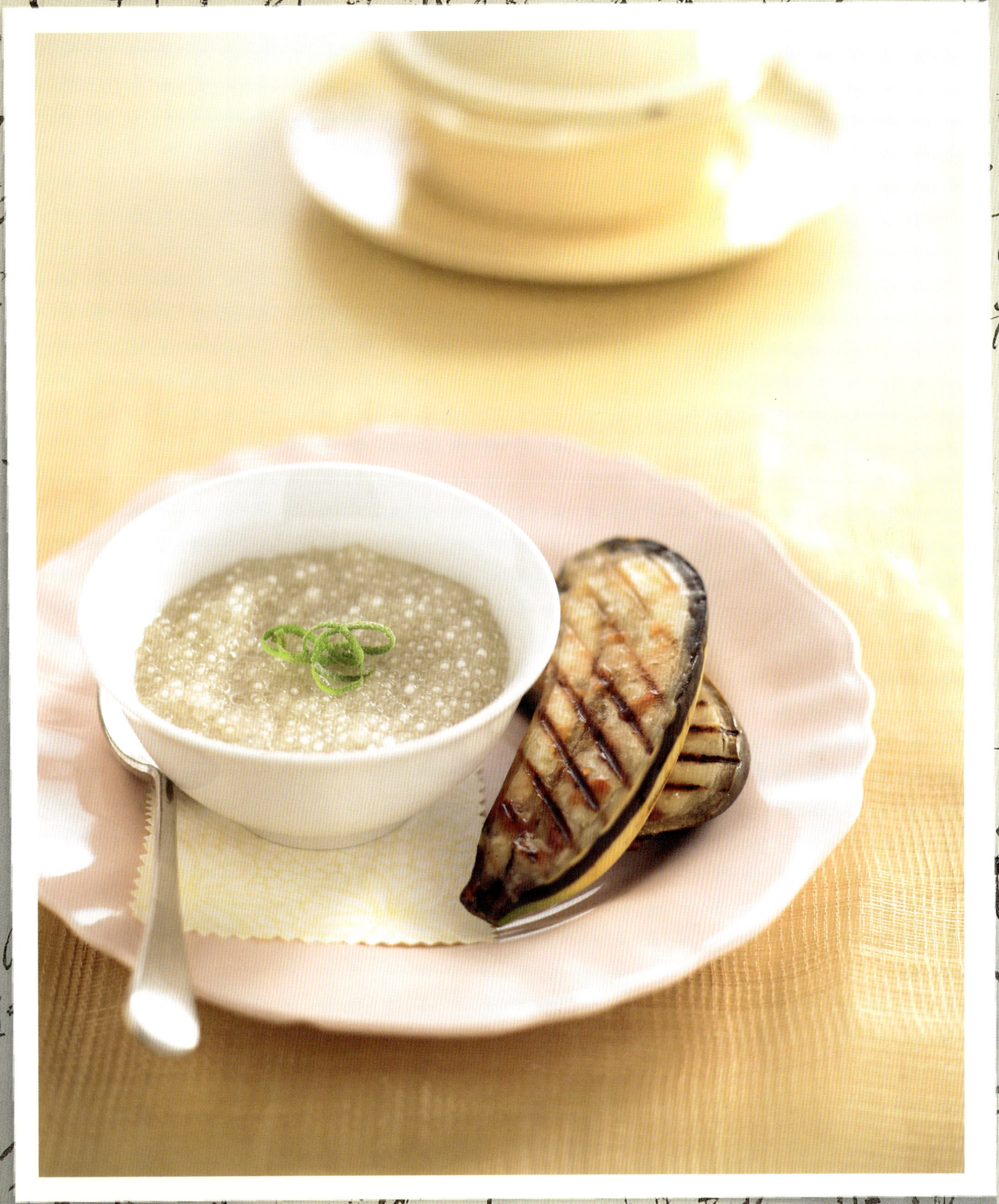

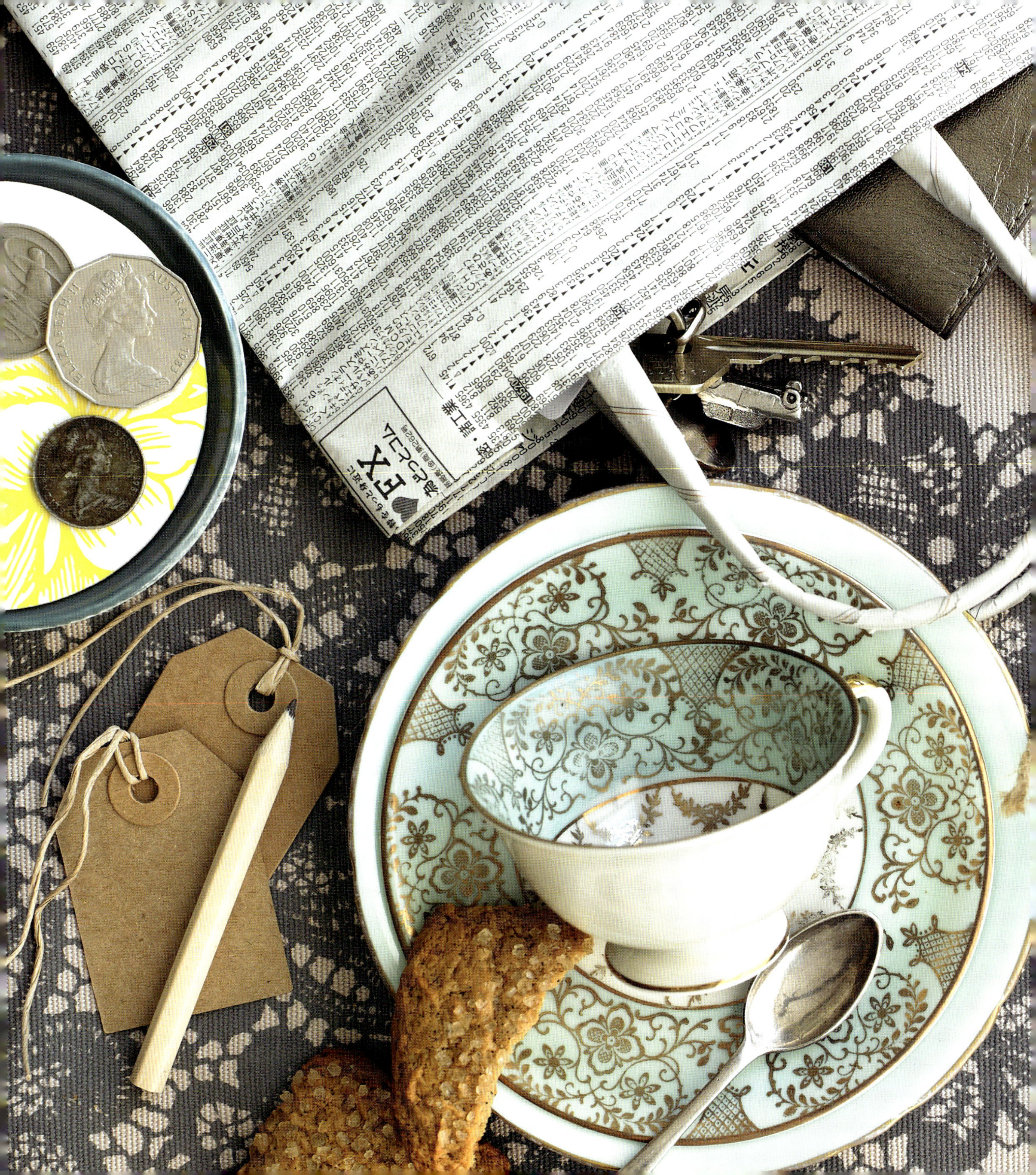
AUSTRALIA
ELIZABETH II
EX

Modern Mums

Mums today still do it all – working inside and often also outside, the home. Quick, low-fuss meals are the order of the day as preparation and cooking starts when mum gets home. The trick is finding the balance between convenience and nutrition.

Lisa Wilkinson

There was no gourmet cooking in our home; it was mostly meat and three-veg. But I still love a home-cooked meal by Mum. Baked beans on toast or piping hot tomato soup were our family's easy go-to meals. I still love Rice A Riso too – it's packet rice, but it's delicious and similar to risotto. Now that I'm a mum, I've added bruschetta to that I'm-too-tired-to-cook menu, as it's the tastiest quickie meal.

Billi and I have similar loves when it comes to food — she has always been great with vegies and salads, and loves her chocolate fix just as much as her Mum. But the trick with this bruschetta recipe is to really load the topping up with plenty of fresh basil and garlic… so you may want to avoid anyone outside the family for a few days. But believe me, it's worth it.

The recipe can work with either sourdough or any kind of French bread, but we always use a grain bread we buy from the local bakery that you cut yourself. And if you want to bulk it up a bit for the boys (who go through it like the world is about to end), you can always crumble goat's cheese on top.

I have fond memories of making slices too. Saturday and Sunday afternoons I would quite often whip up a chocolate coconut slice, as well as recipes that had peanut butter in them. One of the biggest treats though, growing up, was when Mum cooked jam drop biscuits. I knew it was going to be a great afternoon when, as I got closer to the house after walking home from school, I could smell them wafting out of the oven. Mum would always time it so that just as we were getting home, they were coming out of the oven.

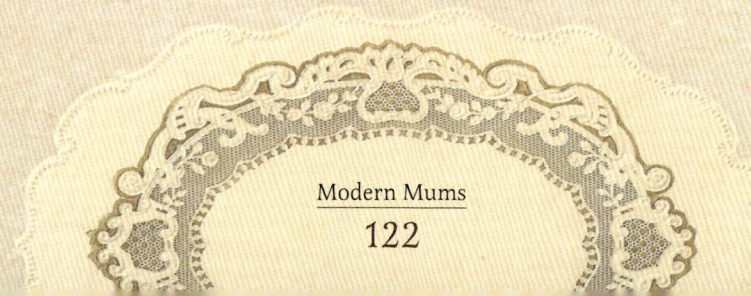

RIGHT: Lisa and her 13-year-old daughter Billi love cooking together.

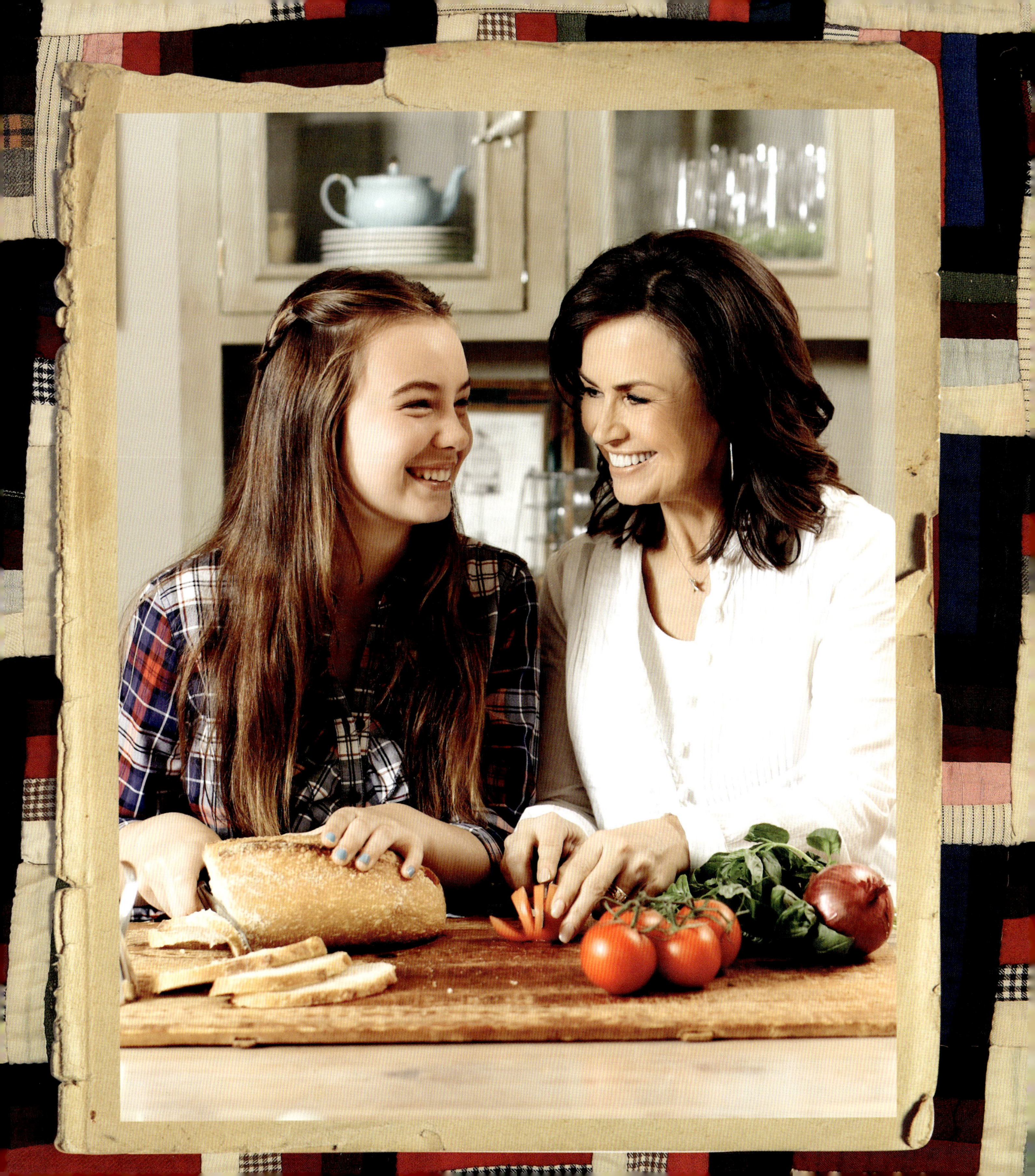

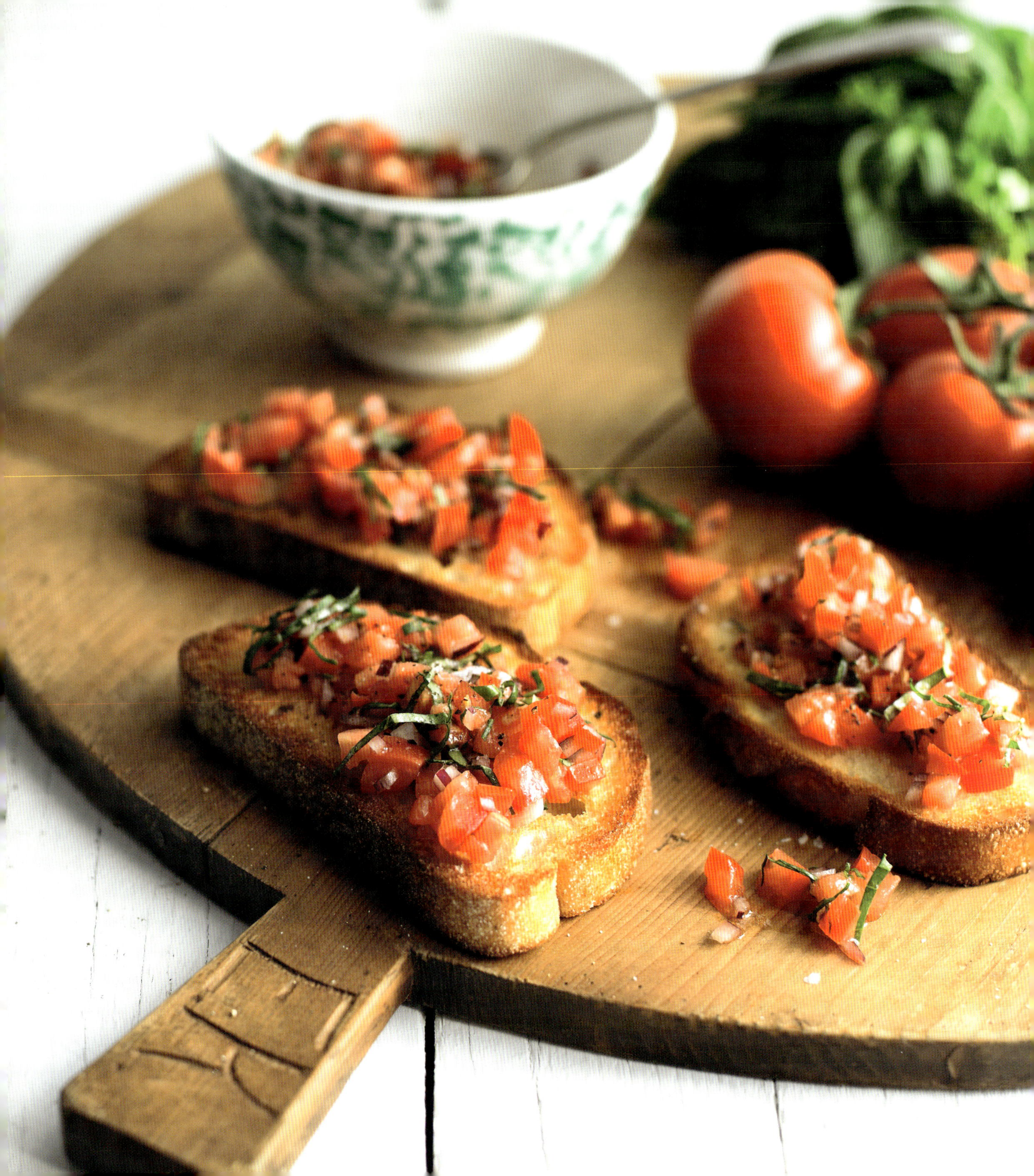

Buddy the doll was bought by my Mum at St. Vincent's De Paul for $2 when our eldest son, Jake, was six months old. He kept it until he was three, then gave it to Louis who had it until he was three, who then gave it to Billi. Buddy now sits on an old antique cupboard.

Bruschetta

2 medium tomatoes (300g), seeded, chopped finely
½ small red onion (50g), chopped finely
1 clove garlic, crushed
1 tablespoon red wine vinegar
2 tablespoons olive oil
4 slices sourdough bread (280g)
cooking-oil spray
2 tablespoons finely shredded fresh basil

1 Preheat oven to 220°C/425°F.
2 Combine tomato, onion, garlic, vinegar and oil in small bowl. Stand 20 minutes.
3 Meanwhile, place bread on oiled oven tray; spray with cooking oil. Toast, in oven (or under grill), until browned both sides.
4 Stir basil into tomato mixture, spoon onto toasted bread.

prep + cook time 10 minutes (+ standing)
makes 4
nutritional count per bruschetta 11.2g total fat (1.6g saturated fat); 1116kJ (267 cal); 32.8g carbohydrate; 6.6g protein; 3.9g fibre

RIGHT: (From left) Lisa, daughter Billi aged 8 months old and Mum, Beryl.

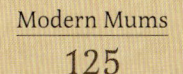

Modern Mums

If you're after a shortcut, you can skip making the tortilla baskets in steps 1 and 2, and simply serve the beef mixture, avocado salsa and accompaniments in warmed tortillas.

Beef burrito baskets

cooking-oil spray
4 x 15cm (6 inches) flour tortillas
2 tablespoons olive oil
600g (1¼ pounds) beef rump steak, sliced thinly
1 medium brown onion (150g), chopped coarsely
1 small green capsicum (bell pepper) (150g), sliced thinly
1 small yellow capsicum (bell pepper) (150g), sliced thinly
1 clove garlic, crushed
1 teaspoon ground cumin
½ teaspoon ground coriander
¼ teaspoon ground cayenne pepper
400g (12½ ounces) canned diced tomatoes
1½ cups (375ml) beef stock
1 tablespoon coarsely chopped fresh oregano
400g (12½ ounces) canned kidney beans, drained, rinsed
1 cup (120g) coarsely grated cheddar cheese
⅓ cup (80g) sour cream
⅓ cup loosely packed fresh coriander (cilantro) leaves

AVOCADO SALSA
1 medium avocado (250g), chopped finely
1 medium tomato (150g), seeded, chopped finely
½ small red onion (50g), chopped finely
1 tablespoon lime juice
1 tablespoon olive oil

1 Preheat oven to 180°C/350°F. Spray four holes of six-hole (¾-cup/180ml) texas muffin pan with oil.
2 Push tortillas carefully into pan holes; bake about 15 minutes or until crisp. Cool in pan.
3 Meanwhile, heat half the oil in large frying pan; cook beef, in batches, over high heat, until browned. Remove from pan.
4 Heat remaining oil in same pan; cook onion, capsicums, garlic and spices, stirring, until onion softens. Return beef to pan with undrained tomatoes, stock and oregano; simmer, uncovered, about 1 hour or until sauce thickens and is reduced by half. Add beans; stir until heated through.
5 Meanwhile, make avocado salsa.
6 Divide beef mixture into tortilla cups; top with cheese. Bake about 5 minutes or until cheese melts.
7 Serve burrito baskets topped with sour cream, avocado salsa and coriander.

avocado salsa Combine ingredients in small bowl.

prep + cook time 1 hour 55 minutes **serves** 4
nutritional count per serving 54.9g total fat (20.7g saturated fat); 3507kJ (839 cal); 30.1g carbohydrate; 52.9g protein; 8.8g fibre

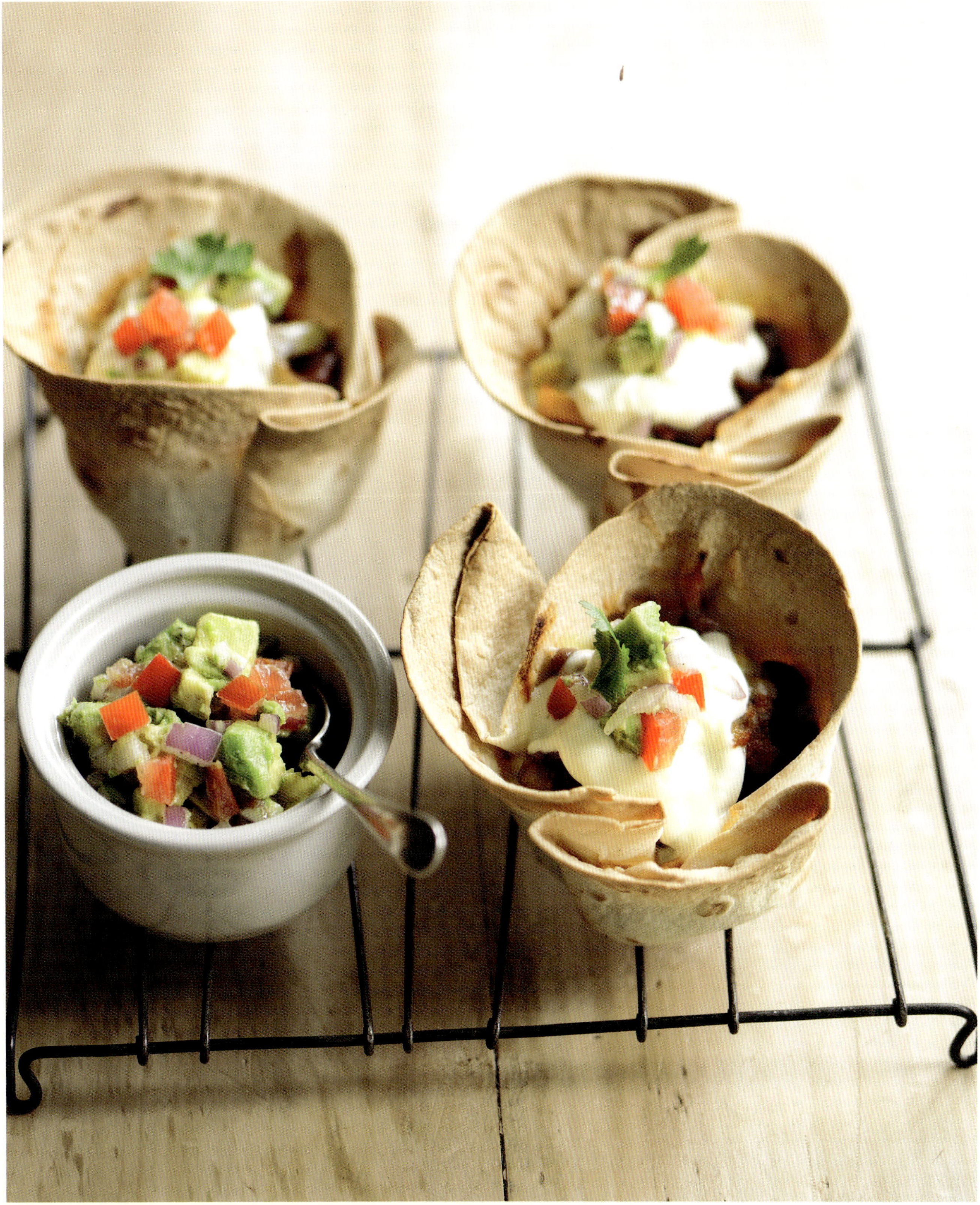

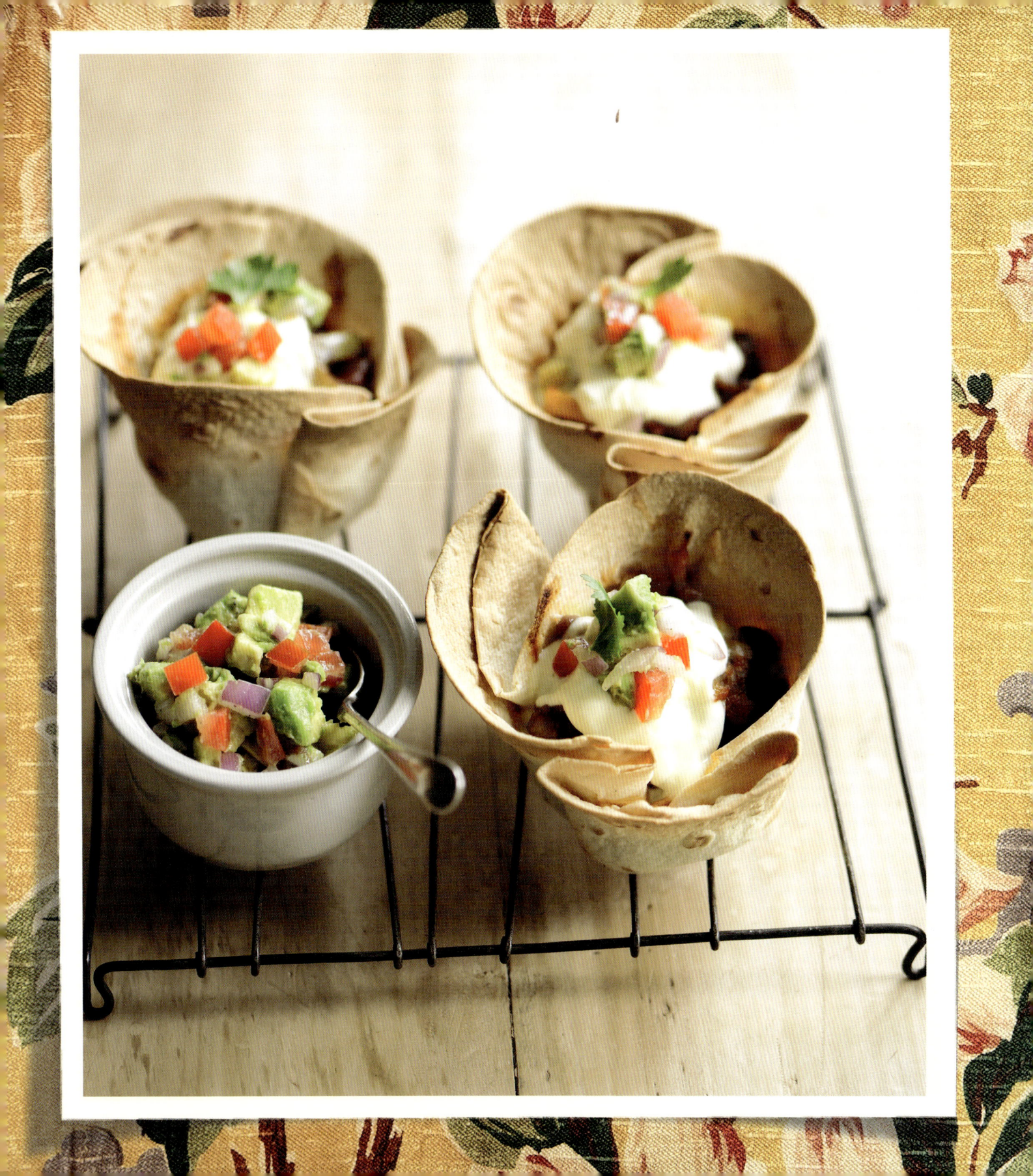

Eggplant, haloumi and rocket pizza

1½ cups (225g) plain (all-purpose) flour
1 teaspoon dried yeast
½ teaspoon salt
¾ cup (180ml) warm water
2 tablespoons olive oil
¾ cup (195g) bottled tomato pasta sauce
2 cloves garlic, crushed
2 small red onions (200g), cut into wedges
1 small eggplant (230g), sliced thinly
250g (8 ounces) haloumi cheese, sliced thinly
¼ cup firmly packed fresh oregano leaves
60g (2 ounces) rocket (arugula) leaves

1 Combine flour, yeast and salt in medium bowl; gradually stir in the water and half the oil. Mix to a soft, sticky dough; turn onto floured surface, knead about 10 minutes or until smooth and elastic. Shape dough into ball; place in large oiled bowl. Cover; stand in warm place 1 hour or until dough doubles in size.
2 Preheat oven to 230°C/450°F. Oil two oven trays.
3 Punch down dough; knead until smooth. Divide dough in half; roll each half on floured surface into two 23cm x 33cm (9-inch x 13-inch) rectangles. Place dough on trays; prick with fork, spread with combined pasta sauce and garlic. Stand in warm place 10 minutes.
4 Meanwhile, combine onion, eggplant and remaining oil in large bowl. Cook, in batches, on heated grill plate (or grill or barbecue) until browned on both sides.
5 Top pizza bases with onion and eggplant mixture, cheese and oregano.
6 Bake pizzas about 15 minutes or until crust is golden brown. Serve topped with rocket.

prep + cook time 40 minutes (+ standing) **serves** 4
nutritional count per serving 21.2g total fat (8.3g saturated fat); 2065kJ (494 cal); 50.9g carbohydrate; 22.1g protein; 5.6g fibre

Smoked salmon and poached egg on rye

4 eggs
170g (5½ ounces) asparagus, halved crossways
4 slices (180g) rye bread, toasted
200g (6½ ounces) smoked salmon
2 tablespoons fresh chervil leaves

1 Half fill large shallow frying pan with water; bring to the boil. Break one egg into cup, slide into pan. Repeat with remaining eggs, when all eggs are in pan, allow water to return to the boil.
2 Cover pan, turn off heat; stand about 4 minutes or until a light film sets over egg yolks. Remove eggs, one at a time, using slotted spoon; place spoon on absorbent-paper-lined saucer briefly to blot up poaching liquid.
3 Meanwhile, boil, steam or microwave asparagus until tender; drain.
4 Divide toast among serving plates; top each with salmon, asparagus then egg. Serve sprinkled with chervil leaves.

prep + cook time 15 minutes **serves** 4
nutritional count per serving 8.8g total fat (2.2g saturated fat); 1175kJ (281 cal); 24.5g carbohydrate; 23.7g protein; 4.1g fibre

Chrissie Swan

Growing up we ate together every night at 6pm; we had a great routine and each had a different duty for meal preparation. Mine was to set the knives and forks on the table – our metal cutlery had little grapevines on the handles. I still have great memories of dinnertime in the 70s.

In the 70s, Mum had a full family to look after. But by the 80s, my sisters were soon to move out and Dad was living in Adelaide, so it was just me and Mum and things became more casual. We'd have curried sausages or ki si min (curried mince and cabbage) and for special occasions, there was beef stroganoff or coq au vin. Mum always believed in a good breakfast and now I'm the same way. So, it'd be scrambled eggs with onion and curly parsley, or a boiled egg with toast. We were one of the first families to always have multigrain bread too: a very new thing back in the 70s.

One thing that I really remember was our cookie jar as a kid. It was a mission brown plastic affair with a mosque-like fluted lid and a big round knob on top. It lived in a pantry with a slatted-timber door and was stocked mainly with Arnott's Family Assorted biscuits.

My favourite recipe of Mum's has always been her steamed golden syrup pudding. She used this fabulous aluminium steamer bowl with a lid; we always got very excited when we saw it. Also, she makes great pikelets. She always used the same jug for the batter and I clearly remember the smell of the frying pan heating up. She would cook each one then flip it onto a plate with a paper towel on it, then cover the pile in a tea towel to keep them moist and warm.

RIGHT: Chrissie forms a mean team in the kitchen with her Mum, Pat Swan.

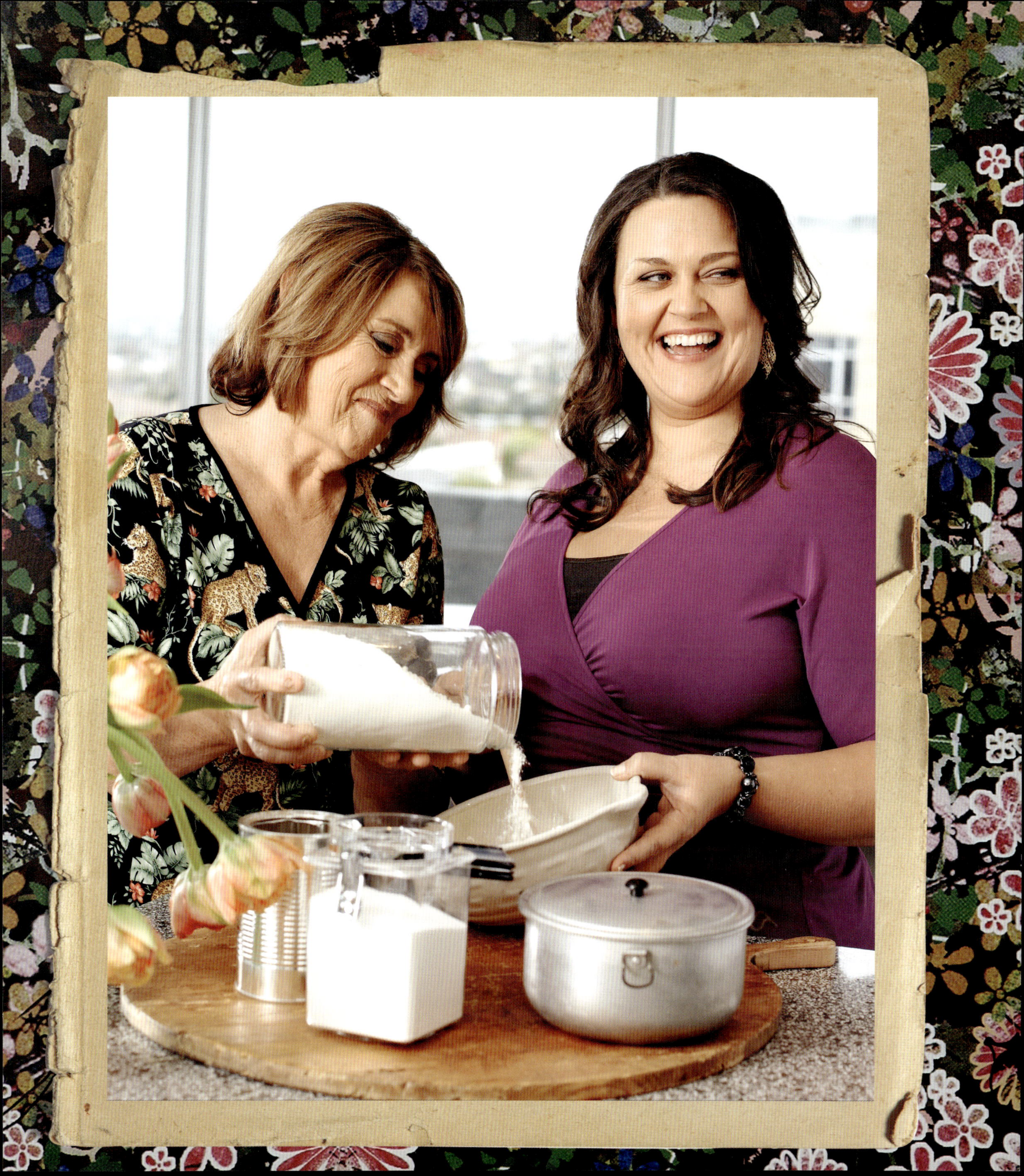

These dumplings are made from a scone-type dough. cooking them in the sauce infuses them with the sweet flavour. You'll need to use a saucepan large enough to allow the dumplings to expand in the simmering sauce. if the dumplings don't expand they won't cook through. If the pan is too large, too much of the sauce will evaporate before the dumplings are added.

This pot is a very old steamed pudding pan. My Mum only used it to make golden syrup pudding and would lose her mind if the lid wasn't returned to it immediately so it was ready to go for 'next time'. It must be 50 years old now. Great memories.

Golden syrup dumplings

1¼ cups (185g) self-raising flour
30g (1 ounce) butter
⅓ cup (115g) golden syrup or treacle
⅓ cup (80ml) milk
SAUCE
30g (1 ounce) butter
¾ cup (165g) firmly packed light brown sugar
½ cup (175g) golden syrup or treacle
1⅔ cups (410ml) water

1 Sift flour into medium bowl; rub in butter. Gradually stir in golden syrup and milk.
2 Make sauce.
3 Drop rounded tablespoonfuls of mixture into simmering sauce; simmer, covered, about 20 minutes. Serve dumplings with sauce and cream or ice-cream.
sauce Stir ingredients in large saucepan over heat, without boiling, until sugar dissolves. Bring to the boil, without stirring. Reduce heat; simmer, uncovered, 5 minutes.

prep + cook time 30 minutes **serves** 4
nutritional count per serving
13.6g total fat (8.7g saturated fat); 2788kJ (667 cal); 128g carbohydrate; 5.6g protein; 1.8g fibre

ABOVE: Chrissie and her Mum in the 1980s.

BELOW: "Here we are at home in East Hawthorn in 1984. I'm in my school uniform and Mum has on lovely designer knitwear!"

Modern Mums

RIGHT: Today, Shelley shares hosting duties across a range of popular primetime television shows.

Shelley Craft

Mum was a good cook but she hardly cooks at all now. Since everyone moved out she must have decided, "Thank God I don't have to do that anymore." It's no wonder; she would prepare a beautiful spaghetti bolognese and someone would say "there's too much onion" or "I don't like mushrooms." We often rotated chicken, spag bol, lamb, steak and Chinese takeaway. A lot of families will probably relate to that menu.

I had absolutely zero interest in cooking. Even now, I'm very good at the preparation but not good at the actual following through. My favourite thing was Coco Pops with ice-cream and every birthday you got to put in a dinner request and roast lamb was always mine. Christmas was pretty much the same menu — a ham, turkey, potato salad – and my dad made the pudding from a family recipe.

ABOVE: Shelley, aged around 14 months is held by her Mother, Sally Caroline Ili

Modern Mums
134

BELOW: Libbi holds three-month-old daughter Dali, while son Che, nearly five years old, plays.

RIGHT: Libbi and son, Che, create the traditional Australian dessert, pavlova.

Libbi Gorr

Family meals were always special in my childhood, around which my extended blended family came together. We'd talk about the day as Mum prepared dinner, after she'd come home from work. Mum made traditional foods but would always adapt the recipe and throw in a surprise. She let us come up with the adaptation sometimes. I still don't follow a recipe methodically, every time. I remember Mum waking up once in the middle of the night after she finally figured out how to cut pinwheel smoked salmon sandwiches to get the swirl of the salmon right. I also loved going fishing with Dad, and then Mum would cook up our flathead. I always made her do patties. On Australia Day every year we have bagels, smoked salmon with barbecued butterfly lamb and Plushkas – a European biscuit. Mum and my aunts also rotate the making of Australian desserts like a lovely fruit-laden pavlova.

Modern Mums
135

Spiced lamb roast with walnut and basil pesto

1½ tablespoons cumin seeds
8 cloves garlic, chopped coarsely
2 tablespoons olive oil
2kg (4 pounds) leg of lamb, trimmed
500g (1 pound) piece pumpkin, cut into thin wedges
2 medium red onions (340g), cut into 6 wedges each
100g (3 ounces) baby rocket (arugula) leaves
2 tablespoons lemon juice
WALNUT AND BASIL PESTO
1½ cups firmly packed fresh basil leaves
½ cup (50g) roasted walnuts
2 cloves garlic, chopped coarsely
⅓ cup (80ml) olive oil
⅓ cup (25g) finely grated parmesan cheese

1 Preheat oven to 180°C/350°F.
2 Dry-fry cumin in small frying pan, stirring, until fragrant. Using mortar and pestle, crush cumin, garlic and half the oil until mixture forms a paste.
3 Place lamb in large shallow baking dish; pierce several times with a sharp knife. Spread paste all over lamb, pressing firmly into cuts. Roast lamb, uncovered, about 1 hour 20 minutes or until cooked as desired.
4 Meanwhile, toss pumpkin and onion with remaining oil in large shallow baking dish; roast, uncovered, in single layer, for the last 20 minutes of lamb cooking time.
5 When lamb is cooked as desired, remove from oven; cover lamb. Increase oven to 220°C/425°F, continue to roast pumpkin and onion, uncovered, about 10 minutes or until tender and browned lightly.
6 Meanwhile, make walnut and basil pesto.
7 Gently combine hot vegetables in large bowl with rocket and juice.
8 Serve lamb with pesto and vegetables.
walnut and basil pesto Blend or process basil, nuts and garlic until chopped finely. With motor operating, add oil in a thin, steady stream; process until mixture is smooth. Add cheese; blend until combined.

prep + cook time 2 hours **serves** 6
nutritional count per serving 39.3g total fat (10g saturated fat); 2654kJ (635 cal); 8.9g carbohydrate; 60.4g protein; 3.5g fibre
tip The lamb and vegetables can be prepared, ready for roasting, a day ahead of time.
serving suggestion Serve with crusty bread.

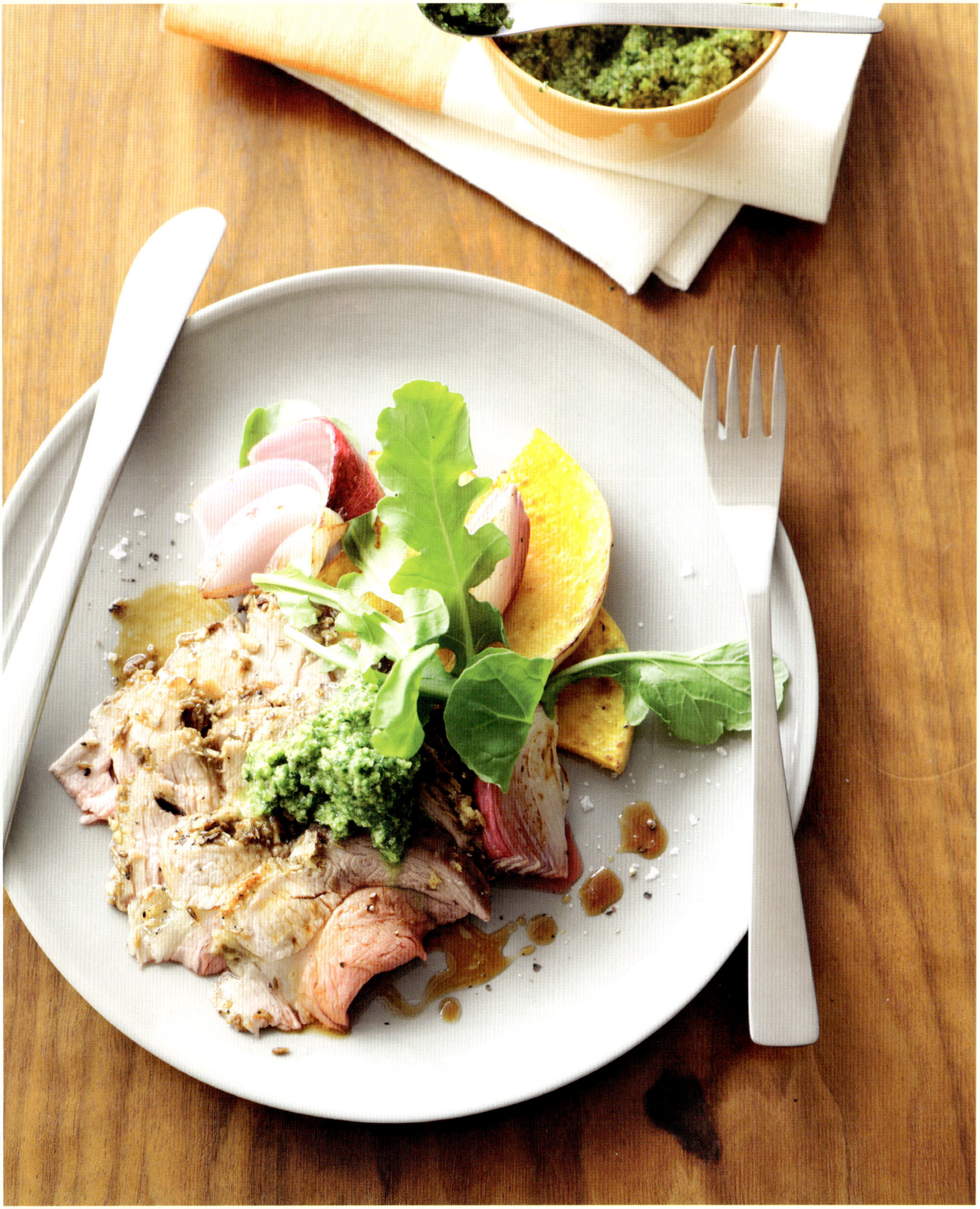

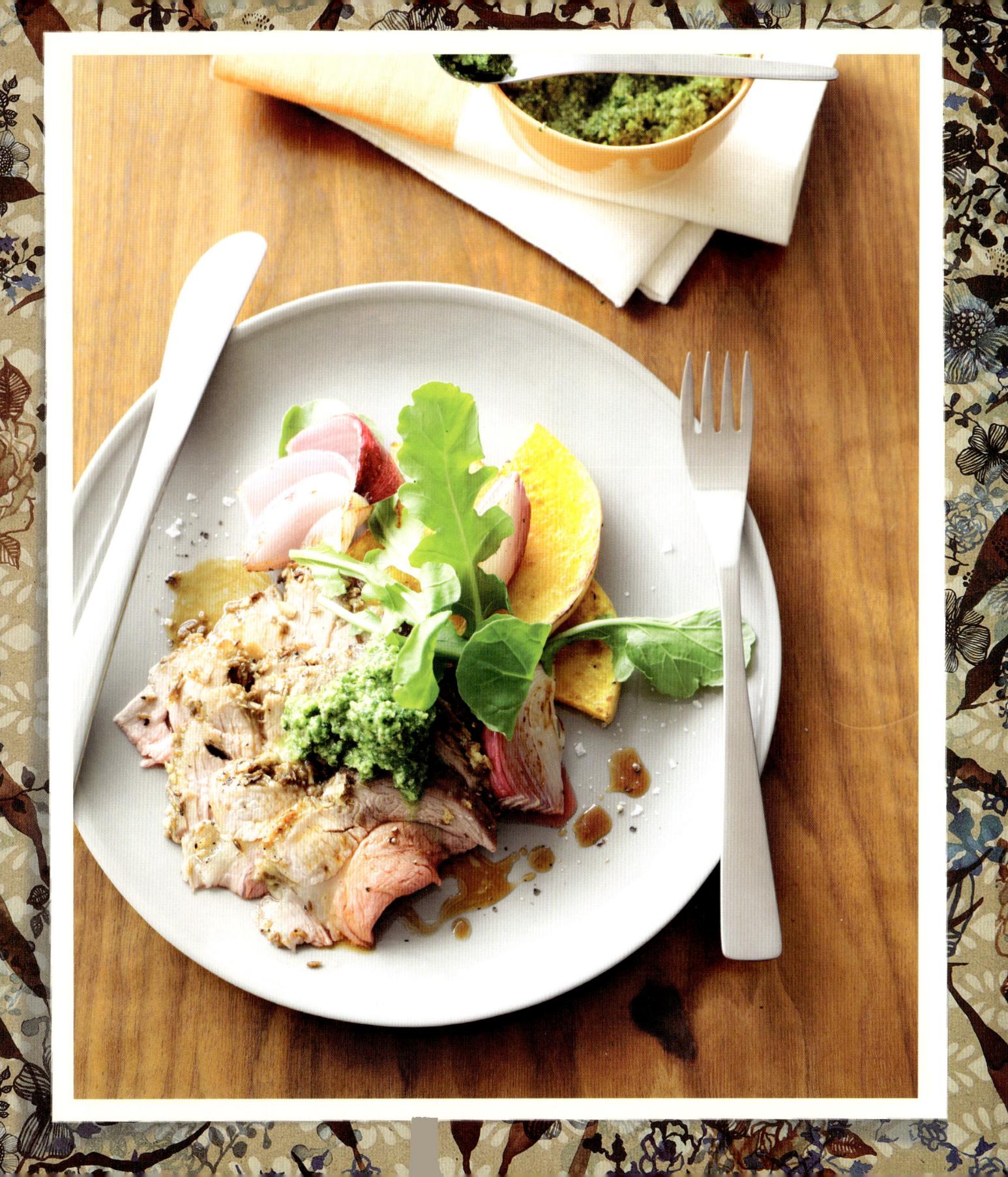

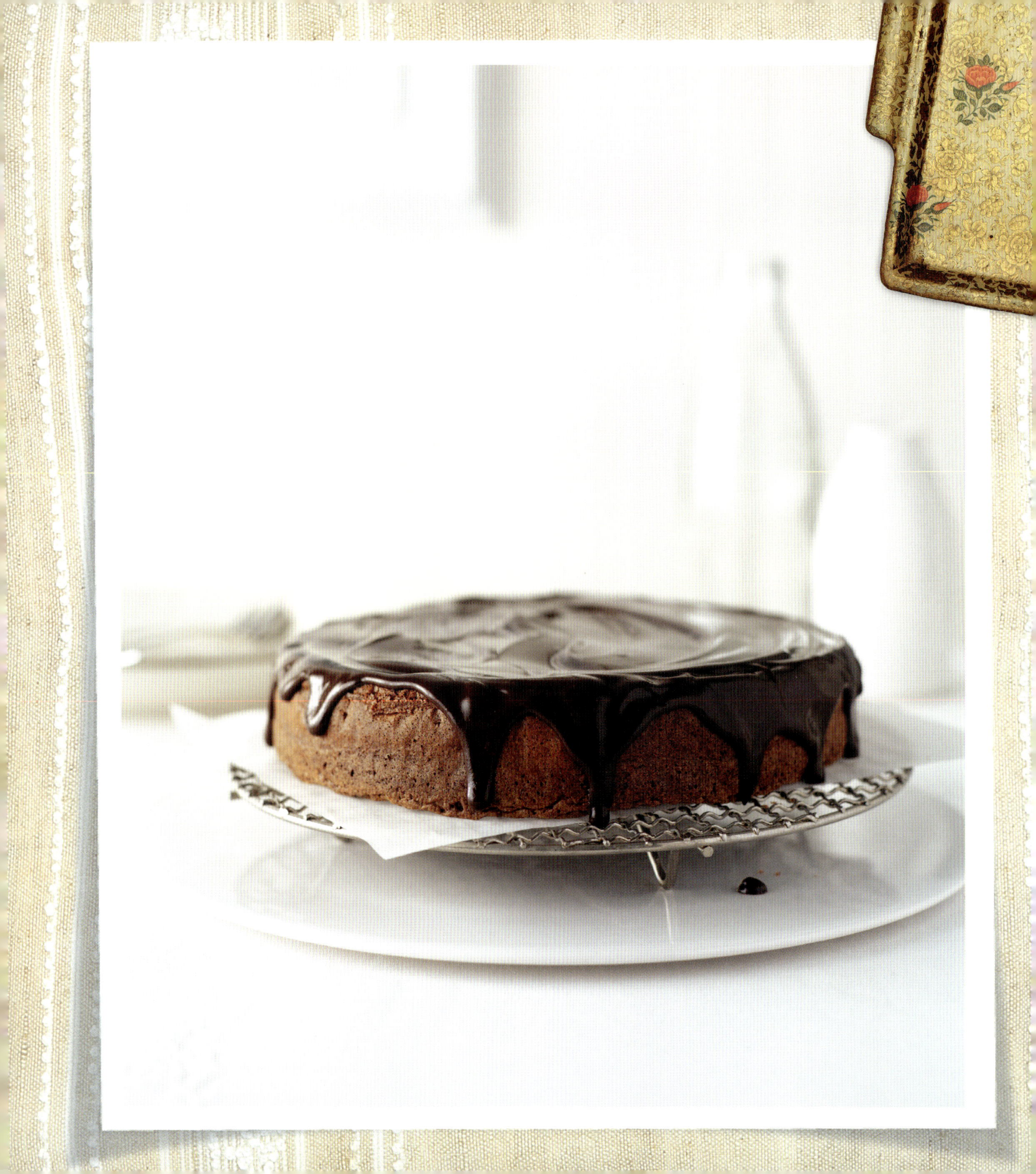

If you can't find ground pecans, simply blend or process 150g (4½ ounces) of roasted pecans until they are finely ground. Be sure to use the pulse button, however, because you want to achieve a flour-like texture, not a paste.

Chocolate and pecan torte

200g (6½ ounces) dark eating (semi-sweet) chocolate, chopped coarsely
150g (4½ ounces) butter, chopped coarsely
5 eggs, separated
¾ cup (165g) caster (superfine) sugar
1½ cups (150g) ground pecans
GANACHE
½ cup (125ml) pouring cream
200g (6½ ounces) dark eating (semi-sweet) chocolate, chopped coarsely

1 Preheat oven to 180°C/350°F. Grease deep 22cm (9-inch) round cake pan; line base and side with baking paper.
2 Stir chocolate and butter in small saucepan over low heat until smooth; cool 10 minutes.
3 Beat egg yolks and sugar in small bowl with electric mixer until thick and creamy. Transfer to large bowl; fold in chocolate mixture and ground pecans.
4 Beat egg whites in small bowl with electric mixer until soft peaks form; fold into chocolate mixture, in two batches. Pour mixture into pan.
5 Bake cake about 55 minutes. Stand in pan 15 minutes; turn, top-side up, onto baking-paper-covered wire rack. Cool.
6 Meanwhile, make ganache.
7 Pour ganache over cake; refrigerate cake 30 minutes before serving.
ganache Bring cream to the boil in small saucepan. Remove from heat; add chocolate, stir until smooth.

prep + cook time 1 hour 20 minutes (+ standing & refrigeration) **serves** 10
nutritional count per serving 42.3g total fat (19.8g saturated fat); 2369kJ (566 cal); 42.8g carbohydrate; 7g protein; 1.7g fibre

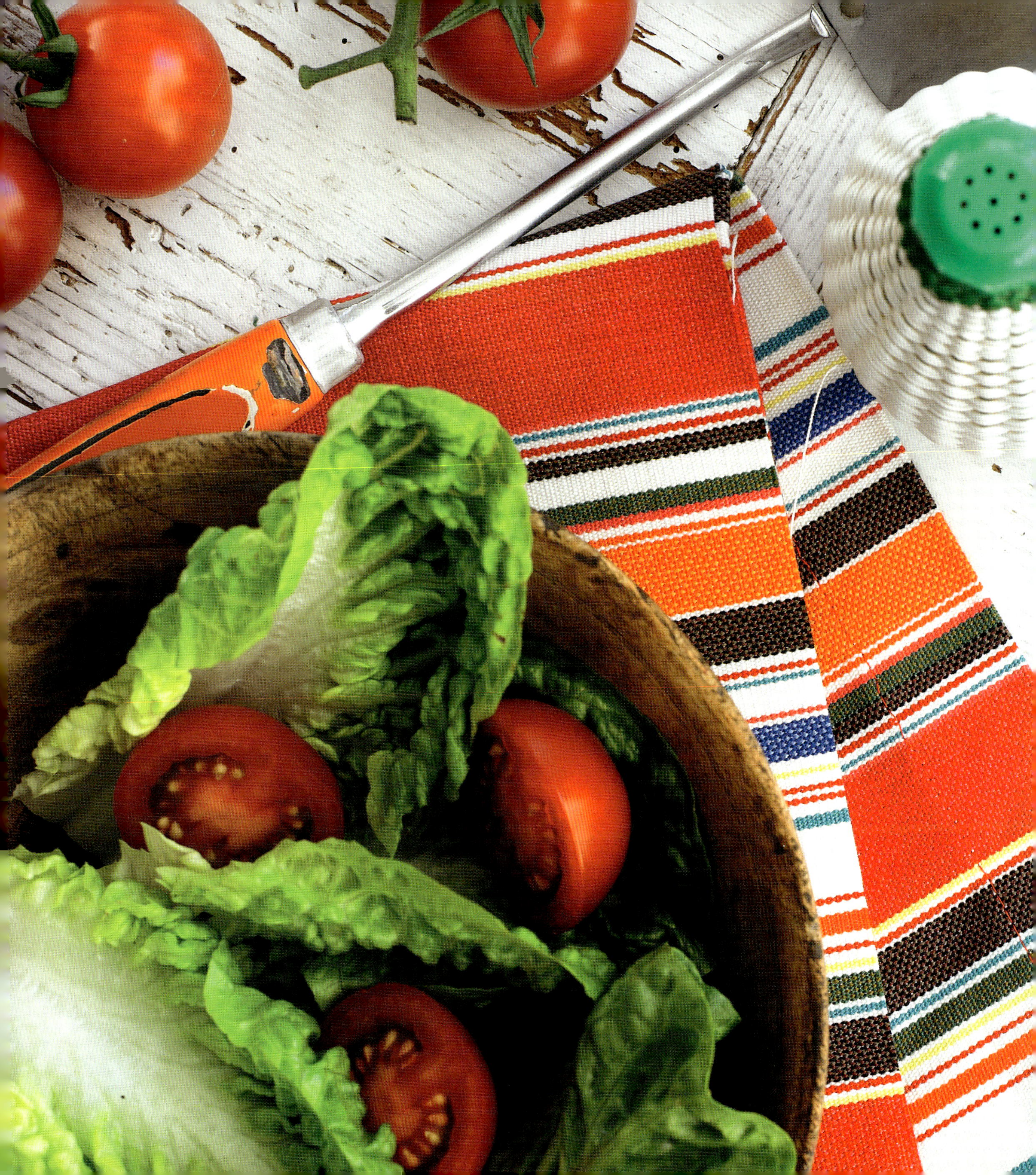

Lazy Sundays

When the weekend rolls around, it's a chance to slow down and enjoy time with family and friends. Fire up the barbecue in summer and feast on snags, seafood and salads – in winter, carve up a roast and serve with plenty of baked vegetables and gravy.

Dr Chris Brown

We always ate very well and Mum was very focused on us eating healthily. She baked for a while till the amount of washing up that ensued put her off the idea of baking again for a couple of years. I know I tormented Mum with the classic *The Australian Women's Weekly* kids' birthday cake cookbook for a number of years.

For about a month before my birthday I'd start to narrow down which cake I wanted, almost Australian Idol-style to the top 12, then six and then to the winner – and I always chose the most complicated, difficult cake she could ever create. Growing up, we had a dog called Penny and being a Boxer, when she jumped up we'd be a similar height. I remember pushing the dog aside to get to lick the beaters from the cake mix. We would be vying for prime position. I'd get to lick the beaters and the dog would get to lick me and everyone was happy!

Mum studied Italian for a number of years so everything we did had an Italian undertone to it. You couldn't cook pasta with bacon: it had to be pancetta or coppa. It had to be your standard, with an Italian twist. There is a lamb dish that I do which is basically lamb with mashed potato; but no – it's lamb, wrapped in prosciutto with semi-dried tomatoes.

For birthdays, besides cake, the tradition was breakfast. You could always choose your own special breakfast. Coco Pops got the early run, but as my teenage years hit, the traditional weekend favourite, the fry up, became popular.

Growing up on the coast in Newcastle, fish was always a big part of our diet, so one of my favourite dishes of Mum's and perfect for a special Sunday dish, was a salt-crusted fish, cooked on the barbecue.

RIGHT: Dr Chris gets a helping hand from Mum, Anne Brown.

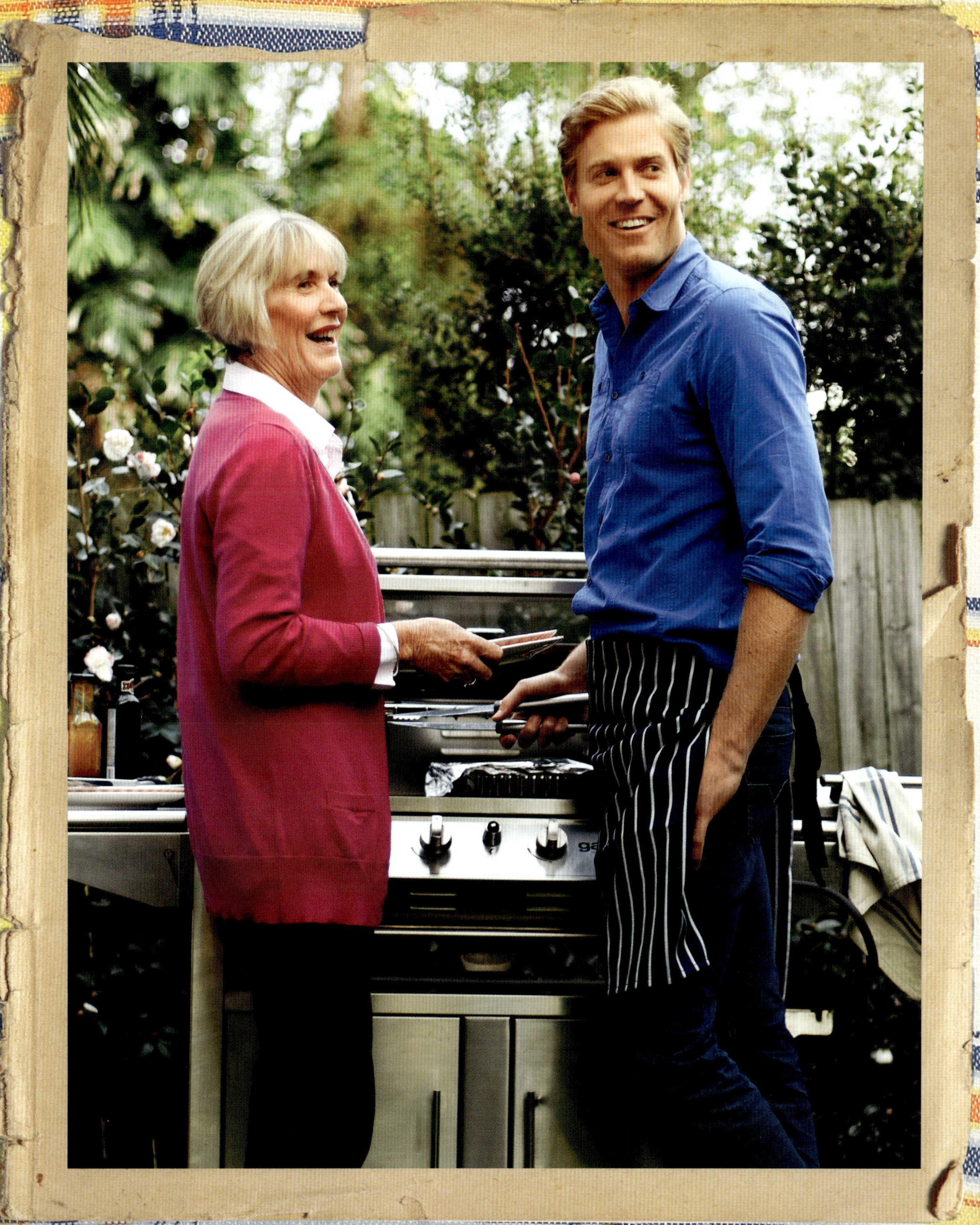

Kaffir lime leaves, also known as bai magrood, look like two glossy dark green leaves joined end to end, forming a rounded hourglass shape. They're available from Asian food stores, greengrocers and some major supermarkets.

Whole fish with ginger and garlic

¾ cup loosely packed fresh coriander (cilantro) leaves, chopped coarsely
10cm (4-inch) stick fresh lemon grass (20g), chopped finely
8cm (3-inch) piece fresh ginger (40g), chopped finely
5 cloves garlic, sliced thinly
4 fresh long red chillies, sliced thinly
3 kaffir lime leaves, shredded finely
60g (2 ounces) butter, melted
4 medium lemons (560g), sliced thinly
4 x 600g (1¼-pound) whole white fish

1 Combine coriander, lemon grass, ginger, garlic, chilli and lime leaves in medium bowl; season.
2 For each fish, layer two sheets of foil that are double the length of the fish, on bench. Brush centre of foil with half the butter; top with lemon slices.
3 Score fish both sides; place on lemon, brush with remaining butter, season. Top each fish with ginger mixture. Gather corners of foil together; twist to enclose fish securely.
4 Cook fish in covered barbecue, using indirect heat, about 35 minutes. Remove from heat; stand 5 minutes before serving.

prep + cook time 50 minutes **serves** 4
nutritional count per serving 19.8g total fat (10.4g saturated fat); 2015kJ (482 cal); 3.7g carbohydrate; 66.2g protein; 4.6g fibre
tips We used barramundi, but you can use any whole white fish. A strip of fresh lime peel may be substituted for each kaffir lime leaf.

BELOW (CENTRE & BOTTOM): Chris, aged 12, with Bridget the cow in 1989. Bridget was Chris's 12th birthday present, after he begged to get her. Although Chris used to show Bridget at all the cow shows "sadly she never won anything!"

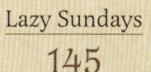

Soak eight bamboo skewers in cold water for an hour before use to prevent them splintering or scorching during cooking. Thick asparagus is best for this recipe.

Haloumi, asparagus and red onion skewers

½ cup (125ml) balsamic vinegar
1 tablespoon honey
1 tablespoon light brown sugar
350g (11 ounces) haloumi cheese, cut into 2.5cm (1-inch) pieces
150g (5 ounces) asparagus, cut into 2.5cm (1-inch) pieces
1 small red onion (100g), cut into thin wedges

1 Stir vinegar, honey and sugar in small saucepan over low heat, without boiling, until sugar dissolves. Bring to the boil; boil, uncovered, about 5 minutes or until syrup thickens slightly, cool.
2 Thread cheese, asparagus and onion onto eight bamboo skewers; season. Cook skewers on heated oiled barbecue (or grill or grill pan) until browned and tender.
3 Serve skewers immediately, drizzled with balsamic syrup.

prep + cook time 35 minutes **makes** 8
nutritional count per skewer 7.8g total fat (4.8g saturated fat); 564kJ (135 cal); 6.1g carbohydrate; 9.8g protein; 0.4g fibre

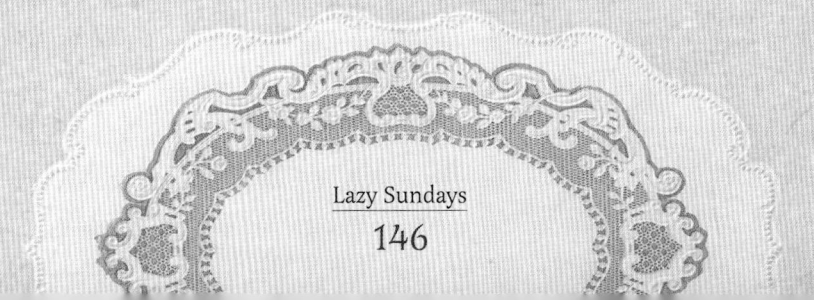

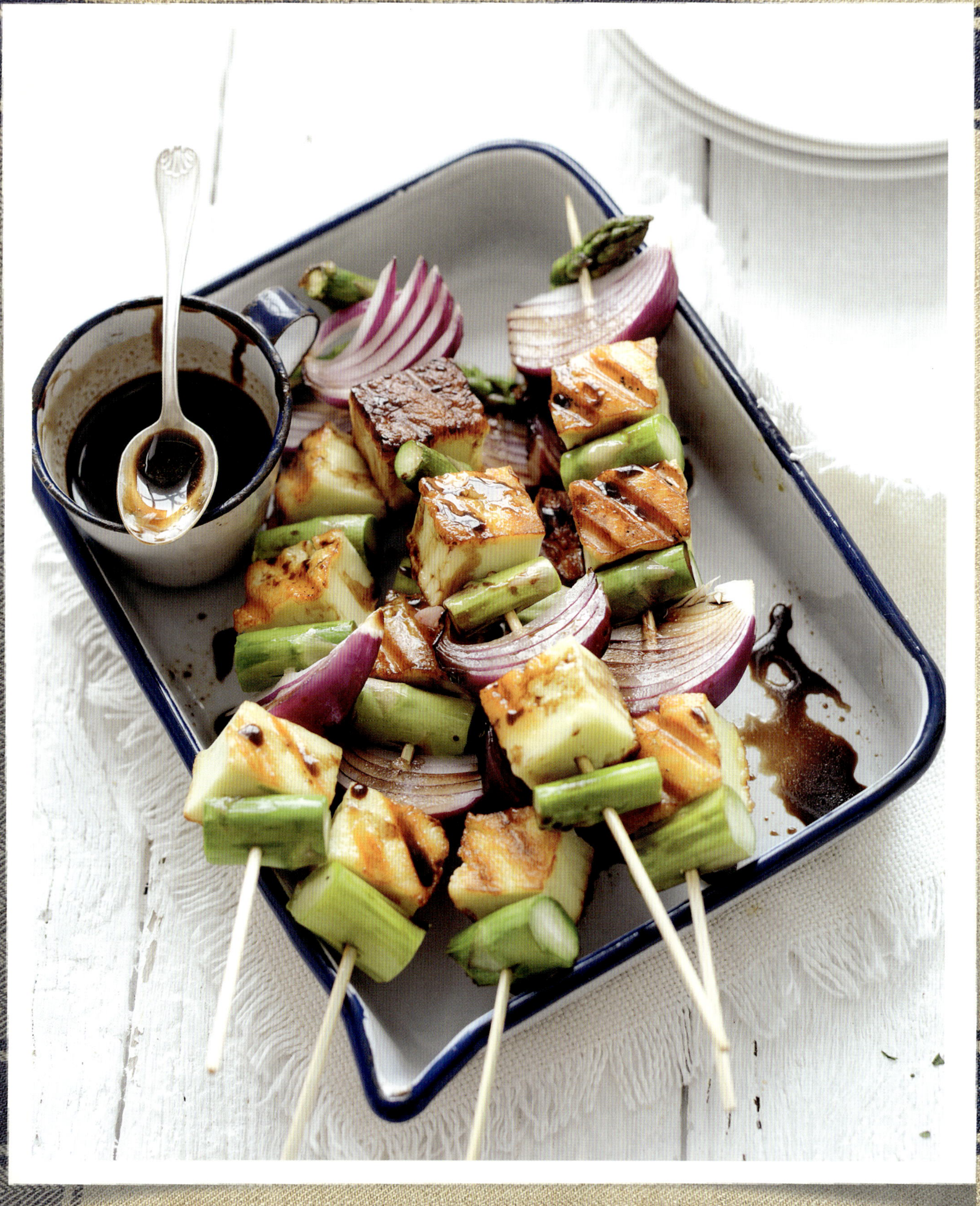

Spicy yogurt chicken drumettes with raita

20 chicken drumettes (1.4kg)
1½ cups (420g) yogurt
½ teaspoon dried chilli flakes
1 tablespoon each ground coriander and ground cumin
2 teaspoons ground turmeric
½ cup each finely chopped fresh mint and fresh coriander (cilantro)
1 clove garlic, crushed
1 tablespoon lemon juice

1 Combine chicken with half the yogurt, chilli and spices in large bowl; season. Cover; refrigerate 30 minutes.
2 Remove chicken from marinade; shake off excess. Discard marinade. Cook chicken on heated oiled barbecue (or grill or grill pan) until cooked through.
3 Meanwhile, make raita by combining herbs, garlic and juice with remaining yogurt in small bowl.
4 Serve chicken with raita.

prep + cook time 35 minutes (+ refrigeration) **serves** 4
nutritional count per serving 15.4g total fat (6.3g saturated fat); 1509kJ (361 cal); 7.9g carbohydrate; 46.4g protein; 0.6g fibre

Herbed beef fillet with kipfler potatoes

1kg (2 pounds) kipfler (fingerling) potatoes
1kg (2-pound) beef eye fillet, trimmed
2 medium red onions (340g), cut into wedges
2 tablespoons olive oil
¾ cup (210g) horseradish cream
¾ cup each loosely packed flat-leaf parsley, dill and tarragon leaves, chopped finely

1 Boil, steam or microwave potatoes until almost tender; drain, then cut in half lengthways.
2 Meanwhile, cook beef on heated oiled covered barbecue (or grill or grill pan) about 15 minutes until browned all over and cooked as desired. Remove from barbecue; cover beef, stand 10 minutes.
3 Combine potatoes with onion and oil in medium bowl. Cook potatoes and onions on heated barbecue about 5 minutes or until potatoes are browned and tender; season. Cover to keep warm.
4 Combine horseradish cream and herbs in medium bowl; season. Spread herb mixture all over beef.
5 Serve beef sliced, with potatoes and onions.

prep + cook time 40 minutes **serves** 6
nutritional count per serving 18.1g total fat (6.6g saturated fat); 1914kJ (458 cal); 30.1g carbohydrate; 40.5g protein; 5g fibre

Lazy Sundays

RIGHT: A love of seafood extends to fishing for Ben. He landed this impressive Pearl Perch off Moreton Island, Queensland.

Ben O'Donoghue

Growing up, food seemed more to just be something of a daily process. It was never the main focus in our family, like it is for some. But Sunday dinner was the major event of the week and we used to relish the thought of Yorkshire pudding and roast beef. My dad is Irish, so we often had potatoes, as well as boiled bacon and cabbage. While my mum used to cook, my Grandma often did too as she and Granddad lived with us and she was always home. I always remember my Grandma kept her meringues and a big tin of golden syrup by the side of the oven and I use to steal the meringues and dip my finger into the syrup.

Christmas was our biggest tradition. Being English immigrants we had the traditional turkey and ham, even when the weather was incredibly hot. As boys, we would just run in and out and grab something both times.

ABOVE: Ben, aged two years old, digs into a hearty bowl of tucker while living in Chingola, Zambia.

BELOW: Three generations come together; (from left) Catriona, her Nan, Riria Seaton, and Catriona's mum, Heather Rowntree.

RIGHT: "Here I am with my Mum, Heather Rowntree, when I was six months old. Strangely we're outside Sydney Airport where I now spend so much of my life!" says Catriona.

Catriona Rowntree

Whilst Mum never obsessed about recipes, food played a vital role in bonding our family. All meals were eaten at the table, be it in the kitchen or dining room for more formal occasions. Every meal involved flat-out conversation – we'd talk about the day, argue with a sibling or wolf down her delicious meals. I may not have inherited her cooking talent, but I feel I make up for it with her witty repartee… well, I try anyway! "Get out! You children are driving me mad," she would say, with four hungry children whipping around her ankles. Meal times usually had Mum cooking for seven as we lived with my Nan, yet to this day her repertoire of sure-fire recipes remain my all-time favourites. I take my hat off to her. Sundays were always full-stopped with a roast, but weekend food was normally about building energy for sport. The highlight was packing the car boot to take to my brother's footy games. It would be filled with pavlovas, chicken sambos, bread rolls, fruit and drinks. Nothing could have made Mum happier.

Lazy Sundays

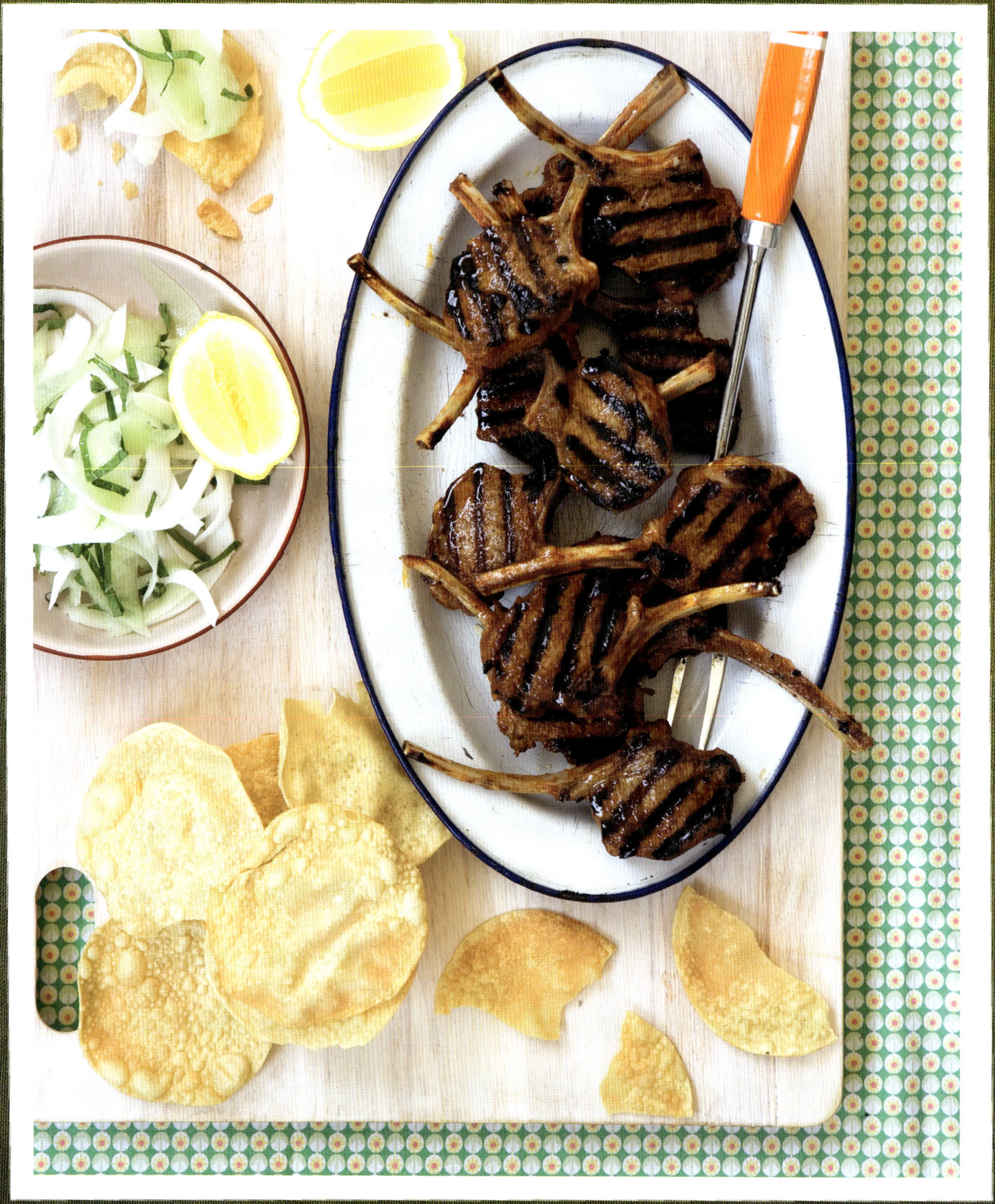

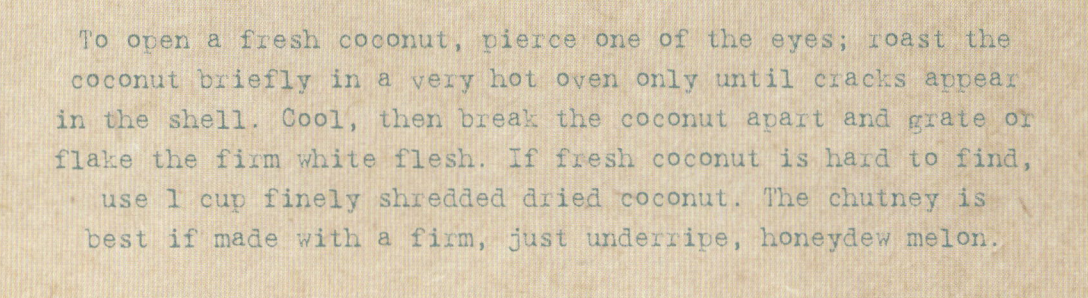

To open a fresh coconut, pierce one of the eyes; roast the coconut briefly in a very hot oven only until cracks appear in the shell. Cool, then break the coconut apart and grate or flake the firm white flesh. If fresh coconut is hard to find, use 1 cup finely shredded dried coconut. The chutney is best if made with a firm, just underripe, honeydew melon.

Tandoori lamb cutlets with fresh coconut and melon chutney

¼ cup (75g) tandoori paste
¼ cup (70g) yogurt
12 french-trimmed lamb cutlets (600g)
FRESH COCONUT AND MELON CHUTNEY
1 cup (110g) shaved fresh coconut
½ large firm honeydew melon (850g), shaved
2 tablespoons finely chopped fresh mint
1 tablespoon lemon juice

1 Combine paste, yogurt and cutlets in large bowl; season.
2 Cook cutlets on heated oiled barbecue (or grill or grill pan) until brown both sides and cooked to you liking.
3 Meanwhile, make fresh coconut and melon chutney.
4 Serve cutlets with chutney.
fresh coconut and melon chutney Combine ingredients in medium bowl.

prep + cook time 30 minutes **serves** 4
nutritional count per serving
27.3g total fat (13.5g saturated fat); 1601kJ (383 cal); 13.2g carbohydrate; 18.9g protein; 5.7g fibre
serving suggestion Serve with pappadums and lemon wedges.

Lazy Sundays

Pete Timbs

We moved house a lot as kids, but one constant was our holiday house at Nelson Bay, just north of Newcastle. It was right on the beach and was always full of people. Mum and Dad were great entertainers and there was always lots of tasty, but simple food around.

There'd be a barbie, a bunch of salads, a leg of ham: things that could feed the masses of hungry kids and adults when we came back from a long day at the beach. Mum also had her staple dishes that she knew everyone loved, which was hard with five fussy children.

Her lasagne is legendary; my wife even stole her recipe. She also makes a killer spaghetti bolognese where she uses tomato soup, instead of tomatoes, to give it a sweetness that we loved. Mum was also very health conscious so after Asian stir fries became trendy, we had them a couple of nights a week. And of course, during summer especially, there were tons of prawns and fresh fish – some of which we would catch ourselves, although Mum always refused to clean them.

But one of her great summer numbers is her crab dip; it was very 70s, but was always on the table when friends visited and was always the first thing finished. It was just crab mixed with some Philadelphia cream cheese, made into a mound and covered with seafood cocktail sauce. It became the taste of summer, for not just our family but all our friends. Every now and then someone will whip it out at a party or on a lazy Sunday with a few wines and we all have a good laugh about it but it is still the first dish finished.

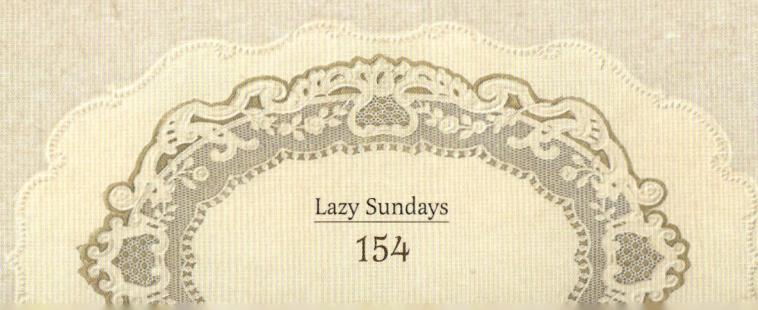

RIGHT: (From left) Pete's Mum, Susan Timbs, Pete's two-year-old daughter, Arabella, Pete and his four-year-old daughter Matilda.

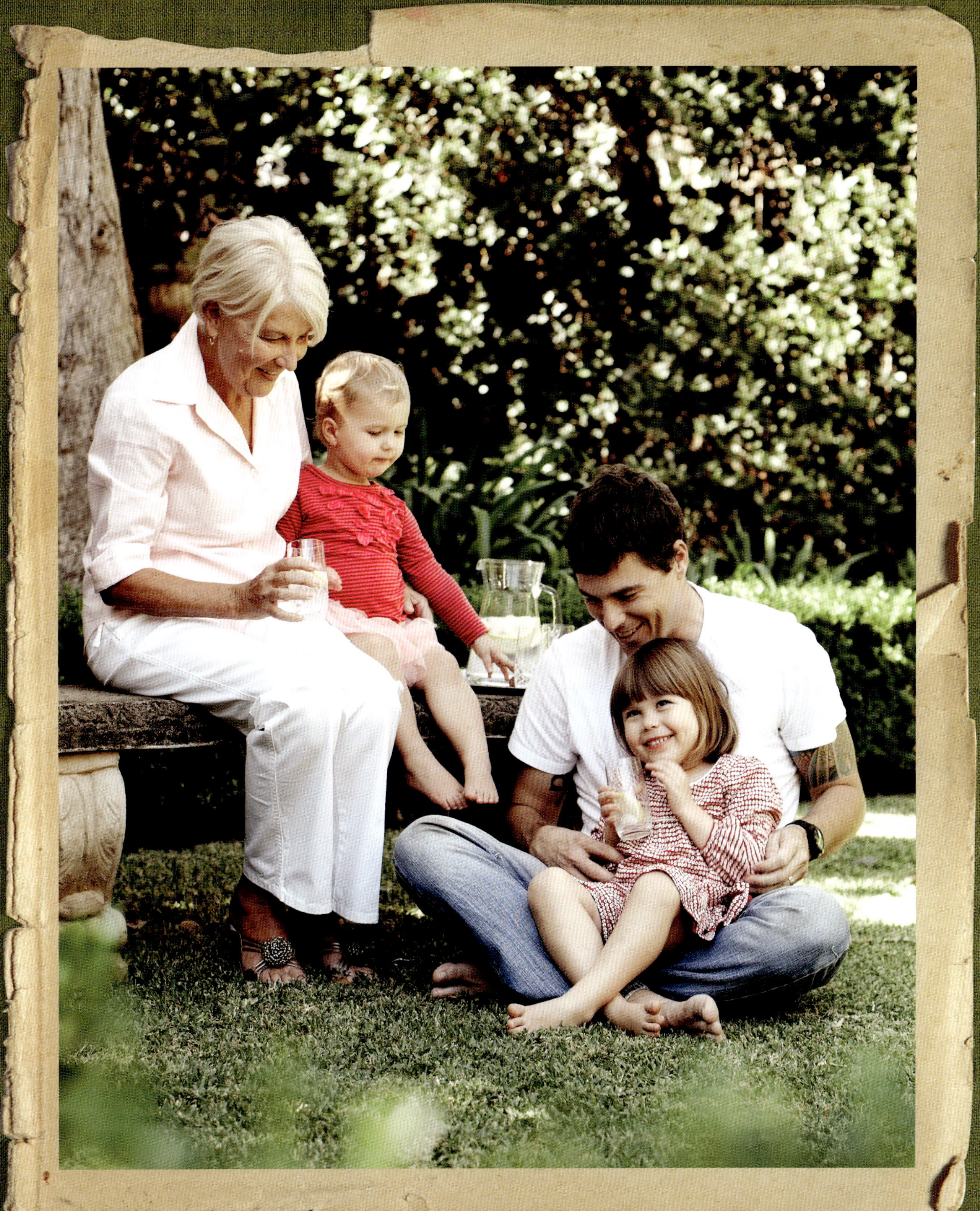

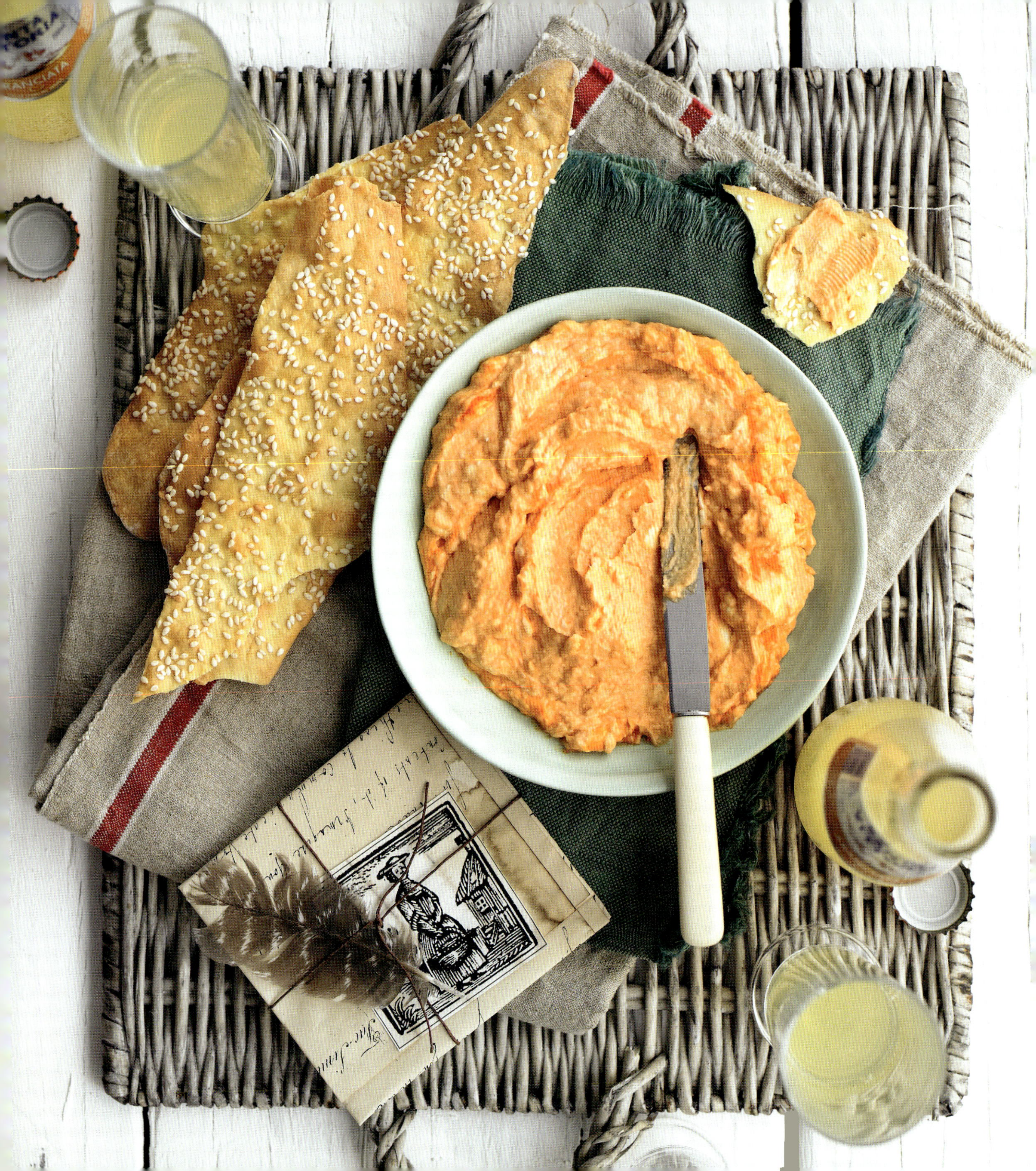

Crab dip

400g (12½ ounces) canned crab meat, drained
250g (8 ounces) cream cheese
250g (8 ounces) cocktail sauce

1 Combine crab, cream cheese and cocktail sauce in small bowl.
2 Cover bowl; refrigerate 15 minutes.
3 Serve dip with bread or crispbreads.

prep time 5 minutes (+ refrigeration)
serves 12
nutritional count per serving
9.5g total fat (4.7g saturated fat); 543kJ (130 cal); 6.8g carbohydrate; 4.8g protein; 0.1g fibre

LEFT: (From left) Pete's Mum, Susan, Pete, and his Dad, Jim, after seven-year-old Pete's first communion in 1979, at Holy Family Primary School, Merewether Beach, Newcastle.

RIGHT: This portrait of one-year-old Pete was taken by a professional photographer.

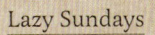

Lazy Sundays

Pumpkin, ricotta and beetroot salad

4 baby beetroot (beets) (100g)
800g (1½-pound) piece pumpkin, unpeeled, cut into eight wedges
2 tablespoons olive oil
40g (1½ ounces) mesclun
1 cup (120g) coarsely chopped roasted pecans
200g (6½ ounces) ricotta cheese, crumbled
LEMON MYRTLE DRESSING
1 tablespoon cider vinegar
1 tablespoon lemon juice
1 teaspoon ground lemon myrtle
2 tablespoons olive oil

1 Preheat oven to 200°C/400°F.
2 Remove unblemished leaves from beetroot; reserve. Peel and halve beetroot.
3 Combine beetroot, pumpkin and oil in large shallow baking dish. Roast, uncovered, turning occasionally, about 40 minutes or until vegetables are tender.
4 Meanwhile, make lemon myrtle dressing.
5 Combine vegetables, beetroot leaves, mesclun, nuts and cheese in large bowl; drizzle with dressing.
lemon myrtle dressing Place ingredients in screw-top jar; shake well.

prep + cook time 55 minutes **serves** 4
nutritional count per serving 37.5g total fat (6.8g saturated fat); 1885kJ (451 cal); 14.7g carbohydrate; 12.2g protein; 3.4g fibre

Ground lemon myrtle is available from specialist spice shops and some gourmet food stores. Lemon myrtle is a small tree that grows in sub-tropical and tropical rainforest areas of Queensland. Ground lemon myrtle is a ground mixture of the dried leaf and flower; it has a strong lemon flavour. If you can't find it, use 1 teaspoon finely grated lemon rind instead.

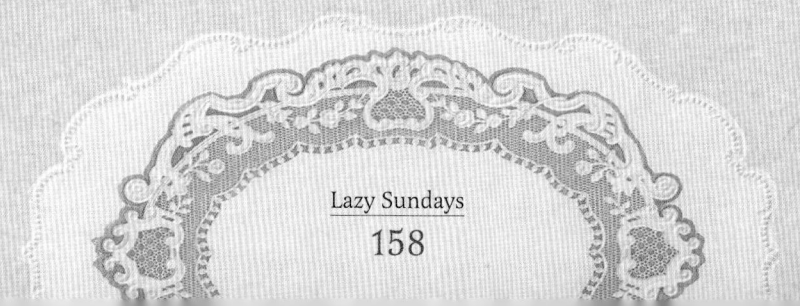

Lazy Sundays

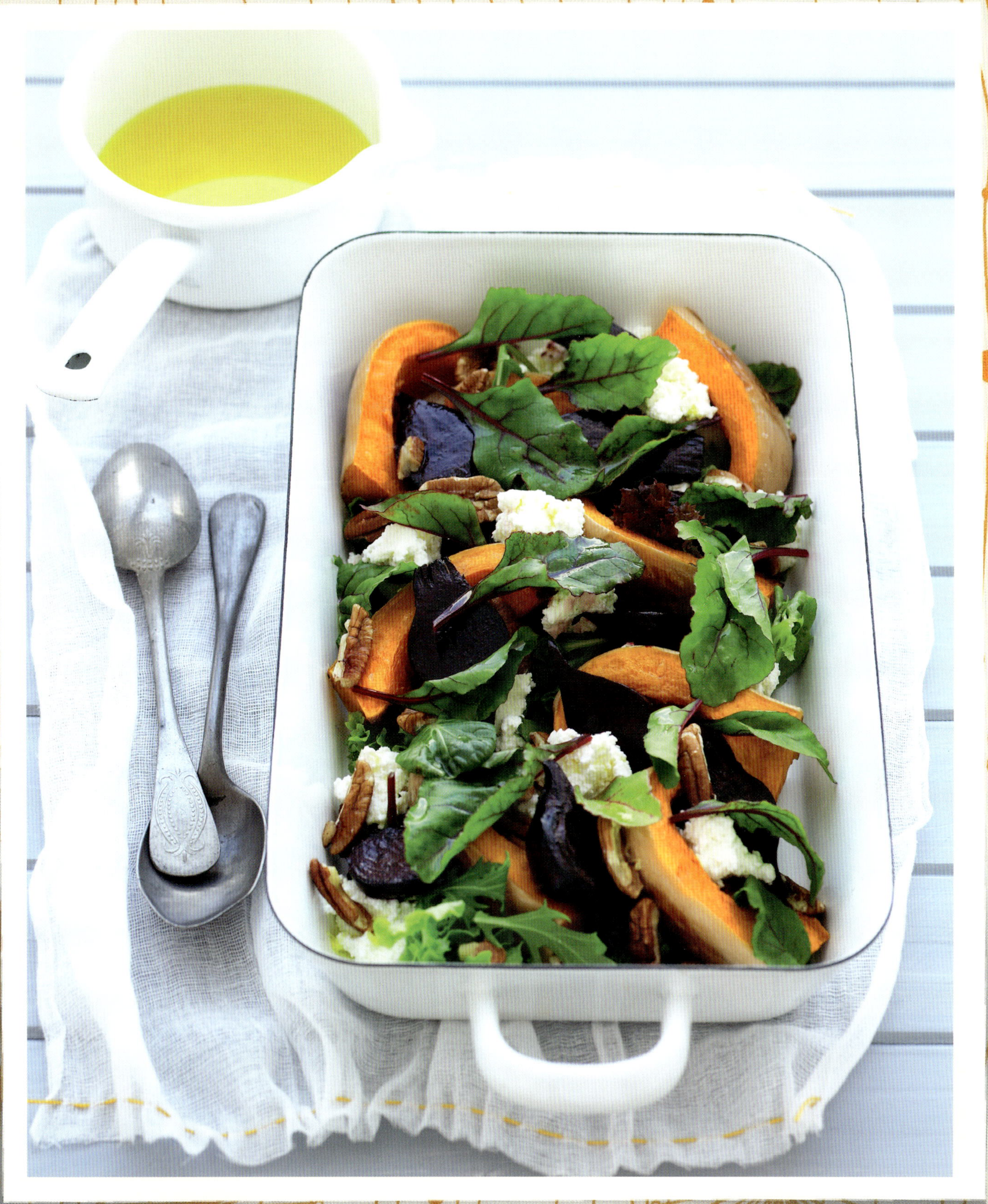

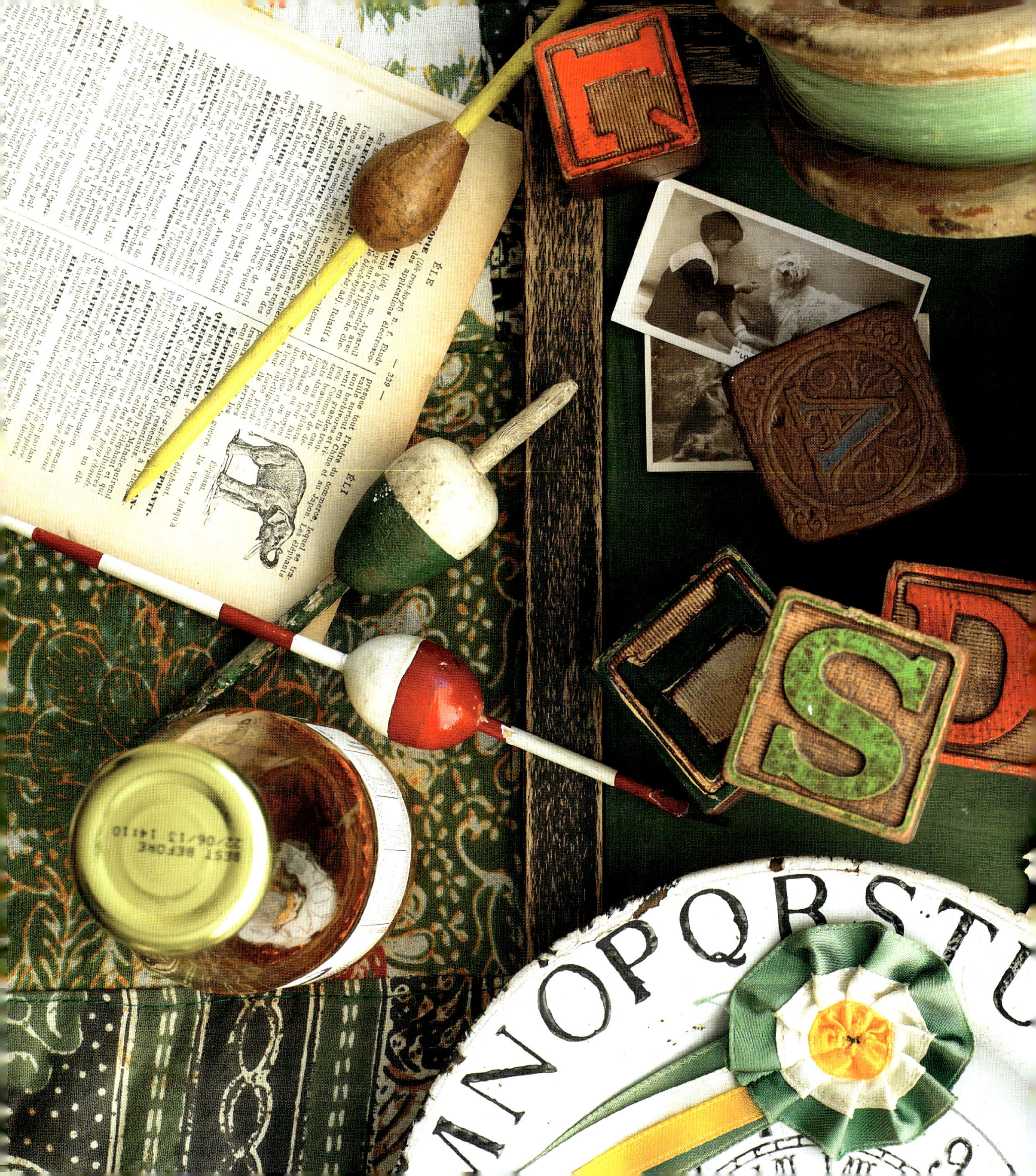
MNOPQRSTU

Lunch Box Days

Packed lunches are a part of every child's schoolyard memories. Each day was a surprise – what treats would be instore? From ham sandwiches to salads, rice paper rolls to hearty soups, lunch box meals are as diverse as the families that prepare them.

LEFT: (From left) Lyndey, aged about two years old, Lyndey's Mum, Isabel Hall, Lyndey's sister, Lesley, aged about six and a half years old, and Santa.

Lyndey Milan

Mum never wasted anything. She was very inventive and could always make something yummy out of leftovers. Dad made our sandwiches for school the night before and kept them fresh under a damp tea towel. I used to shock my friends sometimes with tongue and pickle on a sandwich, which I loved but they thought was weird.

Les Murray

My dad loved his cold meats. He'd bring out a large stick of paprika salami (usually Csabai), a block of cheese, hot capsicum, some bread: then you had a fulsome meal. The standard fare for a school lunch was two slices of bread, spread with lard and sliced onion and sprinkled with powdered paprika, accompanied by a piece of fruit. Things like butter, eggs, ham or salami were too expensive. There was no tuck shop either; in any case, we got no pocket money.

RIGHT: (From left) Les's younger brother, Andrew and a two-year-old Les.

RIGHT: Justine celebrates turning four with delicious cake.

Justine Schofield

In primary school, my lunches were different. I would have leftovers, beautiful salami and a little salad and I'd bring my pasta in a Thermos – everyone else would have their square sandwiches. I'd be excited to tell my friends about what I was eating. In high school they were jealous of it even and would swarm around and try and eat it.

Jason Hodges

For 13 school years I had Vegemite sandwiches. If we were flash, we had ham sandwiches. But that was only on a Friday because we went food shopping on Thursday nights. Devon with tomato sauce was also good; the bread would go all soggy by lunchtime. When I was 11 years old, I got $10 a fortnight and would hit the tuck shop for a sausage roll, two bread rolls and sauce – I'd make two sausage roll rolls.

LEFT: (From left) Jason, aged nearly five years old, brother Keith, nearly 12, and sister Jo nearly 14, line up in February 1975.

Lunch Box Days

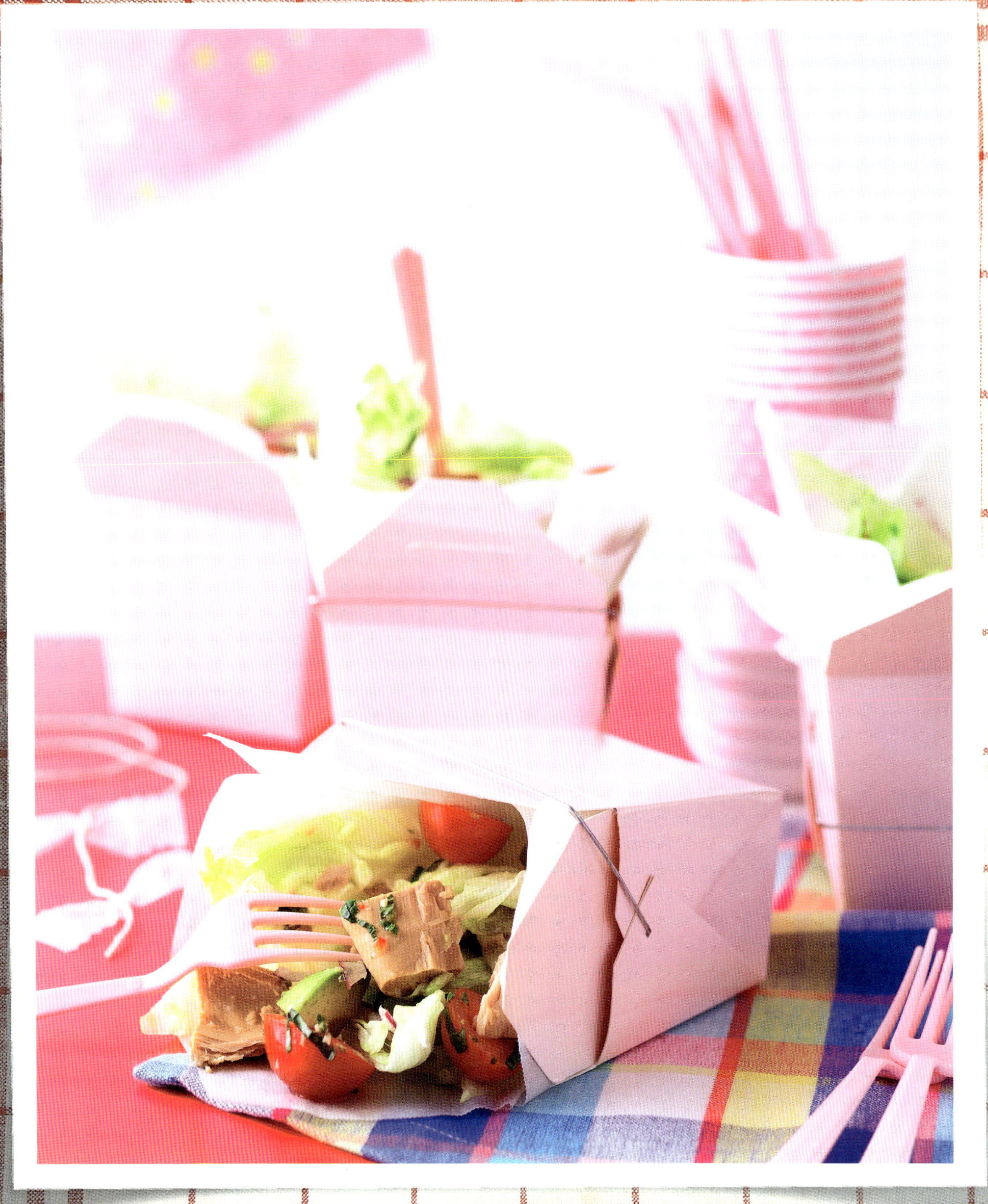

This recipe has a little bit of chilli in it. If you don't like chilli you can leave it out. You can use canned salmon instead of tuna.

Tuna salad

1 lebanese cucumber (130g)
1 medium iceberg lettuce, leaves torn
425g (13½ ounces) canned tuna in springwater, drained, flaked
250g (8 ounces) cherry tomatoes, halved
1 medium avocado (250g), chopped coarsely
1 small red onion (100g), sliced thinly
DRESSING
¼ cup (60ml) olive oil
2 tablespoons white wine vinegar
1 tablespoon lemon juice
2 teaspoons each finely chopped fresh basil and oregano
1 clove garlic, crushed
½ fresh long red chilli, seeded, chopped finely

1 Make dressing.
2 Using a vegetable peeler, slice cucumber lengthways into thin ribbons.
3 Place cucumber in large bowl with dressing and remaining ingredients; toss gently to combine.
dressing Place ingredients in screw-top jar; shake well.

prep time 30 minutes **serves** 4
nutritional count per serving 26.1g total fat (4.9g saturated fat); 1492kJ (357 cal); 4.6g carbohydrate; 24.4g protein; 4.9g fibre

Lunch Box Days

Chicken, celery and avocado sandwich

⅓ **cup (50g) finely shredded cooked chicken**
1 stalk celery (150g), trimmed, chopped finely
¼ **small avocado (50g)**
1 teaspoon lemon juice
2 slices (90g) white bread

1 Combine chicken, celery, avocado and juice in small bowl.
2 Spread chicken mixture on one slice of bread; top with another slice of sandwich bread. Cut into squares or triangles.

prep time 10 minutes **makes** 1
nutritional count per sandwich 14.7g total fat (3.3g saturated fat); 1698kJ (405 cal); 42.8g carbohydrate; 22.6g protein; 4.9g fibre

Honey joys

75g (2½ ounces) butter
⅓ cup (115g) honey
1 tablespoon caster (superfine) sugar
5 cups (200g) corn flakes

1 Preheat oven to 180°C/350°F. Line two 12-hole (⅓-cup/80ml) muffin pans with paper cases.
2 Stir butter, honey and sugar in small saucepan over low heat until smooth.
3 Place corn flakes in large bowl, add honey mixture; stir until corn flakes are well coated. Divide corn flake mixture into cases.
4 Bake 8 minutes. Stand 15 minutes or until firm.

prep + cook time 20 minutes (+ standing)
makes 24
nutritional count per honey joy 2.6g total fat (1.6g saturated fat); 302kJ (72 cal); 11.6g carbohydrate; 0.6g protein; 0.3g fibre
tip Honey joys can be made one day ahead; store in an airtight container at room temperature.

You can store the friands in an airtight container for up to three days. Serve friands dusted with sifted icing (confectioners') sugar.

Mandarin and poppy seed friands

2 large mandarins (500g)
1 tablespoon poppy seeds
6 egg whites
1½ cups (240g) icing (confectioners') sugar
½ cup (75g) plain (all-purpose) flour
185g (6 ounces) butter, melted
1 cup (120g) ground almonds

1 Preheat oven to 200°C/400°F. Grease 12-hole (½-cup/125ml) oval friand pan.
2 Finely grate 1 tablespoon rind from mandarins; squeeze 2 tablespoons juice from mandarins.
3 Combine poppy seeds and juice in small jug; stand 10 minutes.
4 Lightly whisk egg whites with a fork in medium bowl. Sift icing sugar and flour over egg whites. Add butter, ground almonds, rind and poppy seed mixture; stir with a wooden spoon until combined. Spoon into pan holes.
5 Bake friands about 15 minutes. Stand friands in pan 5 minutes; transfer, top-side up, onto wire rack to cool.

prep + cook time 40 minutes **makes** 12
nutritional count per friand 18.7g total fat (8.7g saturated fat); 1262kJ (302 cal); 27.7g carbohydrate; 5g protein; 2g fibre

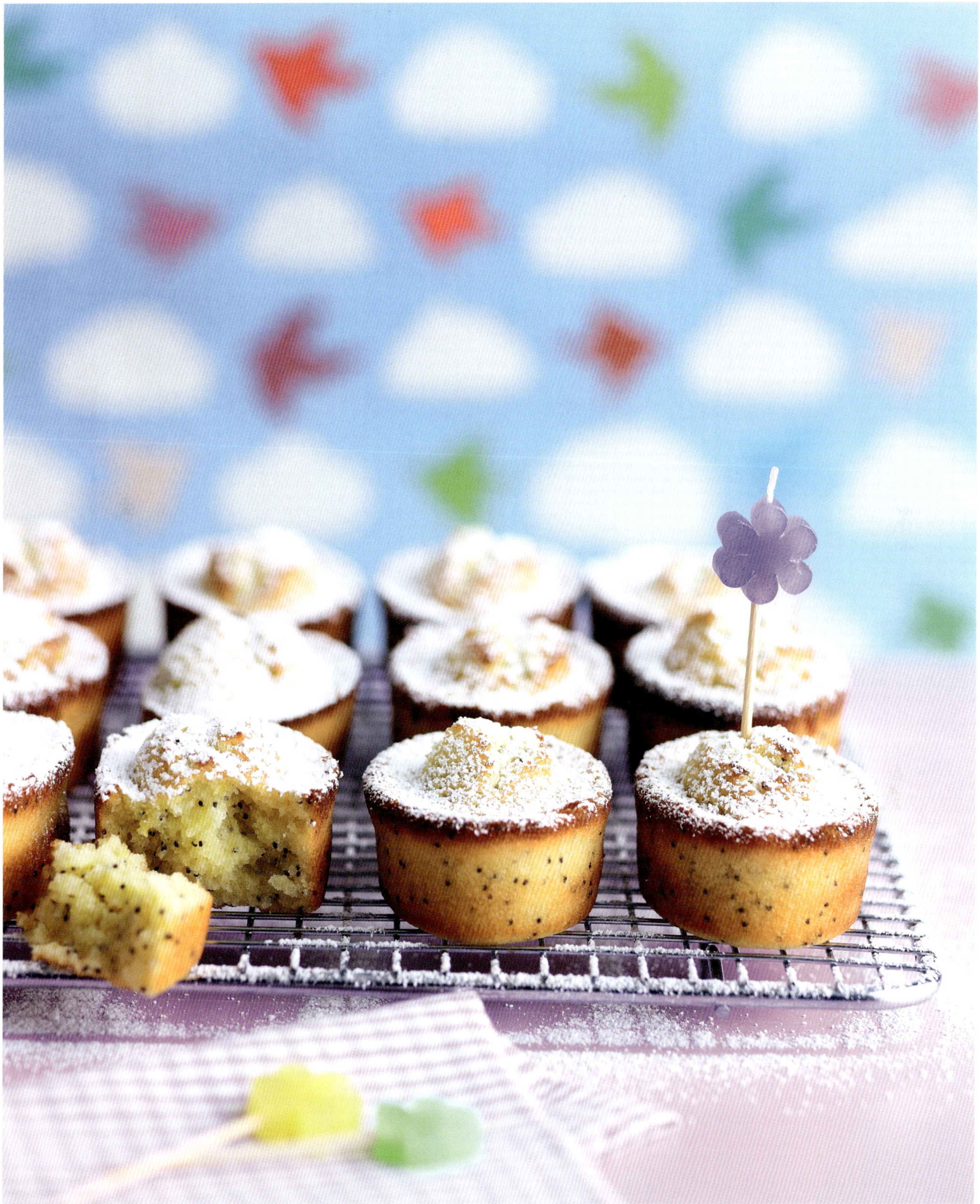

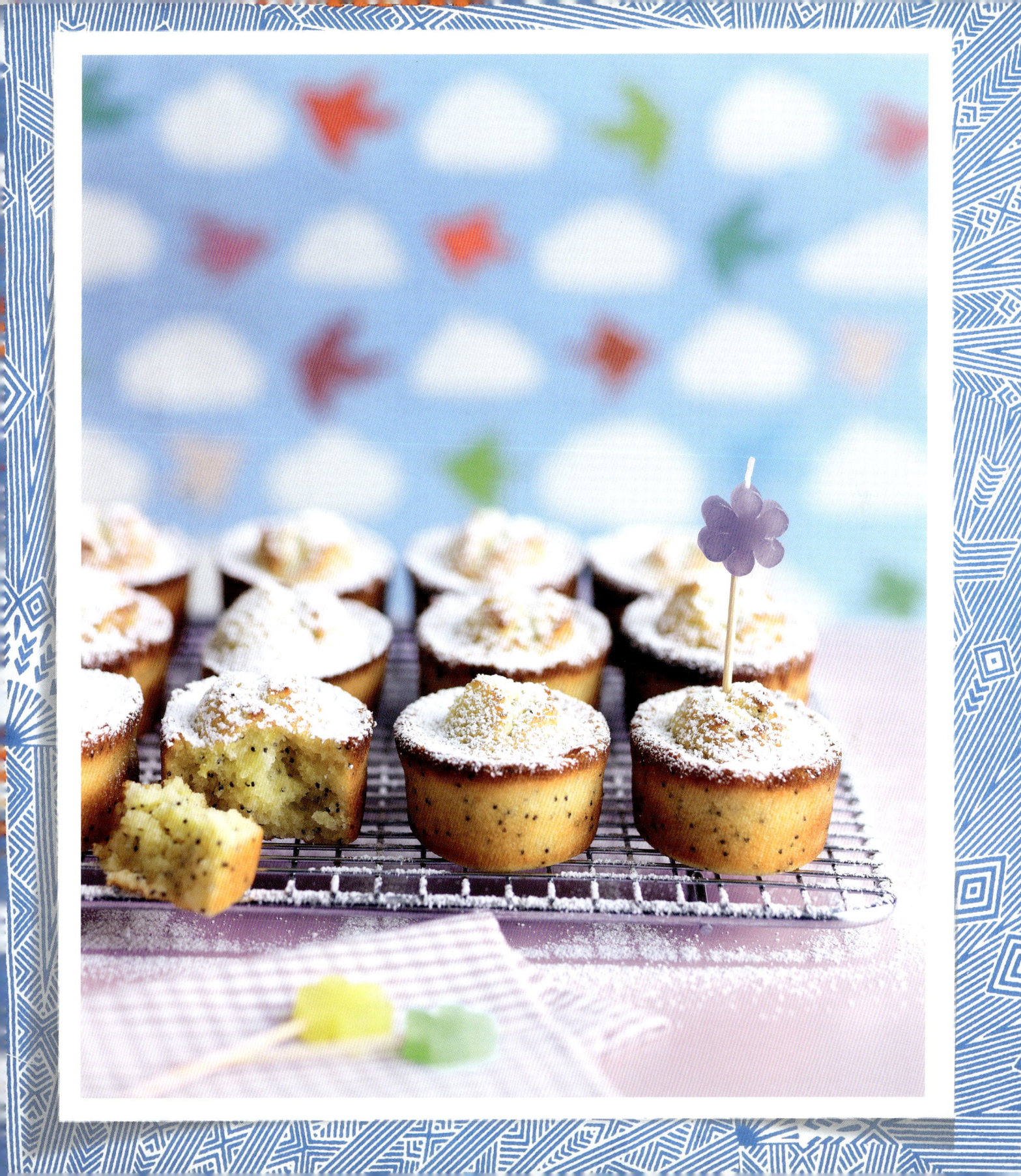

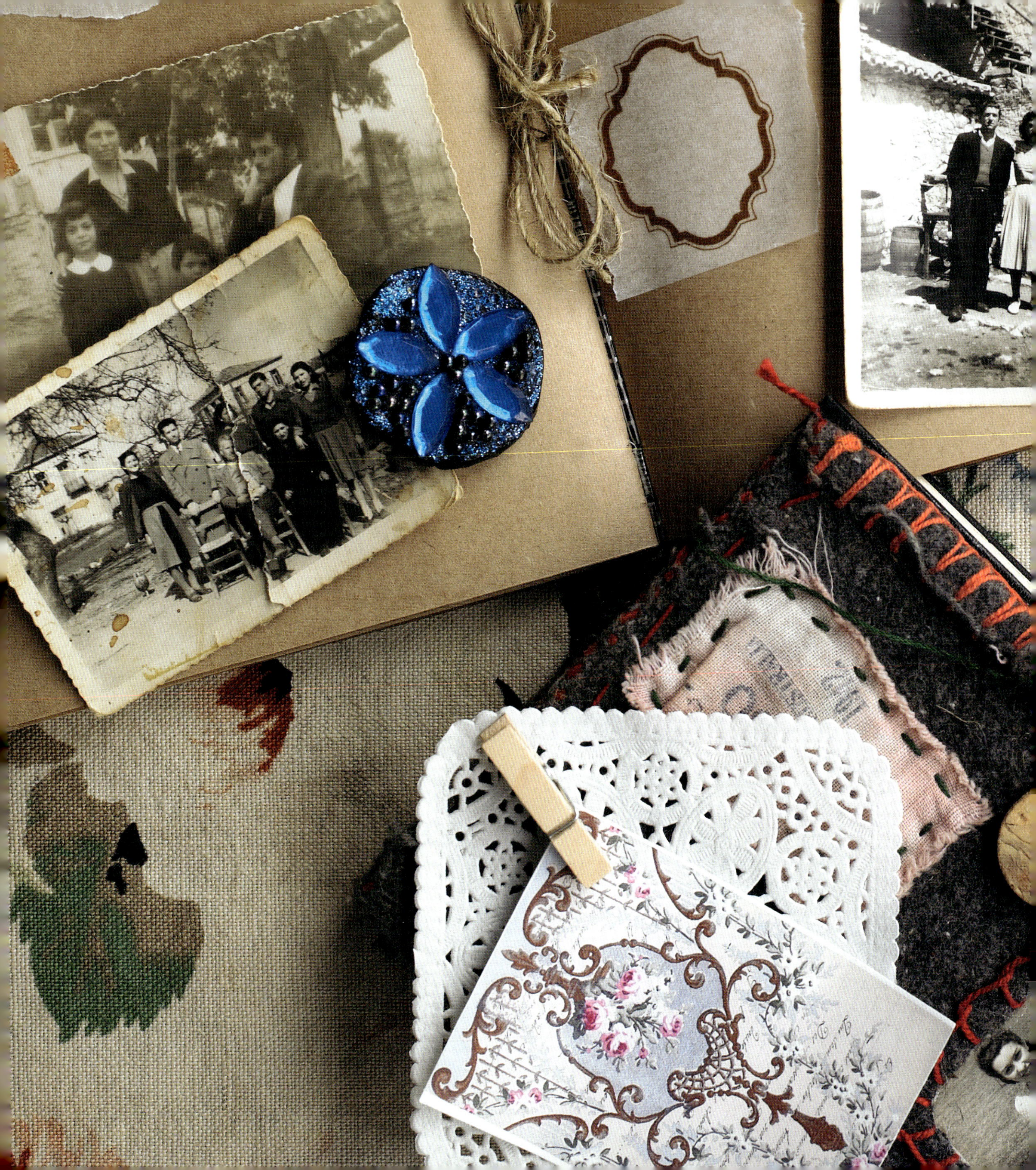

Family Traditions

As a child, you don't realise the culinary habits you adopt in the years ahead will follow in the tried and true footsteps of your mum. Birthdays, Christmas and myriad special occasions all become ingrained through heart-warming customs.

Pete Evans

I think the most important thing and I guess my motto today, is that you cook for love and laughter – and that is what I learnt from my Mother. "It's not the recipes I want you to take: it's how I cook, how much fun you can have and how it can enrich someone's life," she would say. Mum put a lot of passion into her cooking.

I think I got that message more from my Mum, more so than the stuffing recipe or the roast ham. Mum had some great recipes when I was growing up... her spaghetti bolognese is a bit of a legend. She's been on television with me two or three times over the years cooking that dish and I have so many people come up to me on the street, not for my recipe, but for Mum's spaghetti bolognese.

She also does a beautiful tomato sauce, which I just released in my own range and called My Mum's Tomato Sauce Recipe. It's really good to put on your steak sangers, sausages or chips. She's becoming famous for that as well. Mum's always been quite a healthy eater so healthy eating is also one of the great things that I've grown up with. We never had soft drink in the house or hardly anything processed or foods with refined sugars. Treats were in moderation only. She'd also experiment a lot with Asian cuisine, barbecues and seafood especially. Growing up in Queensland, Mum loved seafood and I've carried on that love, along with her love of fresh food and vegies. I believe we can shape our lives from the food we eat.

RIGHT: (From left) Pete's brother, David Evans, Pete's Mum, Joy Evans and Pete.

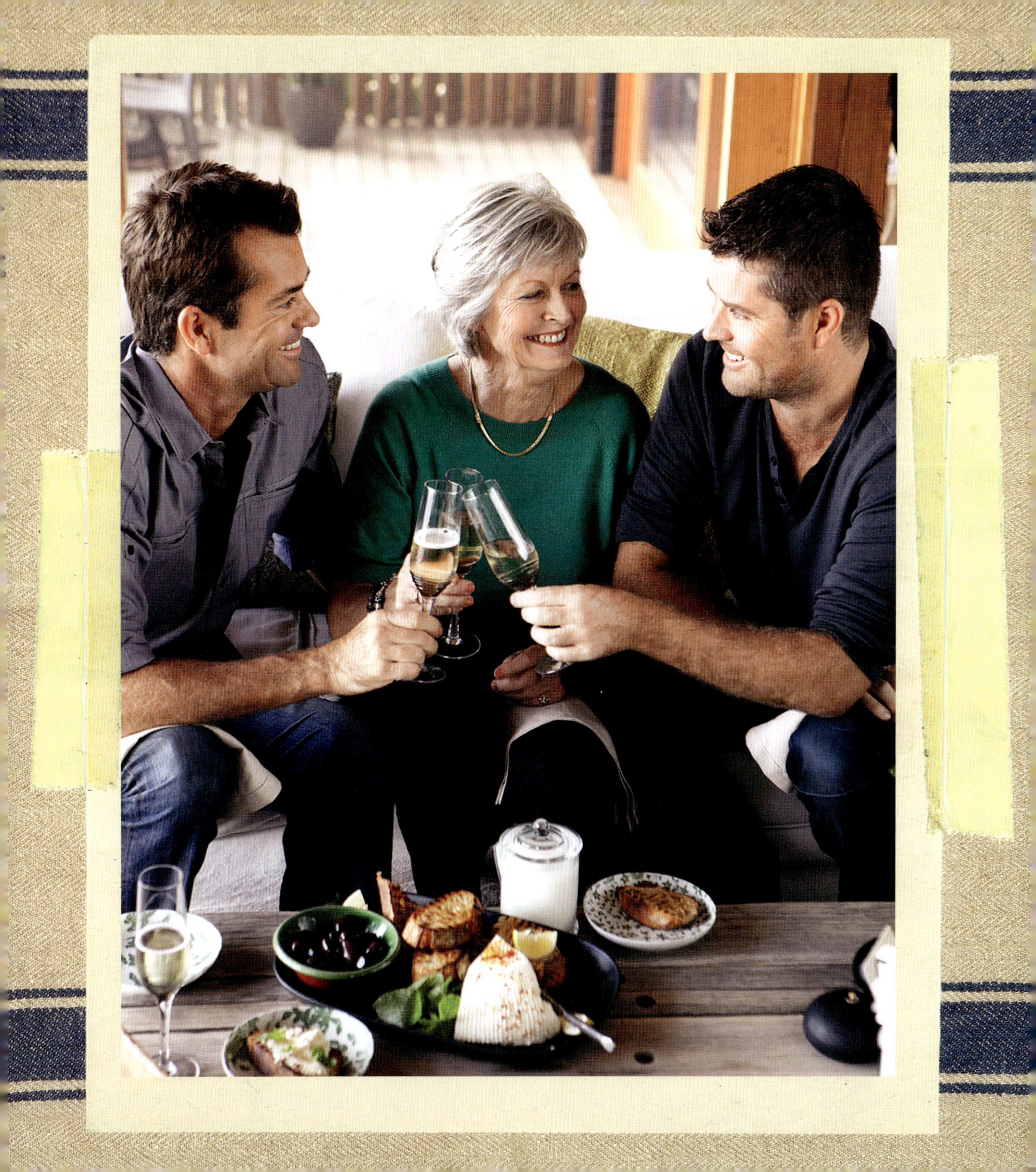

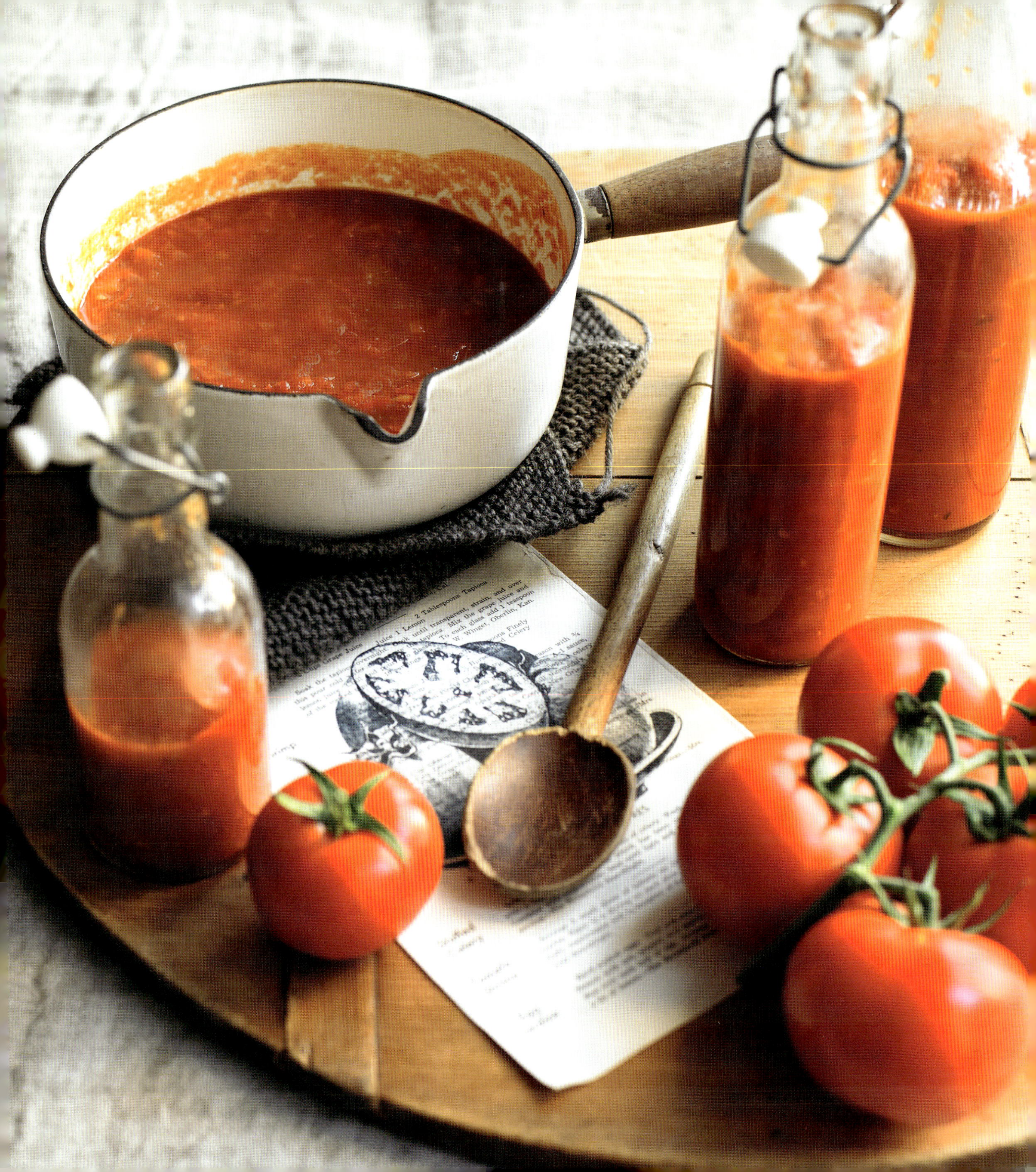

Old-fashioned tomato sauce for bottling

¼ cup (60ml) olive oil
3 medium brown onions (450g), chopped coarsely
2 cloves garlic, crushed
2 teaspoons fresh thyme, chopped
1kg (2 pounds) tomatoes, chopped coarsely
¼ cup (70g) tomato paste
2 tablespoons tamarind paste
1⅔ cup (410ml) tomato sauce (ketchup)

1 Heat oil in large saucepan; cook onion, garlic and thyme, stirring, until onion softens and begins to caramelise.
2 Stir in remaining ingredients; bring to the boil. Reduce heat; simmer, uncovered, 15 minutes. Season to taste. Stand 10 minutes.
3 Blend or process tomato sauce, in batches, until smooth. Cool.
4 Pour sauce into sterilised jars; seal immediately. Keep in a cool place for up to a year.

prep + cook time 45 minutes
makes 2 litres (8 cups)
nutrtitional count per 1 cup (250ml)
7.1g total fat (0.9g saturated fat); 675kJ (161 cal); 20.7g carbohydrate; 3.1g protein; 3.7g fibre

RIGHT: Pete with his Mum, Joy Evans.

RIGHT: A 12-year-old Pete hanging out at home.

Family Traditions

Cream of chicken soup

1.8kg (3½-pound) whole chicken
1 medium brown onion (150g), chopped coarsely
1 medium carrot (120g), chopped coarsely
1 stalk celery (150g), trimmed, chopped coarsely
2 litres (8 cups) water
1 litre (4 cups) chicken stock
40g (1½ ounces) butter
⅓ cup (50g) plain (all-purpose) flour
2 tablespoons lemon juice
½ cup (125ml) pouring cream
¼ cup finely chopped fresh flat-leaf parsley

1 Place chicken, onion, carrot, celery, the water and stock in large saucepan; bring to the boil. Reduce heat; simmer, covered, 1½ hours. Remove chicken from pan; simmer broth, covered, 30 minutes.
2 Strain broth through muslin-lined sieve or colander into large heatproof bowl; discard solids.
3 Melt butter in large saucepan, add flour; cook, stirring, until mixture thickens and bubbles. Gradually stir in broth and juice; stir over heat until mixture boils and thickens slightly. Add cream, reduce heat; simmer, uncovered, about 25 minutes, stirring occasionally.
4 Meanwhile, remove and discard skin and bones from chicken; shred meat coarsely.
5 Add chicken to soup; stir over medium heat until hot. Season to taste. Serve sprinkled with parsley.

prep + cook time 3 hours **serves** 4
nutritional count per serving 59.2g total fat (26.2g saturated fat); 3327kJ (796 cal); 15.7g carbohydrate; 50.7g protein; 2.5g fibre
tip This recipe is not suitable to freeze.
serving suggestion Serve with crusty bread.

Family Traditions

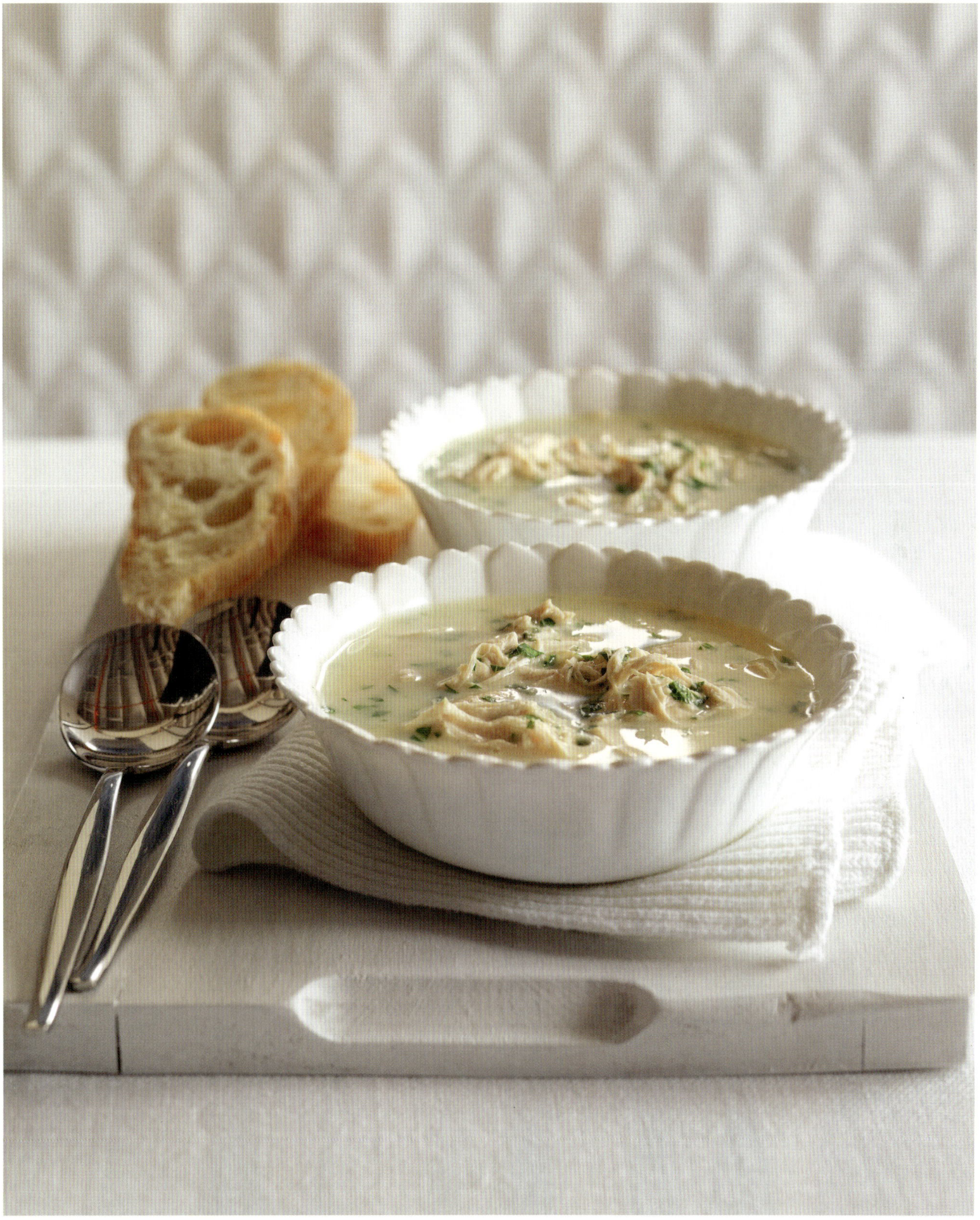

Jason Hodges

For dinner we had our weekly routine. On Monday we had a baked dinner, Tuesdays a BBQ, Wednesdays chicken, Thursdays chops, Fridays fish and chips, Saturdays get your own and Sundays leftovers.

Mum wore an apron all day and used to bake, melt down Mars Bars and make a slice; an Aussie version of chocolate fudge. One of the best experiences was my old man's wood-fired barbecue — he still does it every Tuesday and we sit around it and talk. I reckon I learnt more from sitting down with him doing that, than I learnt at school or from anyone else.

What's funny is that plates come out at Christmas that you don't see any other day. Our Christmas plates have only been used 35 times. And Mum gave me beans and peas so many times, from the age of six I'd negotiate with Dad, "if you take them, I'll take your pumpkin." Mum's tuna bake is also pretty good and she makes a good fried rice.

RIGHT: A two-year-old Jason in March 1975. BELOW: Jason attributes his love for the outdoors to his mum Della and builder dad "Monty".

Family Traditions

Paula Duncan

Food was important in our house because I was brought up in a pub. So when the 'bell' rang we were fed breakfast, lunch and dinner. So my earliest memory in the kitchen was Mum designing the menus at the pub with our chef. I didn't spend a lot of time in the kitchen though — I guess that is why I love cooking. But I did visit my Grandmother most Sundays and she would show me how to make cookies and cakes. We ate several traditional meals that are unforgettable. On Saturdays we had roast dinners; Sundays was snacks and soups (a few of which I cooked); Mondays was my favourite, corned beef and white sauce; Tuesdays was sausages and mash, stews and casseroles; Wednesdays was crumbed cutlets with tomato, onion and capsicum sauce; Thursdays was mixed grills, and Fridays was fish and chips. Cooking was the time that we would all come together. In a busy life that's important for communication. My friends would always want to come over to my place and have dinner.

ABOVE: (From left) Paula and her daughter, Jessica Orcsik visiting The Royal Oak Hotel in Double Bay, Sydney.

RIGHT: (From left) Paula's mum, Rita Duncan and Paula back in the days of her television show Cop Shop, in 1981.

Family Traditions

Shepherd's pie

30g (1 ounce) butter
1 medium brown onion (150g), chopped finely
1 medium carrot (120g), chopped finely
½ teaspoon dried mixed herbs
4 cups (750g) finely chopped cooked lamb
¼ cup (70g) tomato paste
¼ cup (60ml) tomato sauce (ketchup)
2 tablespoons worcestershire sauce
2 cups (500ml) beef stock
2 tablespoons plain flour
⅓ cup (80ml) water
POTATO TOPPING
5 medium potatoes (1kg), chopped coarsely
60g (2 ounces) butter
¼ cup (60ml) milk

1 Preheat oven to 200°C/400°F. Oil shallow 2.5-litre (10-cup) ovenproof dish.
2 Make potato topping.
3 Meanwhile, heat butter in large saucepan; cook onion and carrot, stirring, until tender. Add mixed herbs and lamb; cook, stirring, 2 minutes. Stir in paste, sauces and stock, then blended flour and water; stir over heat until mixture boils and thickens. Pour mixture into dish.
4 Drop heaped tablespoons of potato topping onto lamb mixture.
5 Bake pie about 20 minutes or until browned and heated through.
potato topping Boil, steam or microwave potato until tender; drain. Mash with butter and milk until smooth.

prep + cook time 1 hour **serves** 4
nutritional count per serving 36.2g total fat (20.2g saturated fat); 2976kJ (712 cal); 44.7g carbohydrate; 48.8g protein; 6g fibre

Family Traditions

Roast loin of pork with apple sauce

2.5kg (5-pound) boneless loin of pork, rind on
2 sprigs rosemary
1 tablespoon olive oil
1 tablespoon coarse cooking salt (kosher salt)
APPLE SAUCE
3 large apples (600g)
¼ cup (60ml) water
1 teaspoon white (granulated) sugar
pinch ground cinnamon

1 Preheat oven to 240°C/475°F.
2 Using sharp knife, score pork rind by making shallow cuts at 1cm (½-inch) intervals. Tie pork at 2cm (¾-inch) intervals with kitchen string; tuck rosemary under string. Place pork in large baking dish; rub with oil, then salt. Roast about 40 minutes or until rind blisters. Drain excess fat from dish.
3 Reduce oven to 180°C/350°F; roast pork about 1 hour. Transfer pork to plate; cover loosely, stand 15 minutes before carving.
4 Meanwhile, make apple sauce.
5 Serve pork with apple sauce.
apple sauce Peel and core apples; slice thickly. Place apples and the water in medium saucepan; simmer, uncovered, about 10 minutes or until apple is soft. Remove pan from heat; stir in sugar and cinnamon. Blend or process until smooth.

tip Ask your butcher to roll and tie the pork at 2cm (¾-inch) intervals for you, and to score the rind, if it isn't already done so.

prep + cook time 2 hours **serves** 8
nutritional count per serving 72g total fat (24.1g saturated fat); 3762kJ (900 cal); 7.7g carbohydrate; 56.7g protein; 1.1g fibre

Family Traditions

Classic lasagne

1 tablespoon olive oil
1 medium brown onion (150g), chopped finely
1 medium carrot (120g), chopped finely
1 stalk celery (150g), trimmed, chopped finely
2 cloves garlic, crushed
500g (1 pound) minced (ground) beef
⅓ cup (80ml) dry red wine
850g (1¾ pounds) canned crushed tomatoes
2 tablespoons tomato paste
½ cup (125ml) water
4 slices prosciutto (60g), chopped finely
2 tablespoons coarsely chopped fresh flat-leaf parsley
1 tablespoon coarsely chopped fresh oregano
18 instant lasagne sheets
½ cup (40g) grated parmesan cheese
CHEESE SAUCE
60g (2 ounces) butter
⅓ cup (50g) plain (all-purpose) flour
1 litre (4 cups) milk
¾ cup (60g) grated parmesan cheese
pinch ground nutmeg

1 Heat oil in large frying pan; cook onion, carrot, celery and garlic, stirring, until onion is soft. Add beef; cook, stirring, until browned. Add wine; bring to the boil. Stir in undrained tomatoes, paste and the water. Reduce heat; simmer, uncovered, about 1 hour or until mixture is thick. Stir in prosciutto and herbs; cool slightly.
2 Meanwhile, make cheese sauce.
3 Preheat oven to 180°C/350°F. Oil shallow 3-litre (12-cup) ovenproof dish.
4 Trim six lasagne sheets to fit dish; place in dish. Spread with half the meat sauce; drizzle with 1 cup of the cheese sauce. Repeat layering; top with remaining pasta sheets then spread with remaining cheese sauce and sprinkle with cheese.
5 Bake lasagne about 45 minutes or until pasta is tender and cheese is browned lightly.
cheese sauce Melt butter in heated large saucepan, add flour; cook, stirring, until mixture bubbles and thickens. Remove from heat; gradually stir in milk. Cook, stirring, over heat, until mixture boils and thickens. Remove from heat; stir in cheese and nutmeg. Cool 10 minutes.

prep + cook time 2 hours 50 minutes **serves** 6
nutritional count per serving 32.5g total fat (17.2g saturated fat); 2993kJ (716 cal); 62g carbohydrate; 38.7g protein; 5.6g fibre
tips This recipe can be made up to three days ahead; store, covered, in the refrigerator. It can also be frozen for up to three months.

Family Traditions

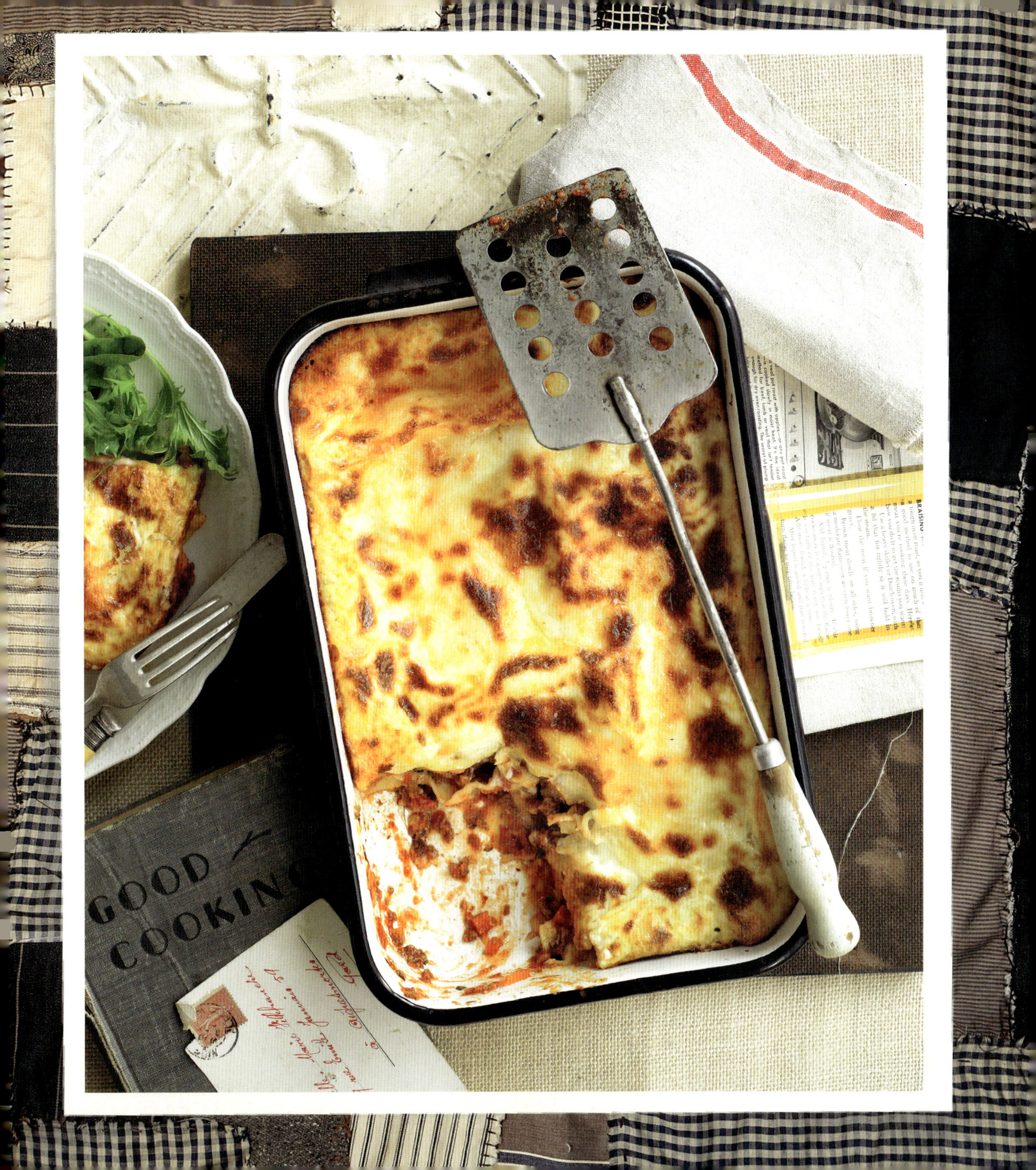
GOOD COOKING

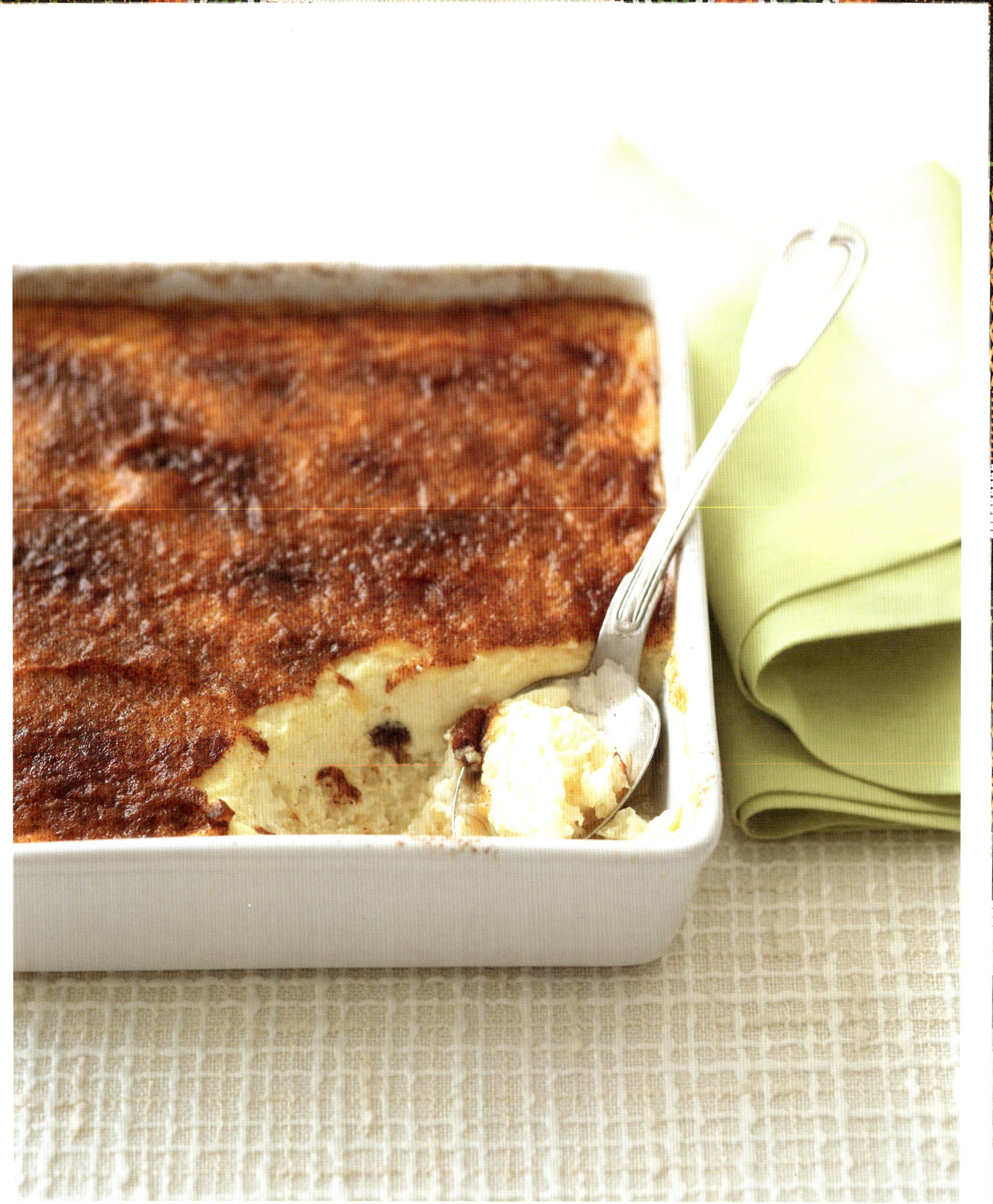

Baked rice custard

4 eggs
⅓ cup (75g) caster sugar
½ teaspoon vanilla extract
2 cups (500ml) milk
1¼ cups (310ml) pouring cream
⅓ cup (50g) raisins
1½ cups (240g) cold cooked white medium-grain rice
1 teaspoon ground cinnamon

1 Preheat oven to 180°C/350°F. Grease 1.5-litre (6-cup) baking dish.
2 Whisk eggs, sugar and extract in medium bowl until combined. Whisk in milk and cream; stir in raisins and rice. Pour mixture into dish.
3 Place dish in larger baking dish; pour enough boiling water into baking dish to come halfway up sides of dish.
4 Bake custard 30 minutes, whisking lightly with fork under skin occasionally. Sprinkle with cinnamon; bake further 20 minutes. Serve warm or cold.

prep + cook time 1 hour **serves** 6
nutritional count per serving 29.1g total fat (17.9g saturated fat); 1613kJ (385 cal); 22.7g carbohydrate; 9.2g protein; 0.6g fibre
tips You need to cook about ½ cup (100g) white medium-grain rice for this recipe. It is fine to use just one 300ml carton of cream for this recipe.

Family Traditions

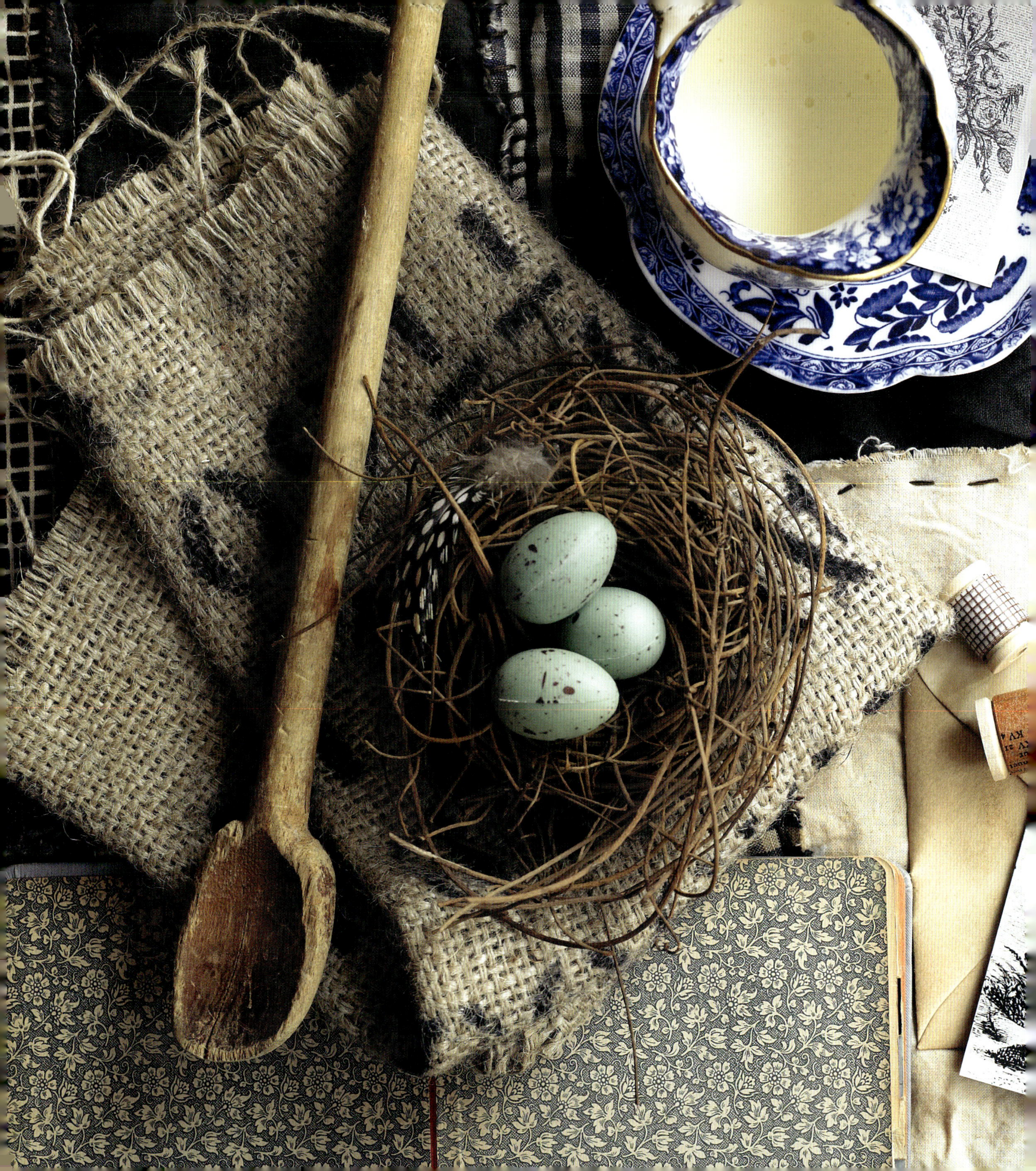

Down on the Farm

Country food is hearty and honest, and uses the best produce the land has to offer. Whether it's wholesome dairy, vegetables, meat or grains, our homestead mums cook it with love, teaching their kids to appreciate the food they eat.

Kylie Gillies

We are not very gourmet in the Mills' household, but Mum's a good cook and even better at cakes and slices and all that CWA stuff. I grew up in the era of meat and three veg; Mum boiled the living daylights out of everything and would add a teaspoon of salt to the water.

But to give her her due, I have grown up to be a great vegetable eater. The next-door neighbour used to grow chokos; I ate so many that it's a wonder I didn't turn into one as a kid.

My grandparents lived on a farm in Coonabarabran, Central West NSW. They had a property with wheat, cattle and sheep on it. We would go kangaroo shooting and that would come back as food for the dogs on the farm.

They had a special slaughterhouse for the sheep. I can tell you what the insides of a lamb look like, no worries at all. We'd watch Granddad cut it all up and then he'd send us back to Tamworth with an Esky full of lamb chops and roasts.

Grandma used to cook with one those big wood stoves: an Aga. She would even open up the little flap on it to cook toast with a fork; we loved that as kids. Grandma was a great cook and would whip up scones with no recipe. She used to make fabulous chocolate sponges with jam on top and coconut.

Mum learnt all her tricks from Grandma and her roast dinner is the best. I don't know how she can cook that for a million people and still have enough potatoes and have it come out hot in a tiny little oven. It's a leg of lamb with gravy and you won't find a better roast dinner.

RIGHT: Kylie with her Mum, Margaret Mills.

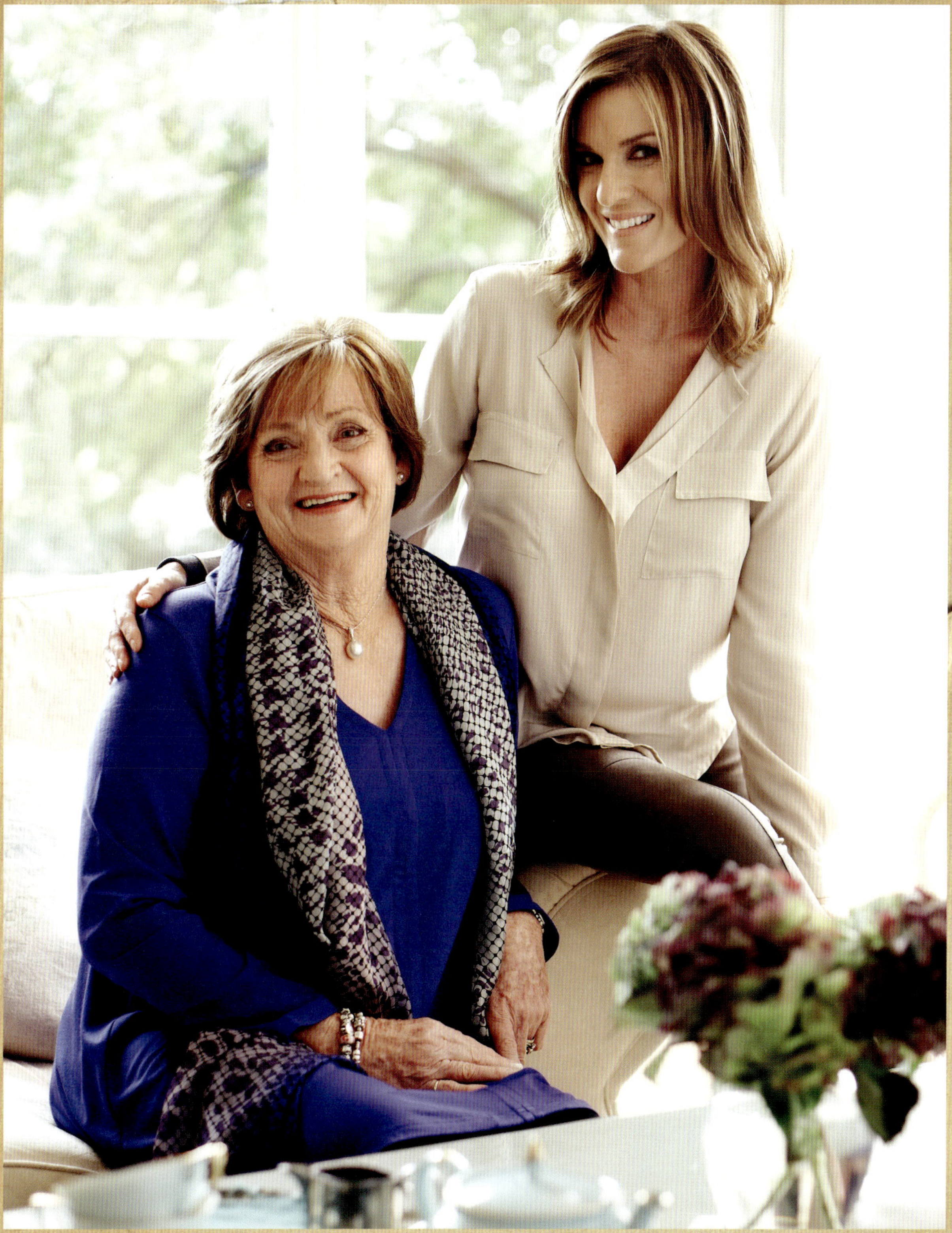

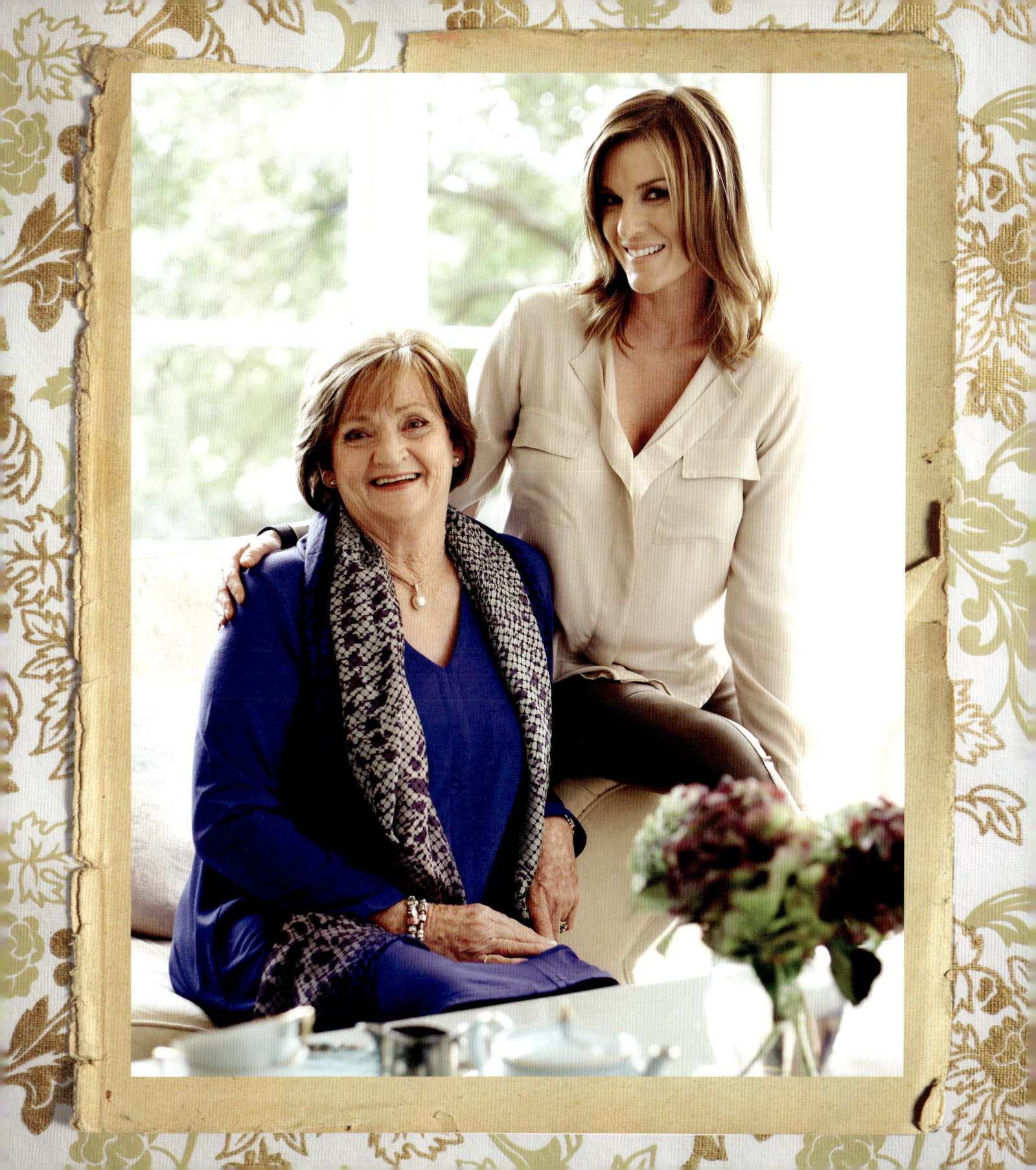

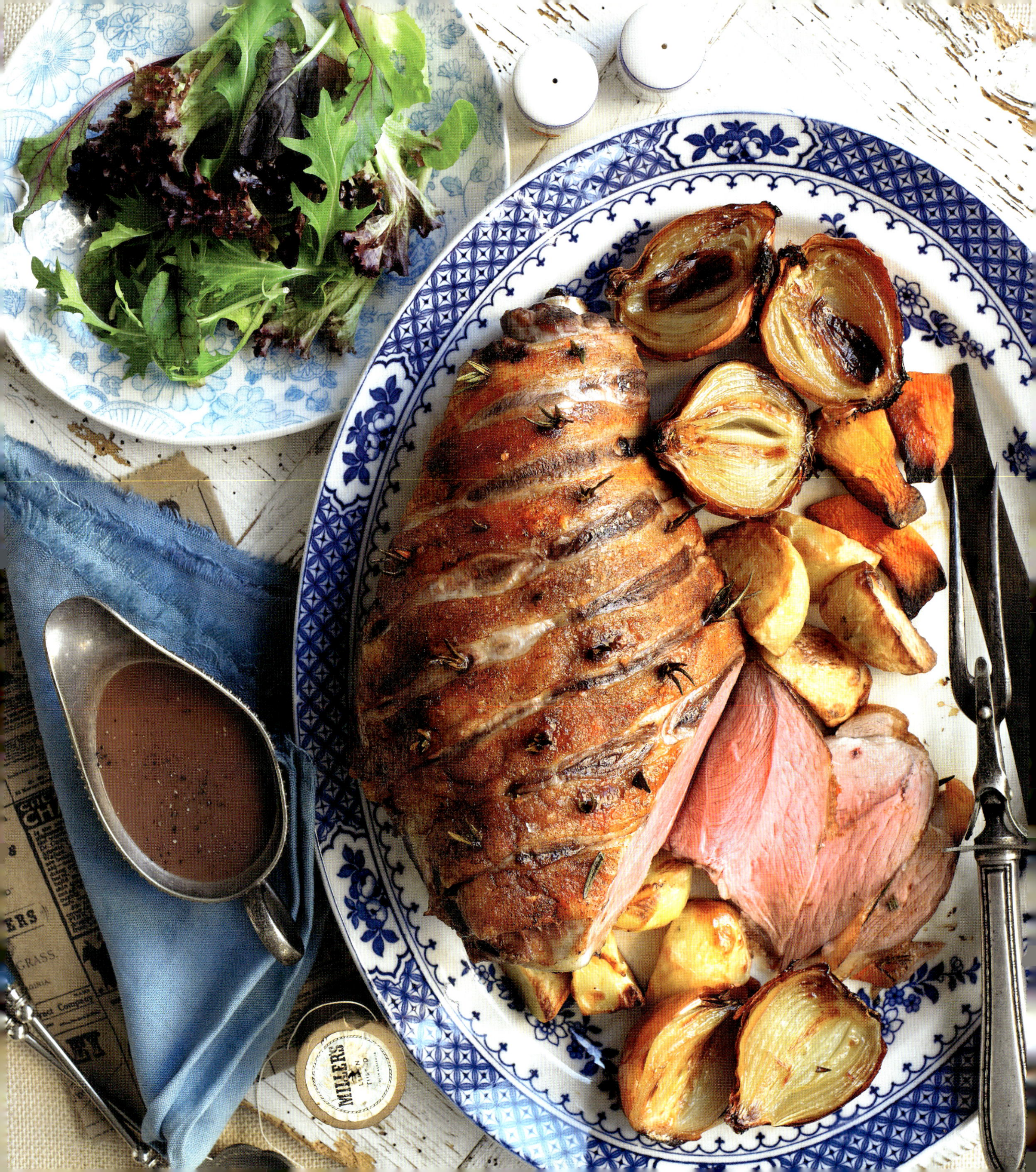

Roast lamb dinner

2kg (4-pound) leg of lamb
3 sprigs fresh rosemary, chopped coarsely
½ teaspoon sweet paprika
1kg (2 pounds) potatoes, chopped coarsely
500g (1-pound) piece pumpkin, chopped coarsely
3 small brown onions (240g), halved
2 tablespoons olive oil
2 tablespoons plain (all-purpose) flour
1 cup (250ml) chicken stock
¼ cup (60ml) dry red wine

1 Preheat oven to 200°C/400°F.
2 Place lamb in oiled large baking dish; using sharp knife, score skin at 2cm (¾-inch) intervals, sprinkle with rosemary and paprika. Roast lamb 15 minutes.
3 Reduce oven to 180°C/350°F; roast lamb about 45 minutes or until cooked as desired.
4 Meanwhile, place potatoes, pumpkin and onions, in single layer, in large shallow baking dish; drizzle with oil. Roast for last 45 minutes of lamb cooking time.
5 Remove lamb and vegetables from oven; strain pan juices from lamb into medium jug. Cover lamb and vegetables to keep warm.
6 Return ¼ cup of the pan juices to baking dish, stir in flour; stir over heat 5 minutes or until mixture bubbles and browns. Gradually add stock and wine; stir over high heat until gravy boils and thickens. Strain gravy into medium heatproof jug.
7 Slice lamb; serve with roasted vegetables and gravy.

prep + cook time 1 hour 30 minutes **serves** 6
nutritional count per serving 7.9g total fat (6.6g saturated fat); 2086kJ (499 cal); 32.3g carbohydrate; 47.7g protein; 5g fibre

LEFT: (From left) Kylie's sister, Stacy, aged 14 months, Kylie's Mum, Margaret, and Kylie, aged two and a half.

Down on the Farm

Sunday fry-up

50g (1½ ounces) butter
300g (9½ ounces) button mushrooms, sliced thickly
8 chipolata sausages (240g)
4 rindless bacon slices (260g)
1 tablespoon olive oil
2 medium tomatoes (300g), halved
4 eggs

1 Melt butter in medium saucepan; cook mushrooms, stirring, 5 minutes or until tender.
2 Meanwhile, cook sausages and bacon in heated oiled large frying pan until bacon is crisp and sausages are cooked through. Remove from pan; cover to keep warm. Drain fat from pan.
3 Preheat grill (broiler).
4 Place tomato halves, cut-side up, onto baking tray. Cook under grill until browned lightly and tender.
5 Meanwhile, heat oil in same frying pan. Break eggs into pan; cook until egg white has set and yolk is cooked as desired.
6 Serve mushrooms, sausages, bacon, tomato and eggs with thick toast, if you like.

prep + cook time 30 minutes **serves** 4
nutritional count per serving 37.6g total fat (17g saturated fat); 1958kJ (468 cal); 4.9g carbohydrate; 26.4g protein; 4.3g fibre

Down on the Farm

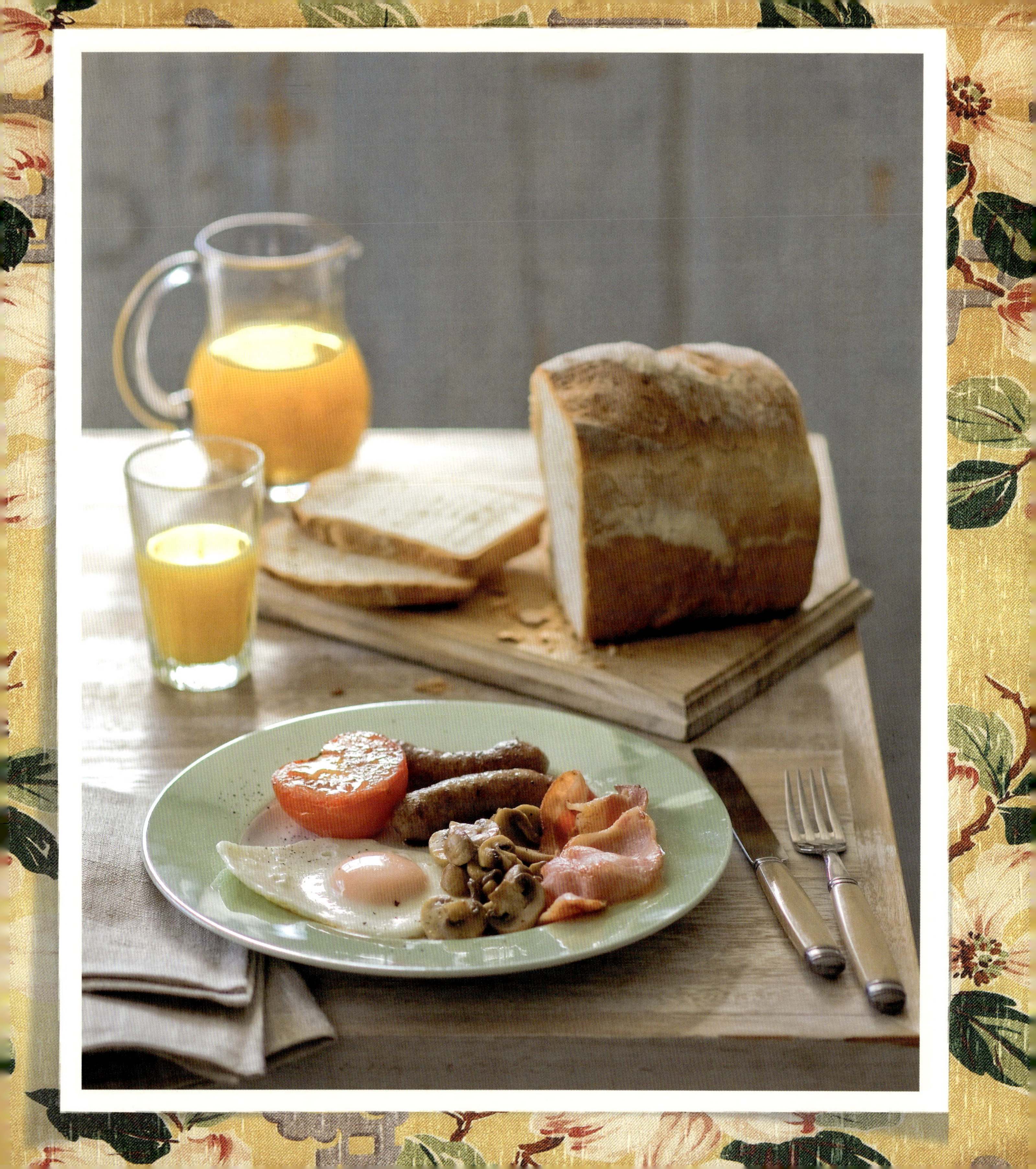

RIGHT: One-year-old Matt with his father, Jim Moran.

Matt Moran

We lived on a dairy farm so we grew up on milk. I remember having buckets of it brought down every morning and we used to walk up through the dairy and get a glass of milk on the way to the bus stop, straight from the vat! I remember having to get up and do our chores like milking and feeding cows and driving the tractor. Growing up it was very much protein and three-veg. Nan lived on another farm nearby and she was more of a home-style cook and made the best date scones in the world. I've asked her for the recipe so many times and all she says is, "I throw in a little bit of this and a little bit of that". It's all done by feel and hand. My Grandfather had lamb and cattle, while we had pigs and chooks and the slaughter is just instilled in you. I remember when I was about four years old, I used to carry the bowl back with all the offal and brains in it.

ABOVE: Once a country boy, today Matt Moran is a well-known chef.

Down on the Farm

Gorgi Coghlin

I grew up on farms in Victoria so it was all about the meat. We would get a beast each year and our butcher would put everything in a huge deep freezer. I remember having to put my whole body in it to get out T-bone steaks, eye fillets, chops and sausages for Mum. Mum has the ability to make a meal out of nothing. She is one of those people who can be told that several people will be dropping in for dinner that night, look in the pantry and improvise. The food Mum cooked was wholesome, simple, and fresh and as a result I have a really healthy attitude towards eating and I love nothing more than a Sunday roast.

My Nana too made wonderful Anzac biscuits, while Grandma raised seven children, so was an economical cook who made delicious pickles with green tomatoes – Mum still uses her recipe and whenever I taste them it brings back memories of her. My favourite recipe of Mum's though is her ginger fluff cake. We made it on The Circle and viewers still tell me they love it.

ABOVE: Gorgi with her 8-month-old daughter, Molly-Rose, in 2011.

ABOVE, RIGHT: "This is Mum, with her Lindy Chamberlain hairstyle, holding my brother Nigel. A two-and-a-half year old me is all smiles on my bike," explains Gorgi.

Down on the Farm

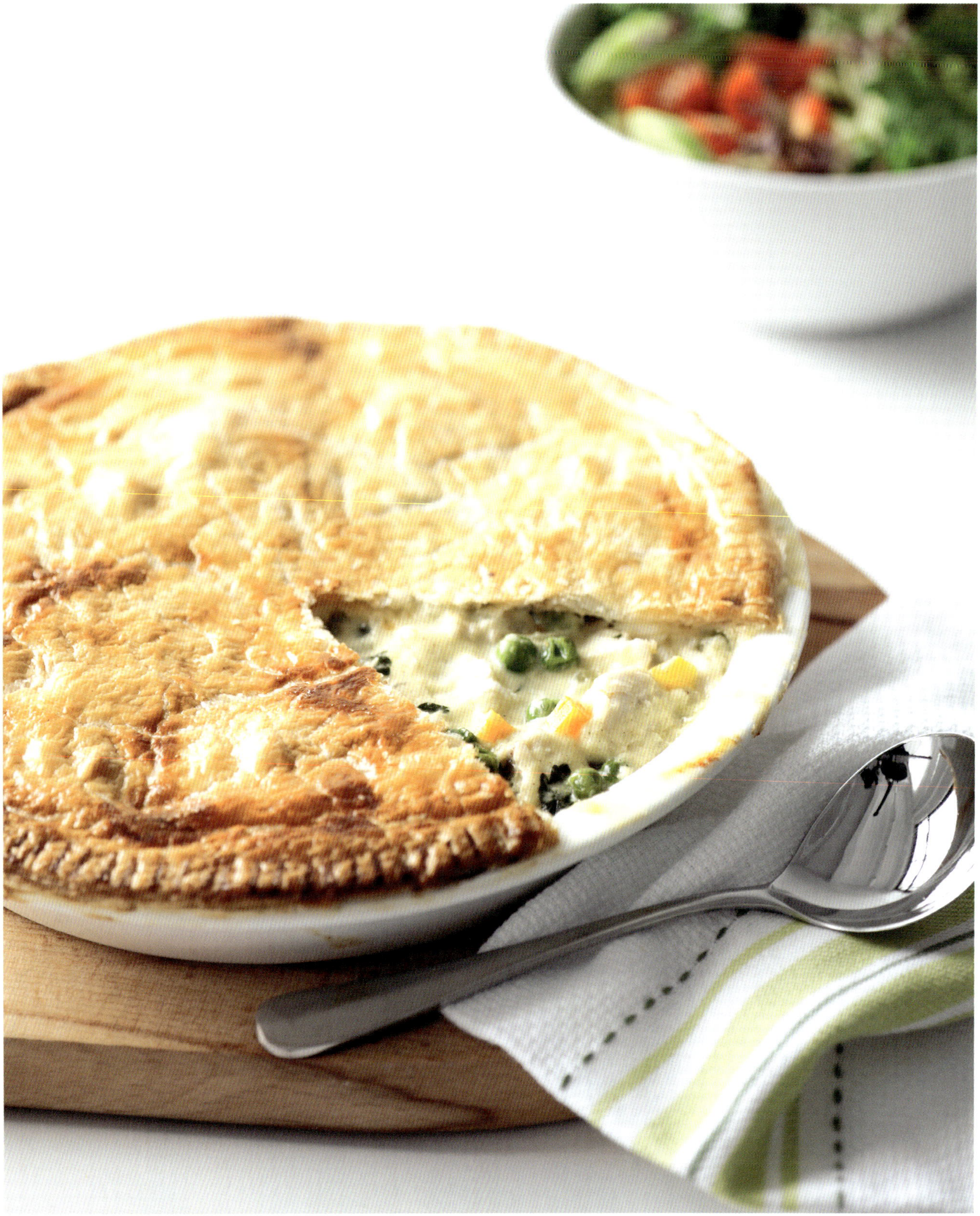

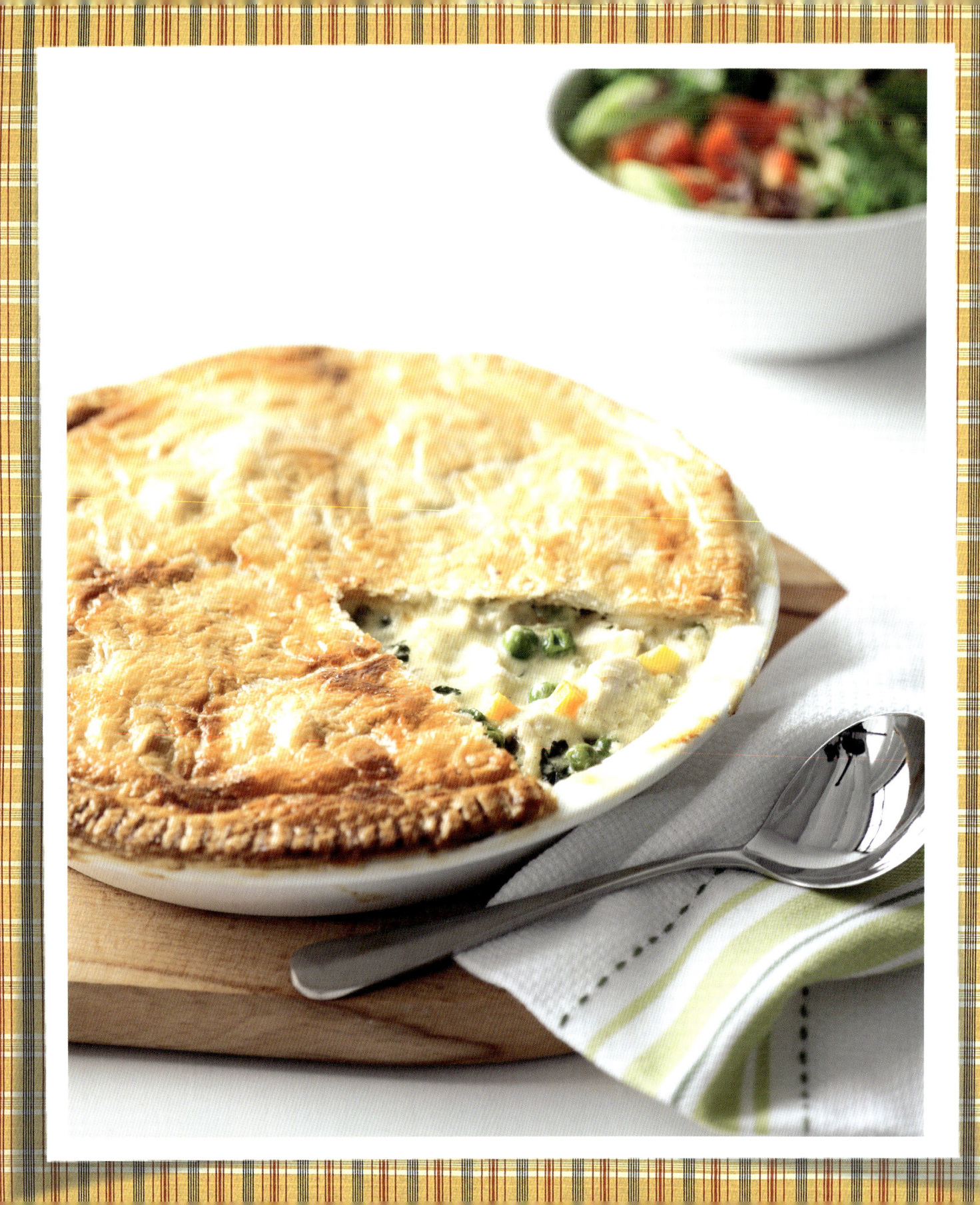

Creamy fish pie

10g (½ ounce) butter
2 teaspoons olive oil
1 small brown onion (80g), chopped finely
1 medium carrot (120g), chopped finely
1 stalk celery (150g), trimmed, chopped finely
1 tablespoon plain (all-purpose) flour
1 cup (250ml) fish stock
500g (1 pound) firm white fish fillets, chopped coarsely
½ cup (125ml) pouring cream
1 tablespoon english mustard
1 cup (120g) frozen peas
½ cup (40g) finely grated parmesan cheese
1 sheet puff pastry
1 egg, beaten lightly

1 Preheat oven to 220°C/425°F.
2 Melt butter with oil in large saucepan; cook onion, carrot and celery, stirring, until carrot softens. Stir in flour; cook, stirring, 2 minutes. Gradually stir in stock, then add fish; cook, stirring, until fish is cooked through and mixture boils and thickens. Remove from heat; stir in cream, mustard, peas and cheese.
3 Spoon mixture into a shallow small 1.5-litre (6-cup) baking dish. Top with pastry; brush with egg.
4 Bake pie about 20 minutes or until browned.

prep + cook time 40 minutes **serves** 4
nutritional count per serving 35.1g total fat (19.1g saturated fat); 2366kJ (566 cal); 23.5g carbohydrate; 37.5g protein; 4.1g fibre

tips It is important you use a shallow baking dish so that the top of the fish mixture is touching the pastry and the pastry is not stuck to the sides of the dish, as this could prevent it from rising.
You can use any firm white fish fillet you like in this recipe, such as blue-eye, ling or snapper.

This is an old-fashioned pickle that is splendid with cold roast lamb or cheddar cheese. For a snack, mix it with grated cheese, pile it on toast and grill. If the jars have been sterilised correctly, unopened pickles will keep for up to 12 months. Refrigerate pickles once the jar has been opened.

Spicy mustard pickles

- ¼ medium cauliflower (400g), chopped coarsely
- 250g (8 ounces) green beans, trimmed, chopped coarsely
- 3 medium brown onions (450g), sliced thickly
- 1 medium red capsicum (bell pepper) (200g), sliced thickly
- ¼ cup (70g) coarse cooking salt (kosher salt)
- 2 teaspoons dry mustard
- 2 tablespoons wholegrain mustard
- 3 teaspoons curry powder
- ¼ teaspoon ground turmeric
- 2 cups (500ml) white vinegar
- 1 cup (220g) firmly packed light brown sugar
- 2 tablespoons plain (all-purpose) flour

1 Combine vegetables and salt in large bowl. Cover; stand overnight.
2 Rinse vegetables; drain. Stir vegetables, mustards, curry powder, turmeric, 1¾ cups of the vinegar and sugar in large saucepan over low heat, without boiling, until sugar dissolves; bring to the boil. Reduce heat; simmer, uncovered, about 10 minutes or until vegetables are just tender.
3 Stir in blended flour and remaining vinegar; stir over heat until mixture boils and thickens. Pour hot pickles into hot sterilised jars; seal immediately.

prep + cook time 50 minutes (+ standing) **makes** 4 cups
nutritional count per tablespoon 0.1g total fat (0g saturated); 113kJ (27 cal); 5.7g carbohydrate; 0.6g protein; 0.5g fibre

sterilising jars Wash the jars and lids in warm soapy water. Rinse well. Place jars in large saucepan and cover with water. Bring to the boil and boil for 10 minutes. Carefully drain water from jars; transfer jars and lids to a baking tray lined with a clean tea towel. Cover with a sheet of foil and place in a low oven until dry. Use straight from oven.

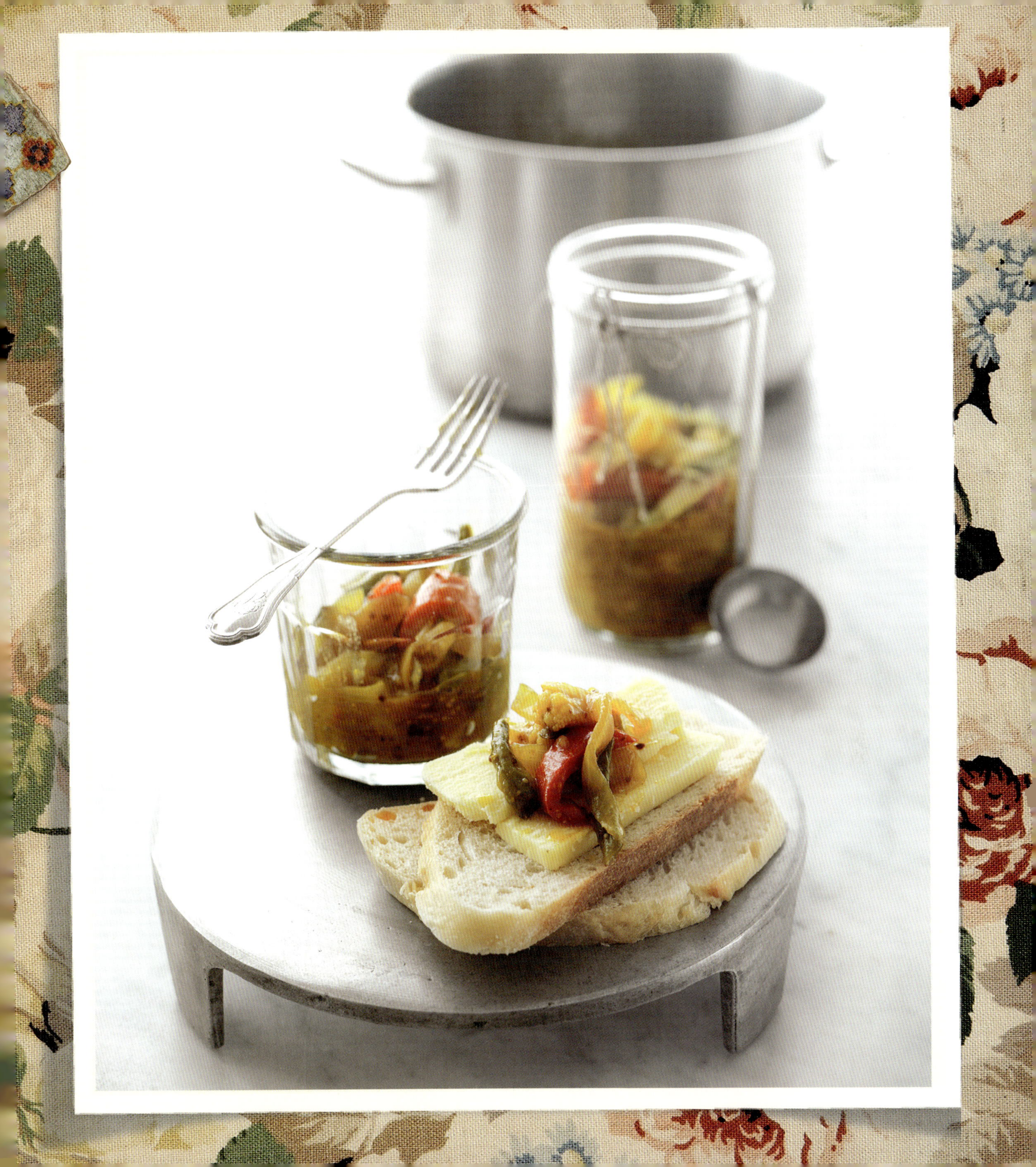

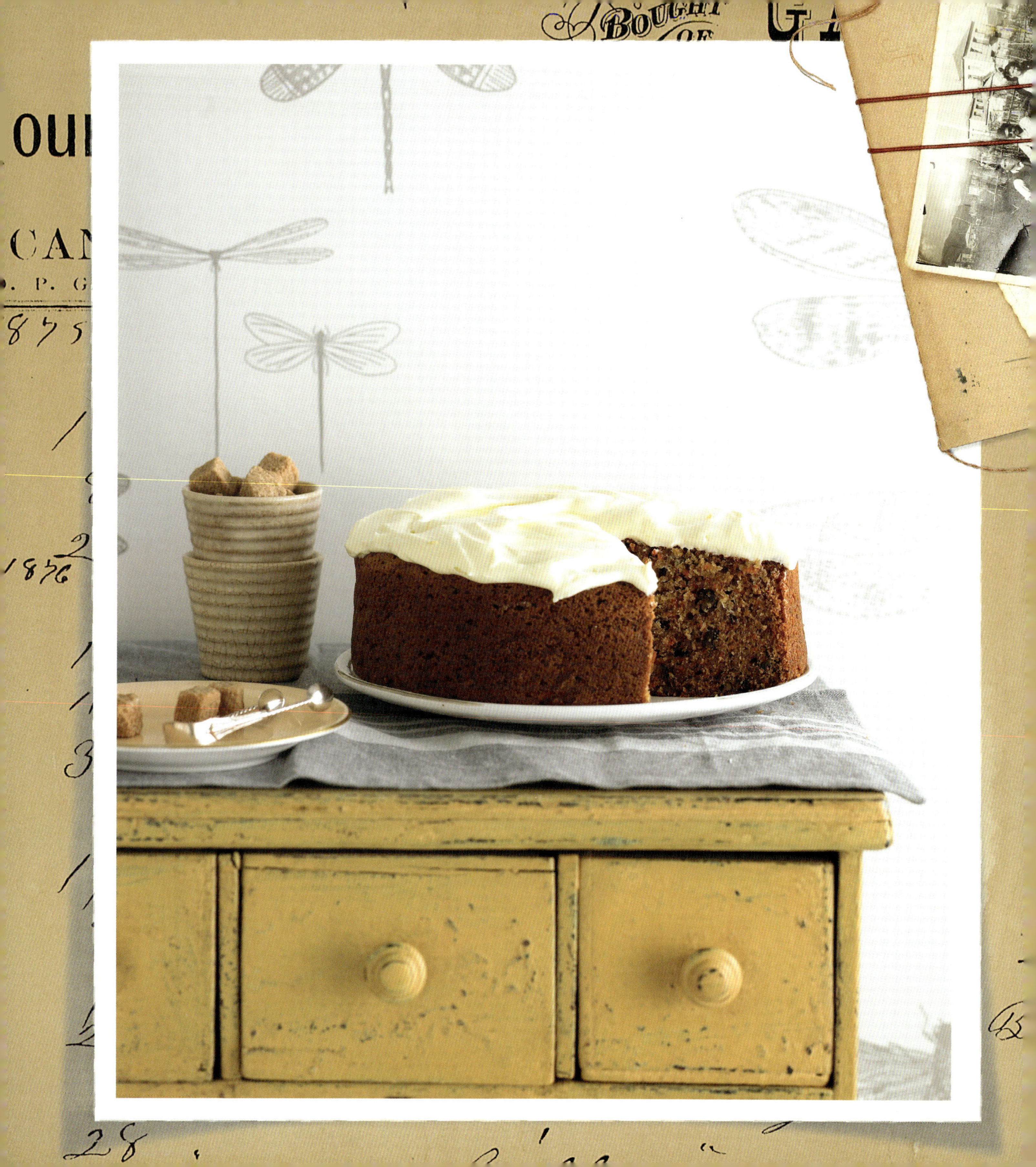
BOUGHT OF

Carrot cake with lemon cream cheese frosting

1 cup (250ml) vegetable oil
1⅓ cups (295g) firmly packed light brown sugar
3 eggs
3 cups (720g) firmly packed, coarsely grated carrot
1 cup (110g) coarsely chopped walnuts
2½ cups (375g) self-raising flour
½ teaspoon bicarbonate of soda (baking soda)
2 teaspoons mixed spice

LEMON CREAM CHEESE FROSTING
30g (1 ounce) butter, softened
80g (2½ ounces) cream cheese, softened
1 teaspoon finely grated lemon rind
1½ cups (240g) icing (confectioners') sugar

1 Preheat oven to 180°C/350°F. Grease deep 23cm (9-inch) round cake pan; line base with baking paper.
2 Beat oil, sugar and eggs in small bowl with electric mixer until thick and creamy. Transfer mixture to large bowl; stir in carrot and nuts then sifted dry ingredients. Pour mixture into pan.
3 Bake cake about 1¼ hours. Stand in pan 5 minutes before turning, top-side up, onto wire rack to cool.
4 Meanwhile, make lemon cream cheese frosting.
5 Spread cake with frosting.

lemon cream cheese frosting Beat butter, cream cheese and rind in small bowl with electric mixer until light and fluffy; gradually beat in sifted icing sugar.

prep + cook time 1 hour 45 minutes **serves** 12
nutritional count per serving 31.4g total fat (6g saturated fat); 2404kJ (575 cal); 67.7g carbohydrate; 6.9g protein; 2.9g fibre
tips You need three large carrots (540g) for this recipe. Cake will keep in an airtight container, in the fridge, for up to four days.

Down on the Farm

Recep

Mum's Little Secrets

Handed down by many a mum, some of the best cooking tricks won't be printed in a book. These pearls of wisdom represent years of experience in the kitchen re-creating dishes and memories for the whole family.

Anthony Field

There were seven kids in our family and Mum was like a miracle-maker. We'd have our friends come over so sometimes there would be 15 kids around and somehow, magically, food would appear. And it wasn't just meat and veg – her food was often European-influenced and she was making her own desserts and ice-cream; she was amazing.

We lived down at Kellyville, Western Sydney, on ten acres. It was a great place to grow up: we had cows, horses and dogs. We even had fresh milk from the dairy next door, although it was warm milk sometimes which was a bit weird.

The boys – there were four boys and three girls – were never interested in the kitchen. I still struggle with toast and have no idea what's going on in the kitchen. I mean, our favourite food was Coco Pops or Fruit Loops! But even those were only allowed once a year at Christmas. During the year we ate all healthy stuff, but once a year we were allowed to lash out.

Mum used to cook this spaghetti that was my Grandmother's recipe and it had real steak, bacon bone and tomato in it. I have never tasted anything like it since. When we used to go back to board at St. Joseph's College after having a Sunday off, we'd have had two or three bowls of it and each one of us went back smelling of garlic. My favourite dish without doubt is the Australian meat pie she cooks, which I think is *The Australian Women's Weekly* recipe from Margaret Fulton. There are no words to describe it – it's like a Van Gogh painting or the Opera House. It's not just food, it's an experience.

RIGHT: A talent and appreciation for music (as well as good food and cooking) runs in the family for Anthony and Mum, Marie Field.

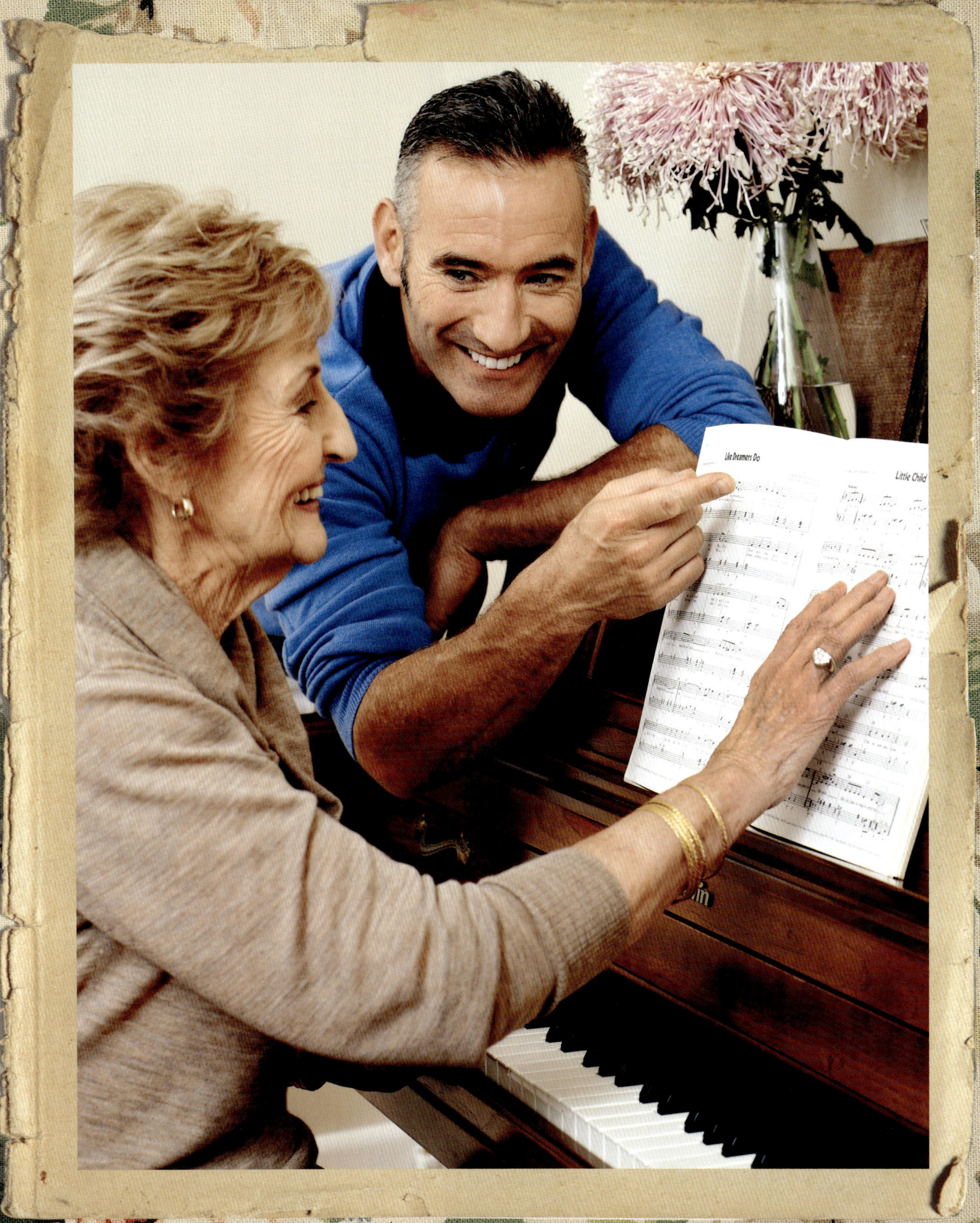
Like Dreamers Do
Little Child

"Mum taught us all those simple basics that they don't often include in cookbooks. They often miss out steps in cookbooks and if you miss out the step, the whole dish is ruined!" **TRACEY SPICER**

"Balance is the key thing I've learnt from my Mum. In Thai cooking, it's important to get the balance of flavours between sweet, sour, salty and spicy." **MARION GRASBY**

"We never had junk food in the house; I'm not talking about recipes as such but more our philosophy on food." **PETE EVANS**

"If you can prepare anything in one bowl, saucepan or frypan, you have less washing up!" **SHELLEY CRAFT**

"When baking, the trick is timing. Have the food coming out of the oven as the kids are coming through the door." **LISA WILKINSON**

"It's definitely all about produce. My Mum will travel anywhere to get the best produce." **JUSTINE SCHOFIELD**

"Mum tried to teach me to be neat in the kitchen. She's a very clean, organised cook whereas I am like a cyclone in the kitchen! I cook and my husband cleans. Mum is super-dooper organised; me not so much." **KYLIE GILLIES**

"Just cook by feel." **MANU FEILDEL**

Mum's Little Secrets

"The underlying thing about growing up on a farm and having fresh produce and fresh lamb, was that we always ate good meals – always." **MATT MORAN**

"My Mum taught me to taste everything and to fiddle with the flavours until they're just right. Now every time I cook I'm looking for that balance of flavours, whether I'm cooking Thai, Italian or anything at all." **MARION GRASBY**

"Out of all my friends, I can cook a really good scrambled eggs. And all it is, is eggs with a splash of milk or cream and don't let it cook too fast or let it burn on the base." **JASON HODGES**

"Mum taught me a portfolio of about four dishes that were all very healthy and would appeal to a wide variety of palates. And the beautiful thing about four dishes is that you can always change the sides with them, so you can probably get another two out of the four and then you've got six. You can otherwise get takeaway one night of the week, so when you put them all on a cycle, randomize them and really — if you've got a serious girlfriend — convince her you could cook for a whole year!" **DR. CHRIS BROWN**

"Buy the best you can afford. We are not a wealthy family by any means, but my mum would make an effort to go somewhere to get a really good quality meat, fresh vegetables or fresh fruit." **JUSTINE SCHOFIELD**

"Everything in moderation, that's the biggest influence." **PETE EVANS**

Mum's Little Secrets

"Mum would send me down to the butcher and if I came back with a piece of steak that was thick at one end and thin at the other, she'd send me back and tell me to learn to watch what the butcher was doing. I was always taking things back. It embarrassed me, but it made me realise that you need to have good fresh food to make good meals." **MARGARET FULTON**

"Nana was particularly good at cooking with eggs which is quite a skill. With scrambled eggs, it's about low heat and gentle slow stirring; with omelettes it's the reverse, medium to high heat and cooking them fast. Poaching is all about the water temperature and low simmering. Mum was also a vinegar user, but I'm not."

PAMELA CLARK

"When making pastry, my Grandma always used lard and butter in hers." BEN O'DONOGHUE

"Cooking is not so much a technique thing, but a palate and a passion thing for my Mum. And I think that's to be said for a lot of great cooks." **MARY COUSTAS**

"Cook off mushrooms without crisping them up and making them nice and soft, by adding a little bit of butter and a little bit of water." **JASON HODGES**

"I learnt to respect food from the start and I think that's really important for children: to learn where things come from."

SUZANNE GIBBS

"Finally in my late 20s when I was living solo overseas, I asked Mum for some recipes. She gave me about half a dozen, but only the most simple versions. I'm sure she thought I was too stupid for the more complex ones."

LES MURRAY

"Stick to tradition: don't change it too much. Mum does not like it if you change her recipes; keep it along the lines it was supposed to be."

JUSTINE SCHOFIELD

"Try things. We didn't eat any seafood because we didn't live near the coast. I thought I didn't like seafood until I was about 15, reason being that I had just never really eaten it."

MATT MORAN

"Mum cooks to taste and she'll know from looking at it when it's ready. She doesn't use a lot of gadgets." **MARY COUSTAS**

"I've grown up with a love affair of healthy eating. I still have the occasional junk food but for me it's very much a treat or a novelty, very much like I might give my kids a lollypop once every couple of months." **PETE EVANS**

"Mum taught me, a long time ago, to clean up as you go. It saves a lot of hassle at the end. She also taught me to teach my own daughters to clean up after themselves. Unfortunately, we are still working on the table manners." **YUMI STYNES**

"When cooking Yorkshire puddings, make it super hot oil for the yorkies: so hot it's dangerous!" **BEN O'DONOGHUE**

"Making up your own recipe is fun! Play with other recipes to create your own take on a dish and make it yours. When presenting it, be inventive and create a story on the plate." **ISABELLA & SOFIA BLISS**

"Mum taught me to never waste anything. I'm pretty good at making things stretch to accommodate unexpected guests and my daughter has the same natural ability." **LYNDEY MILAN**

"Perfect your favourites that you do really well and can pull out of a hat at a moment's notice." **LIBBI GORR**

"Make great meals out of leftovers. Everything tastes good in a fry up." **PETE TIMBS**

"Add a splash of sherry when frying meatballs." **ADRIANO ZUMBO**

"Mum never taught me tricks. In fact she wouldn't be caught dead letting me anywhere near the stove! It wasn't for boys anyway." **LES MURRAY**

"Use butter. Cook simply. Steam your vegies. Make lots and freeze some." **CHRISSIE SWAN**

"My Mum showed me the importance of a well-set table. Flowers, beloved china and correctly-placed cutlery are a Rowntree signature. We eat with our eyes too."
CATRIONA ROWNTREE

"Mum was all about variety. Fish and chips could be grilled John Dory fillets, salmon rissoles, smoked cod, lobster thermidor, curried fish or barramundi pie."
PAULA DUNCAN

"If you feel like making scones for everyone while you are watching the footy, do it! Never mind if you don't have a rolling pin: use an empty champagne bottle."
LIBBI GORR

"Mum taught me to change foods with the seasons; if artichokes were fresh, she'd cook with them. In the summer, tomatoes were beautiful so she'd cook with tomatoes." **ARMANDO PERCUOCO**

"Be persistent! I've inherited my Mum's determination to repeat a recipe it until it's perfected. My Aunty also taught me discipline – whip up delicious dishes with fewer ingredients." **POH LING YEOW**

"Mum had a blackboard in the kitchen so as she cooked I could draw pictures. It was a wonderful way for us to enjoy time in the kitchen together." **GORGI COGHLIN**

Mum's Little Secrets

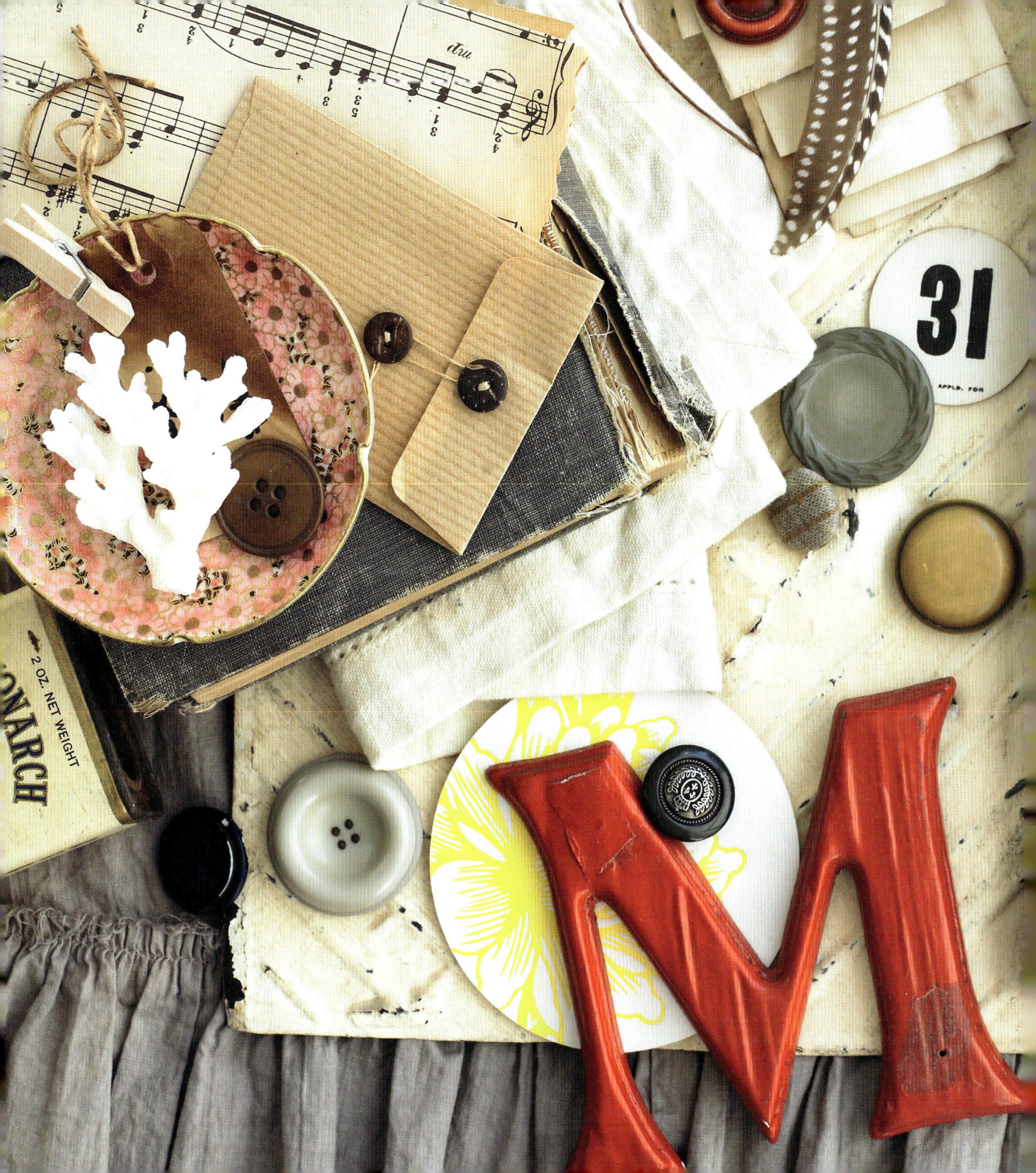
31
APPLD. FOR
2 OZ. NET WEIGHT
ONARCH
M

Recipes to Pass Down

Now it's your turn. The following pages are for you to record your family's culinary treasures for future generations. Special recipes, handy hints, Christmas traditions and fond food memories all deserve to be captured and shared in the years to come.

Recipes to Pass Down

Recipes to Pass Down

215

Recipes to Pass Down

Recipes to Pass Down
217

Glossary

Almonds, ground also known as almond meal.
Cheese
fetta Greek in origin; a crumbly textured goat's or sheep's milk cheese with a sharp, salty taste.
gruyère a hard-rind Swiss cheese with small holes and a nutty, slightly salty flavour. A popular cheese for soufflés.
haloumi a firm, cream-coloured sheep's-milk cheese; somewhat like a minty, salty fetta in flavour. Haloumi can be grilled or fried, briefly, without breaking down. Eat while still warm as it becomes tough and rubbery when cool.
kefalotyri a hard, salty cheese made from sheep and/or goat's milk. Its colour varies from white to yellow depending on the mixture of milk used in the process and its age. Can be replaced with parmesan.
Cinnamon dried inner bark of the shoots of the cinnamon tree; available in stick (quill) or ground form.
Cocoa powder also called unsweetened cocoa; cocoa beans that have been fermented, roasted, shelled, ground into powder then cleared of most of the fat content.
Coconut
cream obtained commercially from the first pressing of the coconut flesh alone, without the addition of water. Available in cans and cartons at most supermarkets.
desiccated concentrated, dried, unsweetened and finely shredded coconut flesh.
milk not the liquid found inside (coconut water), but the diluted liquid from the second pressing of the white flesh. Available in cans and cartons from supermarkets.
Cornflour (cornstarch) used as a thickening agent. Available as 100% maize (corn) and wheaten cornflour.
Cream
pouring also called pure or fresh cream. It has no additives and contains a minimum fat content of 35%.
thickened (heavy) a whipping cream containing a thickener and a fat content of 35%.
Eggplant also called aubergine. Ranges in size from tiny to very large and in colour from pale green to deep purple.

Fish sauce also called nam pla or nuoc nam; made from pulverised salted fermented fish, most often anchovies. Has a pungent smell and strong taste; use sparingly.
Flour
plain (all-purpose) an all-purpose flour made from wheat.
self-raising plain flour with baking powder added in the proportion of 1 cup flour to 2 teaspoons baking powder.
Galangal also called ka or lengkaus if fresh and laos if dried and powdered; a root, similar to ginger in its use. Has a hot-sour ginger-citrusy flavour; used in fish curries and soups.
Ghee clarified butter with the milk solids removed; this fat can be heated to high temperatures without burning.
Golden syrup a by-product of refined sugarcane; pure maple syrup or honey can be substituted.
Horseradish cream a commercially prepared creamy paste made of vinegar, oil, sugar and grated horseradish. Not the same as prepared horseradish, which is preserved grated horseradish root.
Kaffir lime leaves also called bai magrood. Looks like two glossy dark green leaves joined end to end, forming a rounded hourglass shape; used similarly to bay leaves. A strip of fresh lime peel may be used instead for each leaf.
Kecap manis a dark, thick sweet soy sauce. The sweetness is derived from the addition of either molasses or palm sugar when brewed.
Kumara (orange sweet potato) Polynesian name of an orange-fleshed sweet potato often confused with yam.
Lemon grass a tall, clumping, lemon-smelling and -tasting, sharp-edged grass; the white part of the stem is chopped and used. Available fresh, dried, powdered and frozen, in supermarkets, greengrocers and Asian food shops.
Lotus root the crisp, delicately flavoured root of a waterlily. Peel and slice as the recipe directs; place slices in water with a little lemon juice to prevent them from browning. Can be bought canned or frozen and sometimes fresh.
Mirin sweet rice wine used in Japanese cooking; not to be confused with sake.

Mixed spice ground spice mixture generally containing caraway, allspice, coriander, cumin, nutmeg and ginger.

Mushrooms

chanterelle also called girolles or pfifferling; a trumpet-shaped wild mushroom, ranging in colour from yellow to orange. It has a delicate flavour and a chewy texture. Also available dried.

chestnut cultivated mushrooms with a firm texture and strong flavour. They are available only irregularly.

porcini the richest-flavoured mushrooms, also known as cèpes. Expensive but, because they are so strongly flavoured, only a small amount is required for any particular dish.

shiitake, fresh also known as chinese black, golden oak or forest mushrooms. Although cultivated, they are large and meaty and have the earthiness and taste of wild mushrooms.

Muslin inexpensive, undyed, finely woven cotton fabric called for in cooking to strain stocks and sauces; if unavailable, use disposable coffee filter papers.

Nutmeg a strong and pungent spice ground from the dried nut of an Indonesian evergreen tree. Usually bought ground, the flavour is more intense from a whole nut, available from spice shops, so it's best to grate your own.

Oil

peanut pressed from ground peanuts; the most commonly used oil in Asian cooking because of its high smoke point (capacity to handle high heat without burning).

sesame made from roasted, crushed, white sesame seeds; a flavouring rather than a cooking medium.

vegetable any number of oils sourced from plant fats.

Onion

green (scallions) also known as, incorrectly, shallot; an immature onion picked before the bulb has formed, having a long, bright-green edible stalk.

red also known as spanish, red spanish or bermuda onion; a sweet-flavoured, large onion, purple-red in colour.

Oyster sauce Asian in origin, this rich, brown sauce is made from oysters and their brine, cooked with salt and soy sauce, and thickened with starches.

Rice, arborio small round-grain rice; well suited to absorb a large amount of liquid, especially good in risottos.

Sugar

caster (superfine) finely granulated table sugar.

icing (confectioners') also known as powdered sugar; pulverised granulated sugar crushed together with a small amount of cornflour (cornstarch).

light brown a very soft, finely granulated sugar retaining molasses for its characteristic colour and flavour.

palm also called jaggery; made from the sap of the sugar palm tree. Light brown to black in colour and usually sold in rock-hard cakes; use light brown sugar if unavailable.

Tamarind the tamarind tree produces clusters of hairy brown pods, each of which is filled with seeds and a viscous pulp, that are dried and pressed into the blocks of tamarind found in Asian food shops. Gives a sweet-sour, slightly astringent taste to marinades, pastes, sauces and dressings.

Tamarind paste (or concentrate); the commercial result of the distillation of tamarind juice into a condensed, compacted paste.

Tomatoes

canned whole peeled tomatoes in natural juices; available crushed, chopped or diced. Use undrained.

paste triple-concentrated tomato puree used to flavour soups, stews, sauces and casseroles.

puree canned pureed tomatoes (not tomato paste); substitute with fresh peeled and pureed tomatoes.

Turmeric also called kamin; is a rhizome related to galangal and ginger. Must be grated or pounded to release its acrid aroma and pungent flavour. Known for the golden colour it imparts, fresh turmeric can be substituted with the more commonly found dried powder.

Vine leaves preserved grape vine leaves are packed in brine so rinse and dry before use. Soften fresh leaves in boiling water until pliable then dry.

Yogurt we use plain full-cream yogurt in our recipes.

Greek-style plain yogurt that has been strained in muslin to remove the whey and to give it a creamy consistency.

Conversion Chart

measures

One Australian metric measuring cup holds approximately 250ml; one Australian metric tablespoon holds 20ml; one Australian metric teaspoon holds 5ml.

The difference between one country's measuring cups and another's is within a two- or three-teaspoon variance, and will not affect your cooking results. North America, New Zealand and the United Kingdom use a 15ml tablespoon.

All cup and spoon measurements are level. The most accurate way of measuring dry ingredients is to weigh them. When measuring liquids, use a clear glass or plastic jug with the metric markings.

We use large eggs with an average weight of 60g.

dry measures

METRIC	IMPERIAL
15g	½oz
30g	1oz
60g	2oz
90g	3oz
125g	4oz (¼lb)
155g	5oz
185g	6oz
220g	7oz
250g	8oz (½lb)
280g	9oz
315g	10oz
345g	11oz
375g	12oz (¾lb)
410g	13oz
440g	14oz
470g	15oz
500g	16oz (1lb)
750g	24oz (1½lb)
1kg	32oz (2lb)

liquid measures

METRIC	IMPERIAL
30ml	1 fluid oz
60ml	2 fluid oz
100ml	3 fluid oz
125ml	4 fluid oz
150ml	5 fluid oz
190ml	6 fluid oz
250ml	8 fluid oz
300ml	10 fluid oz
500ml	16 fluid oz
600ml	20 fluid oz
1000ml (1 litre)	1¾ pints

length measures

METRIC	IMPERIAL
3mm	⅛in
6mm	¼in
1cm	½in
2cm	¾in
2.5cm	1in
5cm	2in
6cm	2½in
8cm	3in
10cm	4in
13cm	5in
15cm	6in
18cm	7in
20cm	8in
23cm	9in
25cm	10in
28cm	11in
30cm	12in (1ft)

oven temperatures

The oven temperatures in this book are for conventional ovens; if you have a fan-forced oven, decrease the temperature by 10-20 degrees.

	°C (CELSIUS)	°F (FAHRENHEIT)
Very slow	120	250
Slow	150	300
Moderately slow	160	325
Moderate	180	350
Moderately hot	200	400
Hot	220	425
Very hot	240	475

Index

Celebrities

B
Bliss, Isabella & Sofia 62, 211
Brown, Dr Chris 142, 207

C
Clark, Pamela 32, 208
Coghlin, Gorgi 195, 211
Coustas, Mary 76, 208, 209
Craft, Shelley 134, 206

D
Duncan, Paula 179, 211

E
Evans, Pete 172, 207, 209

F
Feildel, Manu 86, 206
Field, Anthony 204
Fulton, Margaret 12, 208

G
Gibbs, Suzanne 12, 208
Gillies, Kylie 188, 206
Gorr, Libbi 135, 210
Grasby, Marion 108, 206, 207

H
Hodges, Jason 163, 178, 207
Houvardas, George 70

K
Kennerley, Kerri-Anne 26

M
Milan, Lyndey 39, 162, 210
Moran, Matt 194, 207, 209
Murray, Les 38, 162, 209, 210

O
O'Donoghue, Ben 150, 208, 210

P
Percuoco, Armando 56, 211

R
Rowntree, Catriona 151, 211

S
Schofield, Justine 163, 207, 209
Spicer, Tracey 44, 206
Stynes, Yumi 110, 209
Swan, Chrissie 130, 210

T
Timbs, Pete 154, 210

W
Wakuda, Tetsuya 98
Wilkinson, Lisa 122, 206

Y
Yeow, Poh Ling 109, 211

Z
Zumbo, Adriano 63, 210

Recipes

A
almonds, ground 218
almond pear flan 29
apple pie slice 35
apple sauce 181
apricot and honey soufflés 53
avocado salsa 126

B
baked lima beans 79
baked rice custard 185
basil and walnut pesto 136
batter (tempura) 192
béchamel sauce 89
beef
   bourguignon 51
   burrito baskets 126
   classic lasagne 182
   corned beef with parsley sauce 19
   herbed beef fillet with
      kipfler potatoes 149
   meatballs napoletana 64
   steak diane 36
   thai beef salad with chilli and lime 105
   wellington 16
brandy yogurt 82
bread and butter pudding 22
bruschetta 125
burrito baskets, beef 126
butter cream 47

C
caesar dressing 48
caesar salad 48

cake
- carrot with lemon cream cheese frosting 201
- dundee 15

carrot cake with lemon cream cheese frosting 201
cassoulet 92
cheese 218
- eggplant, haloumi and rocket pizza 128
- haloumi, asparagus and red onion skewers 146
- pumpkin, ricotta and beetroot salad 158
- sauce 182

cheesecake, italian ricotta 67
chicken
- chicken, celery and avocado sandwich 166
- chicken liver pâté 90
- chicken, mushroom and leek fricassee 41
- chinese chicken wings 113
- cream of chicken soup 176
- karaage 101
- spicy yogurt chicken drumettes with raita 148
- yakitori 104

chinese chicken wings 113
chocolate
- chocolate and pecan torte 139
- icing 21

chutney, fresh coconut and melon 153
cinnamon 218
- milopita 82

classic lasagne 182
cocoa powder 218
- chocolate icing 21

coconut 218
- coconut sago pudding with caramelised banana 118
- fresh coconut and melon chutney 153

corned beef with parsley sauce 19
cornflour 218
crab dip 157
cream 218

creamy fish pie 197
crème caramel 95
custard 22

D
desserts
- almond pear flan 29
- apricot and honey soufflés 53
- baked rice custard 185
- bread and butter pudding 22
- chocolate and pecan torte 139
- coconut sago pudding with caramelised banana 118
- crème caramel 95
- golden syrup dumplings 133
- italian ricotta cheesecake 67
- milopita 82

dip, crab 157
dolmades (stuffed vine leaves) 73
dressing 165
- caesar 48
- lemon myrtle 158
- thai 105

dumplings, golden syrup 133
dundee cake 15

E
eggplant 218
- eggplant, haloumi and rocket pizza 128

eggs
- smoked salmon and poached egg on rye 129
- sunday fry up 192

F
fetta cheese 218
- spanakopita 80

fish curry in lime and coconut 114
fish sauce 218
flan, almond and pear 29
flour 218
fresh coconut and melon chutney 153
friands, mandarin and poppy seed 168
frosting, lemon cream cheese 201

G
galangal 218
ganache 139
ghee 218

golden syrup 218
- dumplings 133

gratin d'endives au jambon (witlof and ham bake) 89
greek salad 74
gruyère cheese 218

H
haloumi cheese 218
- eggplant, haloumi and rocket pizza 128
- haloumi, asparagus and red onion skewers 146

herbed beef fillet with kipfler potatoes 149
honey joys 167
horseradish cream 218

I
icing
- chocolate 21
- passionfruit 35

irish lamb and barley stew 18
italian ricotta cheesecake 67

K
kaffir lime leaves 218
- fish curry in lime and coconut 114

kecap manis 218
kefalotyri cheese 218
kumara 218

L
laksa paste 106
lamb
- cassoulet 92
- dolmades (stuffed vine leaves) 73
- irish lamb and barley stew 18
- mongolian 117
- moussaka 81
- pressure-cooked navarin of lamb 94
- roast lamb dinner 191
- shepherd's pie 180
- spiced lamb roast with walnut and basil pesto 136
- tandoori lamb cutlets with fresh coconut and melon chutney 153

lamingtons 21
lasagne, classic 182
lemon cream cheese frosting 201
lemon grass 218

Index
222

lemon myrtle dressing 158
lima beans, baked 79
lotus root 218

M
mandarin and poppy seed friands 168
meatballs napoletana 64
melting moments 47
milopita 82
mirin 218
mixed spice 218
mongolian lamb 117
moussaka 81
mushrooms 219
    chicken, mushroom and leek
        fricassee 41
    wild mushroom risotto 66
muslin 219

N
nutmeg 219

O
oil 219
old-fashioned tomato sauce for bottling 175
onion 219
oyster sauce 219

P
parsley sauce 19
passionfruit icing 35
pasta
    classic lasagne 182
    fagioli (pasta with beans) 59
    spaghetti with clams 60
pastry 35
pâté, chicken liver 90
pesto, basil and walnut 136
pickles, spicy mustard 198
pizza, eggplant, haloumi and rocket 128
pork
    cassoulet 92
    roast loin of pork with apple sauce 181
potato gratin with caramelised onion 30
prawn laksa 106
pressure-cooked navarin of lamb 94
pudding, bread and butter 22
pumpkin, ricotta and beetroot salad 158

R
rice, arborio 219
rice custard, baked 185
risotto, wild mushroom 66
roasts
    roast lamb dinner 191
    roast loin of pork with apple sauce 181
    spiced lamb roast with walnut and basil pesto 136

S
salad
    caesar 48
    greek 74
    pumpkin, ricotta and beetroot 158
    thai beef salad with chilli and lime 105
    tuna 165
salmon patties 31
salsa, avocado 126
sandwich, chicken, celery and avocado 166
sauce
    apple 181
    béchamel 89
    cheese 182
    old-fashioned tomato sauce for bottling 175
    parsley 19
    white 81
seafood
    crab dip 157
    creamy fish pie 197
    fish curry in lime and coconut 114
    prawn laksa 106
    salmon patties 31
    smoked salmon and poached egg on rye 129
    spaghetti with clams 60
    tuna mornay 50
    tuna salad 165
    whole fish with ginger and garlic 145
shepherd's pie 180
slice, apple pie 35
smoked salmon and poached egg on rye 129
soufflés, apricot and honey 53
soup, cream of chicken 176
spaghetti with clams 60
spanakopita 80
spiced lamb roast with walnut and basil pesto 136
spicy mustard pickles 198
spicy yogurt chicken drumettes with raita 148
steak diane 36
stew, irish lamb and barley 18
sugar 219
sunday fry up 192

T
tamarind 219
tamarind paste 219
tandoori lamb cutlets with fresh coconut and melon chutney 153
tempura batter 102
thai beef salad with chilli and lime 105
thai dressing 105
tomatoes 219
    old-fashioned tomato sauce for bottling 175
torte, chocolate and pecan 139
tuna mornay 50
tuna salad 165
turmeric 219

V
vegetable tempura 102
vine leaves 219
    stuffed (dolmades) 73

W
white sauce 81
wild mushroom risotto 66
witlof and ham bake (gratin d'endives au jambon) 89

Y
yogurt 219
    brandy 82
    spicy yogurt chicken drumettes with raita 148

Published in 2012 by ACP Books, Sydney
ACP Books are published by
ACP Magazines Limited a division of
Nine Entertainment Co.

ACP BOOKS

General manager Christine Whiston
Creative director Hieu Chi Nguyen
Art director & designer Hannah Blackmore
Senior editor Stephanie Kistner
Sales & rights director Brian Cearnes
Acting marketing manager Sonia Scali
Senior business analyst Rebecca Varela
Operations manager David Scotto
Production manager Victoria Jefferys

Published by ACP Books, a division of
ACP Magazines Ltd, 54 Park St, Sydney;
GPO Box 4088, Sydney, NSW 2001
phone (02) 9282 8618; fax (02) 9126 3702
acpbooks@acpmagazines.com.au;
www.acpbooks.com.au

AT MY MOTHER'S KNEE PROJECT TEAM

Consulting editor Emma Nolan
Project editor Pete Timbs
Copy editor Marnie McLean
Celebrity photography Lawrence Furzey
Food photography Julie Crespel
Stylist Kate Nixon
Food preparation Nick Bradbury
Recipe consultant Jordanna Levin
Photo research Thomas Mitchell

To order books
phone 136 116 (within Australia) or
order online at www.acpbooks.com.au
Send recipe enquiries to:
recipeenquiries@acpmagazines.com.au

Printed in China through Phoenix Offset.
Australia Distributed by Network Services,
phone +61 2 9282 8777; fax +61 2 9264 3278;
networkweb@networkservicescompany.com.au
New Zealand Distributed by Southern Publishers Group,
phone +64 9 360 0692; fax +64 9 360 0695;
hub@spg.co.nz
South Africa Distributed by PSD Promotions,
phone +27 11 392 6065/6/7; fax +27 11 392 6079/80;
orders@psdprom.co.za

Title: At my mother's knee / food director Pamela Clark
ISBN: 978-1-74245-101-5 (hbk.)
Notes: Includes index.
Subjects: Cooking
Other authors/contributors: Clark, Pamela
Dewey number: 641.5083

© ACP Magazines Ltd 2012
ABN 18 053 273 546

This publication is copyright. No part of it may be
reproduced or transmitted in any form without the
written permission of the publishers.

Page 109: Poh Ling Yeow image (with her "two mums") by
Randy Larcombe for The Australian Women's Weekly.
Page 135: Libbi Gorr images by David Hahn for Woman's Day.

The publishers would like to thank the Finlay family; the
Stevenson family; the Crawford family; The Olsen Hotel;
Chee Soon & Fitzgerald; Mandalay Flowers; Country Road;
No Chintz; Paper 2; RM Williams; Tommy Hilfiger; Trenery.